WINNING STRATEGIES

Building a Sustainable
Leadership Pipeline through Talent
Management & Succession Planning

Kevin S. Groves, PhD

WINNING STRATEGIES:
Building a Sustainable Leadership Pipeline through Talent Management & Succession Planning

By Kevin S. Groves, PhD

Second River Healthcare
A Healthcare Leadership Publishing Company
26 Shawnee Way, Suite C
Bozeman, MT 59715
Phone (406) 586-8775　|　FAX (406) 586-5672

Copyright © 2017 Kevin S. Groves, PhD

Editor: Tiffany L. Young
Cover Design: Lan Weisberger – Design Solutions
Typesetting/Composition: Neuhaus/Tyrrell Graphic Design
Editing Style: The Chicago Manual of Style – 16th Edition

All rights reserved. No part of this book may be reproduced in any form or by any electronic or mechanical means, or the facilitation thereof, including information storage and retrieval systems, without permission in writing from the publisher, except by a reviewer, who may quote brief passages in a review. Any members of educational institutions wishing to photocopy part or all of the work for classroom use, or publishers who would like to obtain permission to include the work in an anthology, should send their inquiries to Second River Healthcare, 26 Shawnee Way, Suite C, Bozeman, MT 59715

　　Groves, Kevin S.　　WINNING STRATEGIES: Building a Sustainable Leadership Pipeline through Talent Management & Succession Planning / Kevin S. Groves, PhD

　　ISBN-13: 978-1-936406-41-8　(softcover)
　　ISBN-13: 978-1-936406-42-5　(e-book)

　　1. Leadership development　　2. Talent management　　3. Succession planning

　　Library of Congress Control Number: 2017937343

　　First Printing　May 2017

DISCLAIMER: While every precaution has been taken in preparation of this book, the publisher and author assume no responsibility for errors or omissions. Neither is any liability assumed for damages resulting, or alleged to result, directly or indirectly from the use of the information contained herein. If you do not wish to be bound by the above, you may return this book with receipt to the publisher for a full refund.

Innovative Healthcare Speakers, a speaker's bureau and division of Second River Healthcare, provides a wide range of authors and nationally recognized experts for speaking events. To find out more, go to **www.InnovativeHealthcareSpeakers.com** or call (406) 586-8775.

Second River Healthcare books are available at special quantity discounts. Please call for information at: (406) 586-8775 or order from the website: **www.SecondRiverHealthcare.com**

Dedication

To my wife, Jill, for her patience, love, and support throughout this book project and the journey of our blessed life together.

To our daughters, Anna and Kate, whose growth and development as leaders provides my greatest source of joy, pride, and hope for the future.

To my parents, Naida and Robert Groves, for cultivating strong family values of education, work ethic, and faith.

Table of Contents

List of Illustrations vi

Praise for *Winning Strategies* xi

Preface xvii

CHAPTER 1
The Succession Management Challenges of Healthcare Organizations 1

CHAPTER 2
Evidence-Based Model of Succession Management & Talent Development
Best Practices: Talent Management Capabilities (TMCs) 21

CHAPTER 3
Assimilating New Leaders in an Era of Unprecedented Change:
Executive Onboarding at Cleveland Clinic 49

CHAPTER 4
Executing a Best-in-Class Succession Management System:
Talent Review and Succession Planning Practices at Sutter Health 75

CHAPTER 5
Accelerated Executive Development at HCA:
Just-in-Time Development and Placement of Hospital C-Suite Leaders 109

CHAPTER 6
Developing Leadership Talent through Strategy Execution:
Kaiser Permanente's Strategic Leadership Program 135

CHAPTER 7
Assessing and Developing Your Organization's Talent Management
Capabilities (TMCs) 165

Acknowledgments 183

Glossary 187

About the Author 201

Notes 203

List of Illustrations

Figures

1.1: Healthcare Industry Trends & Challenges Driving Urgency for Succession Management 6

1.2: Frequency of Talent Management Practices across Industries 8

1.3: Hospital CEO Turnover Rate 13

1.4: Racial and Ethnic Diversity Representation in Hospital Leadership 17

2.1: Talent Management Capabilities Model 24

2.2: Position Title of Executive Participants in Healthcare Talent Management Survey 2015 37

2.3: Utilization of Talent Management Capabilities (TMCs) for Participating Hospitals & Health Systems 38

2.4: Impact of Talent Management Capabilities (TMCs) on Value-Based Purchasing Performance Domains 44

2.5: Impact of Talent Management Capabilities (TMCs) on Mean Medicare Spending per Beneficiary Episode 45

2.6: Impact of Talent Management Capabilities (TMCs) on Overall HCAHPS Score 45

3.1: Cleveland Clinic Onboarding Phases 52

3.2: Cleveland Clinic Onboarding Framework 54

3.3: First Year Performance Review Ratings for Participants and Non-Participants of Cleveland Clinic's Executive Onboarding Program (EOP) 66

3.4: First Year Employee Engagement Ratings for Participants and Non-Participants of Cleveland Clinic's Executive Onboarding Program (EOP) 66

3.5: First Year Leadership Support Ratings for Participants and Non-Participants of Cleveland Clinic's Executive Onboarding Program (EOP) 67

3.6: New Cleveland Clinic Executives Sourced from External and Internal Talent Pools for 2013 and 2015 68

3.7: Years of Cleveland Clinic Tenure for New Executives Hired for 2013 and 2015 69

3.8: New Cleveland Clinic Executives' Evaluation of the Executive Onboarding Program (EOP) for 2013 and 2015 69

3.9: New Cleveland Clinic Executives' Evaluation of Preparedness and Productivity in their Leadership Role for 2013 and 2015 70

4.1: Sutter Health Talent Strategy 78

4.2: Sutter Health's PSDP Succession Planning: Manager Assessment and Talent Review Worksheet 85

4.3: Sutter Health's Annual Talent Review Process 86

4.4: Sutter Health's Performance and Potential 9-Box Grid 88

4.5: Sutter Health's Internal/External Executive Placement Rate (2011-2015)* 99

4.6: Sutter Health's Executive Leadership Bench Strength (2011-2015) 100

4.7: Sutter Health's Succession Management Depth: Assessment of Critical Positions, Successors, and High-Performing/High-Potential Leaders (2011-2014) 101

4.8: Sutter Health's Executive Gender Diversity (2011-2015) 102

4.9: Sutter Health's Executive Ethnic Diversity (2011-2015) 102

5.1: Executive Development Program Learning Model 114

5.2: EDP Program Phases & Success Factors 118

6.1: Strategic Leadership Program Phases,
Objectives & Learning Activities 141

6.2: Annual Turnover of SLP Alumni versus Comparison Groups
of Kaiser Permanente Leaders (2013-2015) 159

6.3: Annual Promotions of SLP Alumni versus Comparison Groups
of Kaiser Permanente Leaders (2013-2015) 161

6.4: Annual Performance Review of SLP Alumni versus
Comparison Groups of Kaiser Permanente Leaders (2013-2015) 161

7.1: Talent Management Capabilities (TMCs) Assessment Results
& Action-Planning Priorities 172

Tables

1.1: Summary of Key Research Findings on Succession
Planning Practices in Healthcare Organizations 10

1.2: Summary of Key Research Findings on Executive
Development Practices in Healthcare Organizations 12

2.1: Sample of Healthcare Organizations Participating
in Research Projects on the Talent Management Capabilities Model .. 24

2.2: Talent Management Capabilities (TMC) Model:
Top Management Team Support 25

2.3: Talent Management Capabilities (TMC) Model:
Talent Assessment Practices 27

2.4: Talent Management Capabilities (TMC) Model:
Performance Appraisal Practices 28

2.5: Talent Management Capabilities (TMC) Model:
Incentive Pay Practices 29

2.6: Talent Management Capabilities (TMC) Model:
Leadership Development Culture 30

2.7: Talent Management Capabilities (TMC) Model:
Role-Based Leadership Development 32

2.8: Talent Management Capabilities (TMC) Model:
Selection & Onboarding Practices 33

2.9: Talent Management Capabilities (TMC) Model:
Talent Management ROI 34

2.10: Talent Management Capabilities Highly Utilized
by Healthcare Organizations 39

2.11: Talent Management Capabilities Moderately Utilized
by Healthcare Organizations 41

2.12: Talent Management Capabilities Minimally Utilized
by Healthcare Organizations 42

2.13: Impact of Talent Management Capabilities (TMC) on Workforce,
Leadership Development & Leadership Diversity Metrics 46

3.1: Executive Onboarding Success Factors 58–59

4.1: Sutter Health Talent Profiles and Developmental Guide
for Talent Rated as 'Potential for Higher Level' 89

4.2: Sutter Health Talent Profiles and Developmental Guide
for Talent Rated as 'Focus on Current Position' 90

4.3: Sutter Health Talent Profiles and Developmental Guide
for Talent Rated as 'Growth to Larger Position' 91

4.4: Sutter Health's Talent Review & Succession Management
Success Factors 92

5.1: HCA's Core Leadership Competencies 116

6.1: Strategic Leadership Program Success Factors and
Critical Design Elements 149

6.2: Talent Management Taxonomy for Kaiser Permanente Leaders 152

6.3: The SLP Leadership Competencies & Executive Excerpts 155

7.1: Your Organization's Critical Talent Management Challenges............ 167

7.2: Talent Management Capabilities (TMCs) Assessment................168–170

Praise for Winning Strategies

Dr. Groves has done boards and executive management teams a great service with Winning Strategies. *Clearly one of the most challenging responsibilities—many would say the most important responsibility for a board—is succession planning. Given the uniqueness of each situation and the importance of the issue, a cookie-cutter approach won't do. Dr. Groves has given us some basic well-researched principles as well as real life in-depth examples of different approaches to succession planning and how they played out in organizations that are considered leaders in the field of healthcare. Readers will find this not only helpful but very interesting and will be grateful to Kevin for the extensive research and attention to detail he has brought to this project.*

Sister Carol Keehan, DC
President/CEO
Catholic Health Association
Washington, DC

Kevin Groves takes a fresh, evidence-based approach to addressing the myriad talent management challenges facing today's healthcare organizations. Winning Strategies *is a must read for healthcare decision makers who are looking for new thinking and more effective strategies to bolster their organization's talent development and succession management capabilities and grow their leadership pipeline.*

Gary Burnison
Chief Executive Officer
Korn Ferry

Overall Winning Strategies *is a very impressive piece of work. Dr. Groves has certainly provided useful breadth and depth on the topic and I believe it will be successful. I strongly endorse the concept regarding the value of continuity of leadership within an organization and the association that continuity has with success of the organization over time. Just as in medicine itself, increasingly, people come to healthcare leadership positions from various specialized backgrounds (marketing, finance, etc.); as a result, leaders in healthcare today do not have the benefit of having as broad of an experiential background as was once the case when things weren't as specialized. That makes consciously working on talent development even more important today.*

Thomas M. Priselac
President/CEO
Cedars-Sinai Health System
Los Angeles, CA

Every board member and CEO of a hospital or healthcare system should read this important and timely book. Dr. Groves argues persuasively that our industry is far behind most others in developing leaders for today and tomorrow. He provides compelling evidence for why this failure poses grave risks for everyone engaged in organizing and delivering healthcare. He offers enlightening case studies to illustrate how leading healthcare systems prepare young leaders and successfully plan for succession in critical executive positions. Finally, he offers an evidence-based approach to assessing an organization's Talent Management Capabilities(TMC), developed both through his own research and a wide range of engagements with healthcare and non-healthcare leaders alike.

Whether or not you have a leadership development or succession planning process in place, you will benefit from the insights that Dr. Groves provides. His clear writing and thoughtful suggestions can help us all make our organizations stronger.

David M. Lawrence, MD
Chairman and CEO (retired)
Kaiser Foundation Health Plan & Hospitals
Oakland, CA

Winning Strategies *is a must read for healthcare leaders doing combat in today's war for talent. Kevin Groves offers a compelling, evidence-based case for investing in leadership talent that all healthcare leaders should embrace. Founded in best practice, Groves' work offers practical, actionable advice and tools for building an organization's talent management and succession planning capabilities.* Winning Strategies *should be on the reading list of all health and human resources practitioners.*

Debra Canales
Executive Vice President & Chief Administrative Officer
Providence St. Joseph Health
Renton, WA

In Winning Strategies, *Dr. Groves has provided the field with the most comprehensive and evidence-based guide to healthcare talent management to date. His case-study organizations, which include several winners of NCHL's prestigious Best Organizations for Leadership Development award, provide highly practical perspectives on how to get talent management done effectively and at scale. I expect his work to become foundational to the field in the years to come.*

Andrew Garman, PsyD, MS
CEO—**National Center for Healthcare Leadership**
Professor of Health Systems Management
Rush University
Chicago, IL

Dr. Groves has contributed a paramount piece of work to the talent management community. In addition to highlighting some best-in-class leadership programs, the TMC assessment provides a good framework for HR leaders to assist in critical talent discussions.

Jim Dunn, PhD, DHA, DAST
Executive Vice President & Chief Talent Officer
Parkland Health & Hospital System
Dallas, TX

Dr. Groves provides healthcare leaders and human resources professionals with an insightful path to the development of our next generation of leaders. He offers a blend of evidenced-based theory with practical steps to guide practitioners in developing succession and leadership development programs for their own organizations. The case studies from such organizations as the Cleveland Clinic, HCA, Sutter, and Kaiser illustrate both the challenge and complexity in designing, implementing, and sustaining leadership development in complex healthcare organizations. Dr. Groves aptly illustrates that we have no choice. Future success in the healthcare marketplace demands the development of leadership talent and Winning Strategies is the right approach to accomplish this.

Matthew McElrath, EdD
Chief Human Resources Officer
Keck Medicine of USC
Los Angeles, CA

For healthcare C-suite leaders, CHROs, and talent development executives, Dr. Groves has provided us a compelling business case to leverage delivery on strategic goals with a robust talent leadership program. He provides substantial, well-researched evidence of successful health systems and how their strategies on leadership continuity and development drive success in the business and mission of healthcare. For CHROs, it is far more than preaching to the converted as Dr. Groves provides a blueprint to assess your own organization and develop a strategy. To board members and CEOs, Groves articulates clearly how this is an imperative for hospitals and health systems. Indeed it's not only a strategic and operational imperative, but failing to do this well is a significant competitive disadvantage in the marketplace for healthcare talent.

Mike Helm
Former Chief Human Resources Officer (retired)
Sutter Health
Sacramento, CA

Every now and then a book is published that resonates with its readers in a way and at a level that sets it apart. Dr. Groves, in his timely and well-written book Winning Strategies, *masterfully combines rigorous research and real-life best practice approaches to talent management and succession planning by several leading health systems. The result is a book that both frames an important challenge facing our industry and provides inspiration and pragmatic tools for those looking to provide solutions in their own settings. It is a book and a message whose impact will be felt for years to come.*

Jack R. Schlosser
Managing Director
Spencer Stuart
Los Angeles, CA

Succession planning has taken on an ever more important role in identifying the next generation of healthcare leaders. Dr. Kevin Groves has assembled a remarkable resource that melds his own research with healthcare industry best practices to help both experienced leaders as well as students and early careerists better understand this often-overlooked aspect of leadership.

Dan Borton, FACHE
Corporate Director, Leadership Development
McLaren Health Care
Flint, MI

Winning Strategies *is groundbreaking in both its content and insights. While much has been discussed and debated on these topics, no one has more carefully researched these subjects over the last decade than Kevin Groves, PhD. This will be an important resource for leaders responsible for developing talent and building our next generation of leaders.*

James W. Gauss
Senior Vice President, Healthcare and Board Services
Witt/Kieffer
Irvine, CA

I enjoyed Winning Strategies *very much and from a CEO's perspective. I think it hit the spot for an executive level read as well as provides the "how to" component for an organization to incorporate a winning formula for talent management. The case studies were well done and interesting; the perfect match up of process, priorities, and (most important for me) results. The book is timely based on the accelerated pace of change in healthcare and the ever-present debate regarding policy. Get this book published immediately, the industry needs this!*

John Figueroa
Chief Executive Officer
Genoa, a QoL Healthcare Company
Tukwila, WA

Preface

This book represents the culmination of my work with healthcare organizations over the last ten years to identify evidence-based succession management and talent development practices that meet the current challenges of the healthcare environment. I have had the great fortune of partnering with healthcare executives, human resource practitioners, and numerous thought leaders on developing a data-driven business case for talent management practices that meet the unique needs of healthcare organizations. Drawing heavily on my original research projects and consulting work with hospitals and health systems, this book presents the results and best-practice recommendations for developing a sustained pipeline of leadership talent that is prepared to meet the myriad challenges facing today's healthcare executives. Through hundreds of interviews with healthcare leaders, national benchmarking surveys examining the impact of talent management practices on value-based purchasing metrics, in-depth case studies of exemplary healthcare organizations, and numerous consulting engagements, this book is aimed at healthcare executives, board members, and practitioners seeking to establish an action plan for enhancing their organization's talent development and succession management capabilities.

Premise of the Book

Healthcare executives currently face a number of critical business challenges, including the ongoing transition from volume- to value-based performance metrics, the imminent wave of executive retirements, an overall lack of leadership bench strength—percentage of key leadership positions with 'ready now' internal candidates—in critical roles, enhanced physician alignment needs, a strong desire for greater ethnic and gender diversity in executive positions, and continuing consolidation of hospitals and health systems across the country. Given these challenges, there is strong demand for resources and best practices that present an evidence-based approach for designing and implementing a talent management system that drives key performance metrics.

A core theme reinforced throughout this book is the imperative of presenting top management teams and board members with clear and compelling evidence—business performance metrics and verifiable data—that talent development and succession management capabilities are vital investments in the current healthcare environment. Healthcare executives face numerous challenges—the emergence of accountable care organizations (ACOs) or comparable groups of physicians and hospitals providing coordinated patient care, reimbursement degradation, shrinking margins, regulatory changes, increased pressure to reduce costs, and a rapidly aging workforce—that demand new thinking and more effective strategies to demonstrate the ROI of talent management practices. As such, this book provides board members and healthcare executives with accessible, practical, and evidence-based resources and tools, namely the **Talent Management Capabilities (TMC)** framework, for assessing, developing, and sustaining their organization's leadership talent pipeline.

Additionally, succession management and talent development practices must be strategically aligned and clearly positioned to tackle ongoing healthcare reform, workforce demographic changes, and the evolving business environment. With these challenges in mind, this book presents a model of best practices with clear validation data illuminating their impact on: value-based performance metrics (HCAHPS scores or patient sati, Medicare spending per beneficiary episode, etc.) reported by the Centers for Medicare and Medicaid Services (CMS); traditional workforce metrics (annual turnover for nursing staff, executives, etc.), leadership development metrics (bench strength, internal/external hiring ratio for executive positions, etc.), and leadership diversity metrics (gender and ethnicity diversity of C-suite and executive positions); and the alignment of HR systems to a value-based performance environment.

Book Structure & Audiences

This book is written for those seeking to establish, revitalize, or assess their organization's succession management and talent development practices. The content and format of the book have been designed to meet the needs of healthcare practitioners. It also provides useful content and rigorous research findings for thought leaders, academics, management consultants, executive search consultants, and other professionals who are searching for succession management and talent development best practices, and is strongly suited for master's degree courses in human resource management as a practical resource of best practices across leading hospitals and health systems. To enhance the book's accessibility across diverse audiences, a glossary of key terms, common acronyms, and technical language associated with succession management and talent development is provided. The following provides a brief summary of the book's primary audiences:

- Board members who seek greater engagement in their organization's succession management practices, particularly those who serve in board leadership positions (chair), human resource committee positions, and/or roles that are involved in the assessment and development of leadership talent.

- C-suite executives (CEOs, CAOs, COOs, CFOs, CHROs, CNOs, CMOs, etc.) who seek to enhance their respective organization's talent management system to meet the myriad industry challenges and align HR systems with value-based performance metrics.

- Human resource executives and organization development professionals (vice president of talent acquisition, director of corporate university, director of executive development programs, etc.) who are responsible for the design and execution of their organization's talent management system.

- Vice presidents, directors, and managers who seek to become more engaged in the design and execution of their respective organization's talent management practices.

- Coaches, consultants, and academics who help healthcare executives with designing and executing talent management practices, particularly the assessment and development of leadership talent.

- Master of Health Administration (MHA) and Master of Business Administration (MBA) instructors and students who are seeking a practice-oriented resource to complement their readings on human resource practices in healthcare organizations.

The talent development and succession management best practices that were identified via national benchmarking surveys, executive interviews, case studies, and consulting engagements form the structure of this book. Chapter 1 provides a discussion of the key trends driving the surging need for succession management capabilities for organizations both within and outside of the healthcare industry. In this chapter, "The Succession Management Challenges of Healthcare Organizations," I discuss several critical industry trends confronting board members and executive teams, including limited historic investments in succession planning and talent management practices by hospitals and health systems, elevated healthcare CEO turnover, demographic and workforce trends, and the surging demand for clinical leaders. The concluding discussion describes how the **Talent Management Capabilities (TMC)** framework and best practices serve as practical resources for practitioners facing these challenges.

In chapter 2, "An Evidence-Based Model of Succession Management & Talent Development Best Practices," I present a data-driven and validated model of talent management best practices for healthcare organizations. Supported by over ten years of qualitative, quantitative, and case-based empirical studies of hospitals and health systems, the **Talent Management Capabilities (TMC)** framework comprises eight critical sets of talent management practices that distinguish high-performing healthcare organizations, particularly across the performance metrics incentivized by healthcare reform and legislative efforts to enhance clinical outcomes while reducing costs. This chapter illuminates the tremendously positive impact of the **TMCs** on a range of hospital performance outcomes, including value-based purchasing metrics (patient satisfaction, Medicare spending per beneficiary episode, etc.), annual turnover metrics, executive team diversity, leadership bench strength, and other key metrics. As illustrated in this chapter, excellence across talent development and succession management practices translates into outstanding hospital performance. I conclude this chapter by presenting a set of recommendations for how the best-practices model can be leveraged to establish the business case for executive leadership teams and board members.

Chapters 3 through 6 are devoted to showcasing four health systems—Cleveland Clinic Health System (hereafter Cleveland Clinic), Sutter Health, Hospital Corporation of America (HCA), and Kaiser Permanente—via in-depth case studies. While there are certainly a great number of hospitals and health systems that could have been chosen for illustrative case studies of exemplary talent management practices, these four distinguished healthcare organizations were selected for this book in an effort to showcase best practices across a diverse mix of provider organizations—an academic health system (Cleveland Clinic), an investor-owned/for-profit healthcare company (HCA), a private health system (Sutter Health), and a fully integrated national health system (Kaiser Permanente). These organizations have an established track record of excellence in human capital practices—specifically leadership development and executive team transitions—and scored in the top quartile of the semi-annual **Healthcare Talent Management Survey**; they also have been recognized as industry leaders in leadership development practices by the National Center for Healthcare Leadership, The Leapfrog Group, *Modern Healthcare*, and other prominent organizations. Moreover, these exemplary health systems were chosen based upon their well-earned reputation for innovation and effective realignment of human capital practices in a changing business environment.

Chapter 3, "Assimilating New Leaders in an Era of Unprecedented Change: Executive Onboarding at Cleveland Clinic Health System," describes how Cleveland Clinic redesigned its executive onboarding practices to meet the role transition needs of both internal caregivers promoted into leadership roles as well as external candidates placed into executive positions. I describe the primary strategies and practices of the organization's executive onboarding program (EOP), including firsthand experiences of new Cleveland Clinic leaders who completed the program and their respective hiring executives. As part of the evidence-based case for talent management practices, this chapter presents multiple Cleveland Clinic performance outcomes as evidence of the EOP's effectiveness, including the program's impact on newly placed executives' engagement, productivity, and job performance. Finally, I conclude this chapter with a discussion of key lessons learned and a series of practical recommendations for developing exemplary onboarding practices for healthcare leaders.

In chapter 4, "Executing a Best-in-Class Succession Management System: Talent Review and Succession Planning Practices at Sutter Health," I describe Sutter Health's best-in-class succession management system during a critical period of rapid organizational change and numerous leadership transitions. As a regional, 24-hospital health system serving California and Hawaii, Sutter Health has earned numerous distinctions by The Joint Commission, The Leapfrog Group, Truven Health Analytics, and the American Heart Association, while four of its medical centers are rated among the best hospitals in California by *U.S. News & World Report*. Among the most notable medical innovations stemming from Sutter-affiliated research institutes was the world's first heart-lung machine developed by clinicians at California Pacific Medical Center. This chapter describes Sutter Health's talent strategy and succession management framework—key talent assessment practices, talent review sessions, and succession planning processes; it also presents several evidence-based success factors for implementing a best-in-class succession management system, and a series of performance metrics are illustrated as evidence of Sutter Health's highly effective succession management practices, including leadership development metrics (internal/external hiring ratio for executive positions, leadership bench strength, etc.) and leadership diversity metrics (percentage of executive roles occupied by women and ethnic minorities, percentage of female successors to executive positions, etc.). Finally, this chapter concludes with a discussion of lessons learned and best-practice recommendations for developing an exemplary succession management system.

Chapter 5, "Accelerated Executive Development at HCA: Just-in-Time Development and Placement of Hospital C-Suite Leaders," shows how a well-designed executive development program supports the company's strategic agenda during a time of unprecedented industry and workforce changes. HCA enjoys numerous distinctions as one of the country's largest and most impactful healthcare companies and is a recipient of numerous awards and recognitions for the quality of care delivered across its vast network of 250 hospitals and freestanding surgery centers. Central to the chapter's content, HCA has sustained a strong commitment to attracting and developing executive leadership talent by utilizing its Executive Development Program (EDP), a best-in-class executive development program for accelerated development and placement of leadership talent into hospital C-suite roles. The personal experiences and reflections of numerous EDP stakeholders are presented, including HCA's talent management and executive development executives, EDP alumni working in hospital CEO, CFO, CAO, COO, and CNO roles, division presidents, group presidents, and members of HCA's corporate leadership team. Several critical performance metrics are showcased as evidence of the EDP's effectiveness and impact on HCA's business outcomes, including annual turnover of C-suite executives, placement rates of EDP alumni into C-suite roles, and the gender and ethnic diversity of HCA's executive teams. Finally, this chapter concludes with a discussion of lessons learned and best-practice recommendations for developing an effective executive development program for healthcare leaders.

The final case study in chapter 6, "Developing Leadership Talent Through Strategy Execution: Kaiser Permanente's Strategic Leadership Program," showcases Kaiser Permanente, an integrated, non-profit health system with a venerated national reputation for high-quality, accessible, and low-cost healthcare services. The KP system has contributed many innovations to US healthcare, including prepaid health plans that spread costs to increase affordability, physician group practices that focus on preventing illness as much as caring for the sick, and an organized delivery system that places as many services as possible under one roof. Kaiser Permanente's Strategic Leadership Program (SLP), a critical element of their leadership development strategy is one of only two national leadership development programs. The SLP serves a central role in executing Kaiser Permanente's national business strategy across the regions, functions, and facilities. This chapter presents a set of evidence-based success factors for designing a leadership development program that enhances strategic alignment and facilitates the execution of a national business strategy. The personal experiences of numerous SLP stakeholders, including Kaiser Permanente's senior leadership team, talent management and leadership development executives, and SLP alumni and their direct managers, are presented throughout the chapter. Importantly, evidence of the SLP's effectiveness and impact on Kaiser Permanente's performance outcomes are illustrated via turnover, promotion, and job performance rates of program alumni. Finally, I conclude with a discussion of lessons learned and best-practice recommendations for designing a program that develops leadership talent by enhancing the strategic alignment of the organization's regions, functions, and business units.

The concluding chapter 7, "Assessing and Developing Your Organization's Talent Management Capabilities (TMCs)," presents an integrative summary of talent development and succession management principles that characterize healthcare organizations with exemplary performance outcomes. This chapter synthesizes a series of best-practice recommendations for CEOs, executive teams, and board members seeking to enhance their respective hospital or health system's talent management capabilities. As part of this final chapter, readers are encouraged to complete a diagnostic tool that assesses their organization's strengths and development opportunities across the **Talent Management Capabilities (TMCs)** and develop an action plan for improvement.

It is my sincere hope that this book provides you and your colleagues an evidence-based resource for confronting the healthcare industry's unprecedented succession planning and talent management challenges. Distinctive in its focus on healthcare organizations and the unique contextual challenges faced by healthcare executives, the **Talent Management Capabilities** framework provides an evidence-based business case for enhancing your organization's talent development and succession management practices. For human resource professionals seeking to establish stronger strategic partnerships with executive teams and board members, the best practices model and numerous practical examples and recommendations will hopefully serve as valuable resources for your work. In closing, my goal for this book is to communicate the urgency of confronting succession management and talent development challenges and also to offer genuine encouragement for establishing talent management capabilities in your own organization.

Kevin S. Groves, PhD
Groves Consulting Group, LLC
Graziadio School of Business and Management
Pepperdine University
Malibu, California

CHAPTER 1

The Succession Management Challenges of Healthcare Organizations

> *Our data show a continuation of the elevated CEO turnover rates we have seen over the past several years. The continuing trend of consolidation among organizations, the emergence of new models of care, retirement of leaders from the Baby Boomer era, as well as movement of CEOs within health systems, may all be contributing factors. The high level of change taking place in hospital C-suites underscores the importance of organizations having well-developed succession plans to ensure success in today's environment.*
>
> Deborah J. Bowen, FACHE
> President & CEO
> American College of Healthcare Executives

The executive teams and boards charged with leading our nation's $2.9 trillion healthcare industry confront a litany of daunting challenges that demand decisive action. Spearheaded by the Affordable Care Act and the industry's transition from volume- to value-based care, the healthcare reform movement has spurred both unprecedented challenges as well as opportunities for developing more effective and sustainable healthcare-delivery organizations. The results of the 2016 national presidential election have only amplified the uncertainty of healthcare reform efforts and added another layer of complexity for healthcare provider organizations. While the formidable challenges of leading hospitals and health systems in the current era of healthcare reform have been widely discussed and debated, including reimbursement degradation and shrinking margins, the viability of accountable care organizations, the rapidly aging workforce, and the imminent wave of executive retirements, the opportunity to leverage succession management and talent development capabilities to overcome these challenges has been largely overlooked. With an estimated $1.5 million total cost of CEO turnover at a single hospital[1] and approximately 75 percent of healthcare CEOs anticipating retirement in the next ten years,[2] hospitals and health systems with underdeveloped or nonexistent succession management practices incur incredibly high costs and instability across leadership teams.

Often keenly aware of these stark realities and the implicit value of identifying and developing leadership talent, executive teams and board members demand a compelling, evidence-based business case. Given the uncertainty of the healthcare environment and limited organizational resources—financial, know-how, and executive team attention—the normative case for investing in leadership development and succession planning practices is insufficient. Why should succession management capabilities be a priority for healthcare organizations given the myriad challenges facing executive teams and boards? What is the hard evidence that succession planning and talent development best practices drive hospital performance outcomes that are critical in the current business environment?

The development of succession management and talent development capabilities represents a vital investment for healthcare organizations as they navigate unprecedented industry changes. Hospitals and health systems must contend with the alignment of human resource systems to a value-based performance environment while also carefully managing the expected surge of executive turnover due to Baby Boomers exiting the workforce. While the healthcare industry overall has historically lagged most other industries and sectors in terms of developing talent management capabilities,[3] there is now compelling evidence that supports the business case for investing in succession management practices to address many of the industry's challenges. Each chapter of this book offers a practical, evidence-based resource and a data-driven business case for investing in and enhancing your organization's talent management capabilities while strategically aligning your hospital or health system to tackle the twin challenges of an aging workforce and an evolving business model.

This introductory chapter summarizes a series of industry trends that highlight the criticality of succession management capabilities for organizations competing in the evolving healthcare environment. First, I summarize the growing evidence that talent management practices impact an impressive range of business outcomes, including financial, operational, and workforce performance metrics. Next, this chapter discusses the primary succession management challenges facing healthcare organizations and the workforce trends driving the urgency for investing in talent management best practices. Finally, I conclude with a brief review of how hospitals and health systems can successfully overcome these challenges by implementing best practices in succession planning and talent development.

Succession Management Trends

Of the many trends driving the importance of succession management capabilities for addressing the challenges faced by healthcare organizations, perhaps none are more fundamental than the development of talent management as a validated field of human resource (HR) practices. Organizations across industries and sectors have sought to strengthen the alignment of traditional HR practices, including employee recruitment, selection, development, and retention, to the business strategy and an evolving business environment. Of the many definitions of talent management that are employed across industries,[4] this book adopts the following definition by Silzer and Dowell:[5]

> *Talent management is an integrated set of processes, programs, and cultural norms in an organization designed and implemented to attract, develop, deploy, and retain talent to achieve strategic objectives and meet future business needs.*

For healthcare organizations seeking to align HR practices with an evolving business model, the strategic alignment of core talent management practices—assessing high-potential leadership, onboarding leaders into critical roles, developing leaders via organization-wide programs or academies—is critical to their long-term impact on business outcomes. While this book focuses on talent management practices for leadership talent, specifically succession management practices, organizations across industries and sectors are successfully implementing talent management across talent pools and employee levels. Overall, an important albeit broad trend that healthcare executive teams and boards should recognize is that talent management is a formal field of study and practice that is supported by rigorous research findings.[6]

The Strengthening Business Case

A fundamental issue for executive teams, board members, and HR professionals alike—irrespective of industry or sector—is articulating the business rationale for investment in succession management capabilities. Across industries, sectors, and organization sizes, what is the hard evidence that talent management practices impact business performance outcomes? Consider the following brief review of the growing research findings to date:

- **Financial Outcomes:** The link between highly developed succession management capabilities and financial performance outcomes has strengthened. Research studies show that succession management and talent development best practices are associated with substantially higher total shareholder return;[7] average profit or net revenue per employee;[8] and return on equity.[9] One illustrative example is a McKinsey & Company study concluding that companies with superior talent management practices outperform their respective industry's mean return to shareholders by 22 percent.[10]

- **Leadership Continuity:** The research findings also illustrate strong evidence for the impact of succession management capabilities on leadership continuity across management levels. Companies with highly developed succession management and talent development practices enjoy much stronger continuity in leadership roles due to the depth of succession plans across management levels;[11] substantially higher internal/external executive placement rates;[12] and lower rates of executive failure or derailment.[13] For example, a national benchmarking survey conducted by Pepperdine University and Groves Consulting Group reported that organizations with strong succession management capabilities achieved a 68 percent internal/external executive placement rate (percentage of open executive-level positions sourced with internal candidates) compared to only 21 percent for companies with less developed capabilities.[14]

- **Workforce Metrics:** The research evidence also demonstrates a strong relationship between excellence in talent management practices and a range of employee and workforce performance metrics. Organizations with highly developed succession management capabilities benefit from much stronger leadership bench strength[15] lower annual turnover;[16] and higher leader and employee engagement.[17] An illuminating example of how succession management capabilities effectively drive employee performance outcomes is a Bersin by Deloitte study which found that companies with the most advanced internal leadership development practices realized a 480 percent improvement in leader engagement and retention.[18]

Research findings also suggest that the risks and costs associated with organizations that fail to develop a robust succession management process are appreciably rising. The Center for Creative Leadership reports that 40 percent of external hires to executive roles will fail within eighteen months[19] while the overall turnover risk for such hires after three years is three times higher than the turnover risk for internal candidates promoted into executive roles.[20] For companies listed in Standard & Poor's 500, over one third of CEOs were external hires,[21] which increases both the costs and risks of failure associated with the leadership transitions. Along a similar vein, *Liberum* reports that the average tenure of a public CEO is approximately 5.3 years, while fewer than 50 percent of boards in the Standard & Poor's 500 are 'very confident' about their organization's succession plans.[22] Overall, these research findings and trends underscore the urgency with which companies should invest in robust succession management capabilities.

Healthcare Succession Management Challenges

In addition to the financial and operational impact of succession management capabilities, several alarming healthcare industry trends are intensifying the business case for hospitals and health systems. The stakes are undoubtedly high for all stakeholders—inside and outside of healthcare—as the $2.9 trillion healthcare industry represents approximately 18 percent of GDP.[23] For executive teams, boards, and HR leaders of healthcare organizations, the following key trends paint a vivid picture of the high costs and risks associated with underdeveloped succession management and talent development practices (figure 1.1).

Changes in Senior Leadership Team Composition: Research confirms that the senior leadership teams of healthcare organizations are experiencing significant changes in size and composition. According to a 2014 American College of Healthcare Executives (ACHE) study,[24] the senior leadership teams of freestanding community hospitals have added new roles to their executive teams to match the growing complexities of healthcare delivery. Given the focus on physician alignment as part of the transition to value-based payment models, the roles most frequently added to senior leadership teams included physician leadership roles such as chief medical officer and medical director. Based on a survey of 469 hospital CEOs, the ACHE study asked the executives to describe the effectiveness of their senior leadership team. The hospital CEOs reported that their team's least effective practice was 'preparing internal leaders for future senior leadership positions.' Overall, the study's authors assert that the "greatest opportunity for improvement in [the effectiveness of senior leadership teams] was associated with preparing internal leaders for future senior leadership positions." Additionally, a 2016 ACHE survey of forty-three healthcare executive search firms reported 'increased demand for physician leadership' as the top trend influencing the manner in which healthcare organizations are constructing their senior leadership teams.[25] More than half of the survey executive search firms reported that their healthcare clients had significantly changed the roles on their senior leadership teams while most changes included more physician leadership roles and greater integration of physician leadership into the top management team.

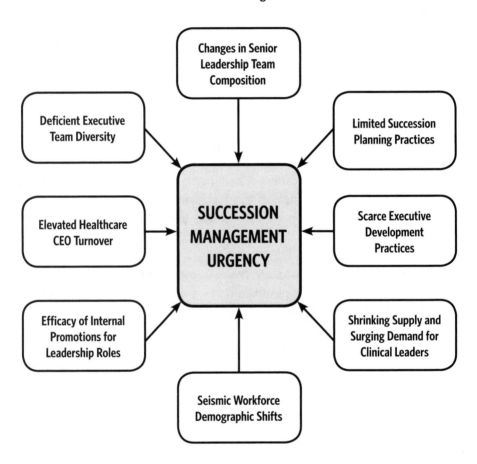

Figure 1.1
Healthcare Industry Trends & Challenges Driving Urgency for Succession Management

The ACHE study findings are also consistent with the 2016 American Hospital Association Environmental Scan,[26] which reported an 'unprecedented' number of physician practices that are being integrated with hospitals and health systems as partners. As part of this massive transition toward more integrated and accountable delivery organizations, the AHA's report advises hospitals and health systems to "rethink and engage the leaders of these medical enterprises in new roles, including their participation in physician organization governance."

As greater numbers of physicians are integrated across healthcare leadership roles, including senior leadership teams, excellence in succession management and talent development practices will prove invaluable for hospitals and health systems.

Seismic Workforce Demographic Shifts: According to the U.S. Bureau of Labor Statistics, millennials became the majority generational cohort in the US workforce in 2015 and will comprise 75 percent of the workforce by 2030.[27] Born between the early 1980s and early 2000s, the nation's 80 million millennials are the children of Baby Boomers. This massive demographic shift impacting the current and future workforce of healthcare organizations demands a new 'employment deal' that emphasizes greater workplace flexibility and work/life balance, an engaging work environment, and—perhaps most importantly—a clear career path that emphasizes educational opportunities, frequent performance feedback, and leadership development. Widely reported in academic studies and popular media outlets, the millennials generally value fulfillment at work and in their personal lives more than compensation.[28] Compared to other generational cohorts, they expect to work at multiple organizations throughout their career and are more willing to depart their employers for organizations that meet their career development needs and emphasize well-being. The key implication of these trends is that healthcare organizations must focus on engaging millennial employees through robust succession management practices such as internal leadership academies, job rotations, mentoring programs, stretch assignments, and community development opportunities.

Limited Succession Planning Practices: In comparison to other industries and sectors, healthcare organizations have generally neglected to develop robust succession management capabilities. An influential research report by the IBM Institute for Business Value and Human Capital Institute (HCI) concluded that by comparison to other industries, the healthcare industry is "a laggard in developing human resource and talent management innovations. Hospitals and health systems have devoted too little time to creating a legacy of leadership… many have no formal plans to identify and develop individuals for future roles, nor do they have a transition strategy should leaders make a planned or unplanned departure," according to the report author Allan Schweyer.[29] The study assessed over a dozen industries on the basis of their execution of core talent management practices such as talent acquisition, onboarding, talent retention and engagement, and training and development. Illustrated in figure 1.2, the research findings demonstrate that the healthcare industry executes significantly fewer talent management practices than most other industries. In fact, healthcare, educational institutions, and government agencies were identified as the *least* likely industries to implement talent management best practices. Of the many talent management practices assessed, succession planning and leadership development capabilities were called out as specific gaps for healthcare organizations. The study identified several specific practices as lacking in healthcare compared to other industries, including the identification of high-potential employees and programs to retain them and succession management capabilities that drive the development of leadership talent. In a sobering analysis of the IBM/HCI research findings, Schweyer offers the following conclusion:

> *The healthcare industry may be unique in the enormity of the talent challenges that confront it. If there ever were a 'perfect storm' related to talent management, it is most acute in healthcare. While it is true that the aging population restricts talent for all industries, it is only in healthcare and life sciences that it so profoundly impacts demand at the same time.*

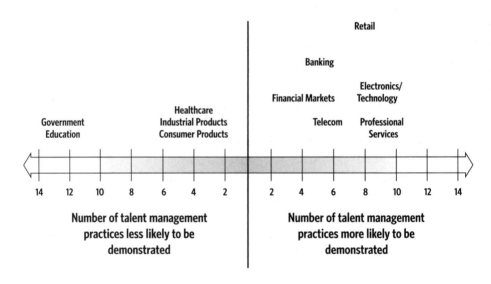

Figure 1.2
Frequency of Talent Management Practices across Industries

Notes: Industries listed to the left of the line represent those where four or more talent management practices are not practiced at a statistically significant level. Industries listed to the right of the line represent those where four or more talent management practices are practiced at a statistically significant level.

Source: IBM Institute for Business Value/Human Capital Institute (2008)

The results of a 2014 ACHE survey of community hospital CEOs indicate that only 52 percent of hospitals routinely conduct succession planning for the CEO position.[30] While these results represent an improvement from a 2007 ACHE survey showing that only 21 percent of freestanding hospitals regularly conduct CEO succession planning, there remains ample room for improvement given the growing complexity of top leadership roles and the elevated rate of CEO turnover. Deborah Bowen, ACHE's president and CEO, asserts that "in today's healthcare environment…an increase in CEO turnover at our nation's hospitals…means if we aim to create high-performing organizations that consistently deliver on patient outcomes, we must put the practice of succession planning front and center."[31] Regrettably, the 2014 ACHE survey results also show that only 43 percent of the responding CEOs had one or more successors identified for their positions. For the 57 percent of CEOs reporting that they have no identified successors, the top two barriers to succession planning at their organization were 'succession planning was not a high priority for the board right now' and 'there were no internal candidates who could be prepared for the position.' Summarized in table 1.1, these survey results and key findings from several additional prominent studies indicate that succession planning represents a critical improvement opportunity for the senior leadership teams and boards of many of our nation's hospitals and health systems.

Scarce Executive Development Practices: While the consistency and depth of succession planning represents a clear development opportunity for many healthcare organizations, a similar pattern emerges for the prevalence of robust executive development practices. A comprehensive survey of US health systems found that only 52 percent reported having an executive leadership development (ELD) program.[32] Similarly, an ACHE-sponsored study[33] of succession management practices at US health systems found that only 36 percent of system CEOs and 28 percent of hospital CEOs believe that their organization's approaches to preparing and developing successors to the CEO role were either 'effective' or 'very effective.' With respect to developing internal candidates for the CEO role, the two factors that were the strongest predictors of an effective succession process included a greater depth and breadth of succession planning practices across the health system and a larger number of leadership development activities as part of the process. The most commonly reported development activities for CEO successors included mentoring (including one-on-one meetings with the current CEO), stretch assignments, structured socialization (e.g., stakeholder meetings), and formal education and training programs. However, the percentage of hospitals and US health systems utilizing leadership development activities is alarmingly low. For example, only 34

Table 1.1

Summary of Key Research Findings on Succession Planning Practices in Healthcare Organizations

Author(s) & Year	Title & Publication	Key Findings
American College of Healthcare Executives (2014)	2014 Hospital CEO Survey on Succession Planning (Healthcare Executive)	▪ 52% of community hospital CEOs report that their hospitals routinely conduct succession planning for the CEO position. ▪ 43% of CEOs reported that one or more successors had been identified for their positions. ▪ Major barriers to naming a successor include no internal candidates who could be prepared for the position and succession planning was not a board priority.
American College of Healthcare Executives (2011)	Improving Leadership Stability in Healthcare Organizations (American College of Healthcare Executives)	▪ 7% of senior healthcare leaders report that their organizations are well positioned for the sudden departure of a key executive. ▪ 25% of senior healthcare leaders report that their organizations are fully committed to succession planning. ▪ 43% of senior healthcare leaders describe the leadership pipeline at their organizations as 'inadequate.'
Andrew Garman & J. Larry Tyler (2007)	Succession Planning Practices & Outcomes in U.S. Hospital Systems: Final Report (American College of Healthcare Executives)	▪ Among CEOs hired internally, only 40% of health system CEOs and 26% of member hospital CEOs were identified in advance. ▪ 49% of system CEOs reported that successor candidates have been identified for their position and succession planning was routinely practiced at the system level of their organization. ▪ 44% of system CEOs and 32% of hospital CEOs reported that their CEO succession planning practices were either effective or very effective.
Amir A. Khaliq, Stephen Walston & David M. Thompson (2006)	The Impact of Hospital CEO Turnover in U.S. Hospitals: Final Report (American College of Healthcare Executives)	▪ 25% of US hospitals take between six months and one year to fill a vacant CEO position. ▪ 77% of chief medical officers, 52% of chief operating officers, and 42% of chief financial officers depart the hospital or health system within one year of a new CEO transition.
Linda Wilson (2005)	Inner Strength: Top-Performing Hospitals are More Apt to Promote from Within (Modern Healthcare)	▪ 50% of CEOs at top performing hospitals were promoted from within compared to 37% at hospitals with average clinical and financial performance outcomes. ▪ Top performing hospitals are 35% more likely to promote an insider CEO candidate compared to hospitals with average or below average clinical and financial performance outcomes. ▪ 36% of executives (other than CEOs) at top performing hospitals were internal candidates compared to 21% at hospitals with average performance outcomes.

percent of hospital CEOs and 17 percent of health system CEOs reported that their organizations utilize formal education or training programs, such as ELD programs. Similarly, highly effective leadership development activities such as 360-degree feedback and job rotations are generally underutilized by health systems. Less than half of community hospital CEOs reported that their organization utilizes structured socialization, 360-degree feedback, formal education or training programs, and job rotations. Presented in table 1.2, these research findings suggest that many hospitals and health systems are missing critical opportunities to develop leadership talent and ensure smooth transitions into the CEO positions and other senior leadership team roles.

Efficacy of Internal Promotions for Leadership Roles: The accumulating research evidence strongly indicates that organizations across industries should promote internal candidates for leadership roles. Numerous studies of CEO successors placed into their roles across various types of selection methods (e.g., promotion, external placement) illustrate the many benefits of promoting internal candidates. According to researchers Zhang and Rajagopalan,[34] internal candidates who had been identified and purposely developed for the CEO position are far more effective in their CEO roles compared to both outside successors and internal candidates who were selected via a 'horse race' that pits multiple insiders for the CEO position. Rigorous research also illustrates the sharp differences in job performance between internal versus external CEO candidates. A Booz & Company analysis[35] of multiple industries demonstrated that compared to external CEO candidates, internal CEO candidates delivered significantly higher market-adjusted shareholder returns, remained in their CEO roles for two years longer, and were substantially less likely to be involuntarily terminated. The many benefits of developing internal leadership talent for CEO successions extends to healthcare organizations, as top performing hospitals are 35 percent more likely to promote an insider CEO compared to hospitals with average performance on clinical and financial outcomes.[36] For healthcare executives and boards seeking to establish clear priorities for their hospitals and health systems, the research evidence to date presents a clear business case for the development of internal candidates via strong succession management capabilities.

Elevated Healthcare CEO Turnover: Mirroring the increasing complexity of the healthcare industry and the challenges posed to senior leadership teams, healthcare CEO turnover remains historically high with an expected surge in CEO transitions over the next ten years. The American College of Healthcare Executives (ACHE) annual survey of hospital CEO turnover reports an elevated hospital CEO turnover rate since 2009.[37] Illustrated in figure 1.3,

Table 1.2

Summary of Key Research Findings on Executive Development Practices in Healthcare Organizations

Author(s) & Year	Title & Publication	Key Findings
American College of Healthcare Executives (2014)	*2014 Hospital CEO Survey on Succession Planning* (Healthcare Executive)	• Community hospital CEOs report low utilization of many common leadership development activities for CEO successors. • Structured socialization (47%), 360-degree feedback (40%), formal education or training (24%) are utilized by less than half of the survey respondents. • Mentoring (regular one-on-one meetings with the current CEO) (78%) and stretch assignments (61%) are highly utilized by community hospitals for developing CEO successors.
Tim Ringo, Allan Schweyer, Michael DeMarco, Ross Jones & Eric Lesser (2008)	*Integrated Talent Management (Part 3): Turning Talent into a Competitive Advantage: An Industry Review* (IBM Institute for Business Value/Human Capital Institute)	• Cross-industry analysis concludes that the healthcare industry lacks sufficient development of two talent management capabilities: (a) attract and retain talent and (b) motivate and development talent. • Leadership development practices found lacking in healthcare include identifying high potential employees and delivering programs to retain them, succession management capability that guides the development of leadership talent, and training managers to demonstrate people management skills.
Ann Scheck McAlearney (2008)	*Executive Leadership Development in U.S. Health Systems: Exploring the Evidence* (American College of Healthcare Executives)	• 52% of US health systems reported having an executive leadership development (ELD) program. • ELD programs are most commonly developed to strengthen the link between leadership development and the organization's strategic goals, enhance succession planning, and provide local development opportunities to leaders.
Andrew Garman & J. Larry Tyler (2007)	*Succession Planning Practices & Outcomes in U.S. Hospital Systems: Final Report* (American College of Healthcare Executives)	• 28% of hospital CEOs and 36% of health system CEOs believe that their organization's approaches to preparing and developing CEO successors were either 'effective' or 'very effective.' • 34% of hospital CEOs and 17% of health system CEOs reported that their organizations utilize formal education or training programs, such as ELD programs. • Mentoring (regular one-on-one meetings with the current CEO) is highly utilized by hospital CEOs (68%) and health system CEOs (84%) for developing CEO successors. • Over half of hospital CEOs (59%) and health system CEOs (56%) utilize 'stretch' assignments for developing CEO successors. • Leadership development activities such as 360-degree feedback (38%) and job rotations (11%) are underutilized by health systems.

hospital CEO turnover was 18 percent in 2015 and a range of 16 to 18 percent over seven years (2009-2015). Alarmingly, for most US states, hospital CEO turnover is much worse. Twenty-three US states report an annual hospital CEO turnover rate of at least 20 percent, including the two highest populous states—California (20 percent) and Texas (23 percent). Underscoring the implications of these trends, ACHE's president and CEO Deborah Bowen says, "the continuing trend of consolidation among organizations, the emergence of new models of care, retirement of leaders from the Baby Boomer era, as well as movement of CEOs within health systems, may all be contributing factors" to the sustained CEO turnover rate. Importantly, Bowen identifies succession management capability as a fundamental need for today's healthcare organizations. "The high level of change taking place in hospital C-suites underscores the importance of organizations having well-developed succession plans to ensure success in today's environment," says Bowen.

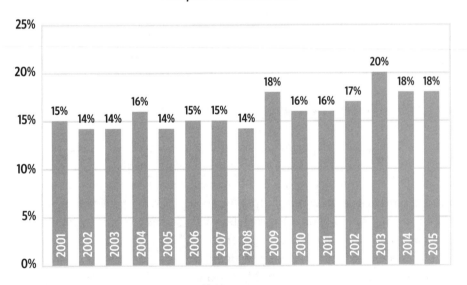

Figure 1.3
Hospital CEO Turnover Rate

Notes: Survey of CEOs at non-federal, short-term general medical and surgical hospitals. Beginning with the 2011 turnover rate, ACHE's calculations exclude known interim CEOs.

Source: American College of Healthcare Executives (2016)

The short- and long-term implications of elevated CEO turnover for healthcare organizations are immense. The immediate impact of frequent executive team transitions is the high cost associated with replacing a senior leader with an external candidate, which is conservatively $50,000 per position.[38] Expectedly, the costs of CEO turnover are sharply higher, according to research reported in Hospitals & Health Networks.[39] Overall, hospitals and health systems can expect to "spend at least two and a half times more than the departing CEO's salary in severance, recruitment expenses, and upping the new CEO's salary," according to the report. Taking into account the senior leadership team turnover that follows an exiting CEO, the total cost of CEO turnover at a single hospital is conservatively $1.5 million. The compounding effects of lagged turnover amongst senior leadership team members is not only costly but also potentially devastating to the hospital's ability to maintain high levels of patient care. Indeed, an ACHE-sponsored study by scholars at the University of Oklahoma[40] concluded that hospital CEO turnover spurs incredibly high turnover of senior leadership team members within one year of the CEO's departure, including 77 percent of chief medical officers, 52 percent of chief operating officers, and 42 percent of chief financial officers. Furthermore, hospital CEO turnover and consequential departures amongst the senior leadership team contributes to an organizational inertia that often halts advances in patient care and quality. According to the survey findings, multiple hospital initiatives and activities are either postponed or halted as a result of the CEO's departure, including strategic planning (30 percent), the development of new services (29 percent), physician recruitment (25 percent), purchasing new equipment (24 percent), and construction projects (23 percent).

Shrinking Supply and Surging Demand for Clinical Leaders: The long-term implications of elevated hospital CEO turnover rates and insufficient investment in succession management capabilities are incredibly challenging for healthcare organizations. Research estimates that nearly 75 percent of healthcare CEOs are planning to retire in the next ten years while 60 percent of chief nursing officers anticipate transferring to new positions in the next four years.[41] Compounding the challenges associated with succession management is a shrinking pool of clinical leadership, particularly nurse and physician leaders, who are essential for facilitating the transition from volume- to value-based healthcare. As reported by the Health Resources and Services Administration[42] and AMN Healthcare,[43] research indicates that 52 percent of registered nurses are older than fifty years of age. Of those nurses over fifty-four years of age, 62 percent are expecting to retire in the next three years. Equally concerning for healthcare executive teams and boards is the steady increase in annual nursing turnover, and the resulting losses in clinical and financial performance. With the highest levels of direct patient contact of all healthcare employees and the increasing importance of patient experience measures that determine reimbursement via value-based purchasing contracts—50 percent by 2016 according to the 2016 AHA Environmental Scan[44]—nurses and nurse leaders play an increasingly critical role in determining a hospital's payments for Medicare and Medicaid patient services. Alarmingly, the financial cost of turnover for a single nurse is substantial—approximately twice the nurse's annual pay while each percentage increase in nurse turnover is estimated to cost the average hospital about $300,000 per year.[45]

The labor market landscape is similarly challenging for physicians and the pool of potential physician leaders. According to the American Medical Association's Physician Masterfile,[46] 42 percent of practicing physicians in the US are fifty-five years or older. Illustrating the critical challenges posed by shifting workforce demographic trends, AMN Healthcare's 2016 Survey of Physicians 55 and Older[47] confirm that 52 percent plan to retire within the next five years while a paltry 23 percent are involved in a succession plan as part of their hospital, medical group, ACO, or other entity. In addition to the diminishing pool of physicians and potential physician leaders, the necessity of physician leadership roles in the ongoing transition toward health system integration will add to the complexities of succession management. Futurescan™ 2015, a national survey of ACHE's CEO members and senior, provider-based members of the Society for Healthcare Strategy and Market Development, reports that between 2015 and 2020 the need for primary care physicians will surge while the role of physicians will evolve toward leadership of team-based care.[48] While the majority of primary care physicians deliver direct patient care, ongoing healthcare reform and the sharp increases in patients covered through managed care products will demand a team-based approach that includes pharmacists, medical assistants, nurses, and health educators. As part of the report, Dr. Michael Hochman predicts that physicians will be able to prioritize their time on leading primary care teams and addressing the most complex medical situations. "Physicians, particularly those with strong leadership skills, will also increasingly be called on to serve in leadership roles and to help improve systems of care," says Hochman. Overall, these trends in physician age demographics and the evolving role of physician leaders will place increasing pressure on healthcare organizations to employ succession management practices, including the assessment of physician leadership potential, physician leadership development, and succession profiles for critical physician leadership roles.

Deficient Executive Team Diversity: The final key industry trend intensifying the business case for succession management and talent development capabilities is the overall lack of executive team diversity in healthcare organizations. The persistent underrepresentation of women and ethnic minorities on healthcare executive teams has driven the American Hospital Association to adopt the elimination of such disparities in the governance and management of hospitals organizations as a core advocacy issue.⁴⁹ Indeed, the disproportionate number of women and ethnic minorities in top executive roles is not unique to the healthcare industry, as the paltry 4 percent of women CEOs of Fortune 500 companies attests. However, the predominance of women throughout the ranks of healthcare organizations and particularly in clinical roles suggests that the career advancement and leadership development practices of our nation's hospitals and health systems stand much to gain for identifying and developing high-potential women and minority leaders.

Many healthcare organizations have sought to implement various strategies for ensuring that their workforce and management teams reflect the gender, ethnic, and cultural backgrounds of their patients and local communities. Regrettably, the overall results have been disappointing. Research reports by ACHE and AHA illustrate the current status and numerous challenges associated with enhancing the diversity of healthcare management teams. In an ACHE survey study assessing the career attainments of men and women executives, the findings revealed that women achieved CEO positions at approximately 50 percent of the rate at which men achieved the top executive role.⁵⁰ When applying survey controls for prior healthcare management experience, approximately 11 percent of women executives achieved CEO positions compared to 22 percent of male survey respondents. The representation of women CEOs in healthcare organizations has worsened since the previous 2006 ACHE survey, which showed women achieving CEO positions at 63 percent of the male rate. Consistent with prior studies, a far lower percentage of women executives (37 percent) aspire to the CEO position compared to 66 percent of male executives. The report asserts that a key explanation for the observed disparities between the career outcomes of men and women is their employer's policies and practices—or lack thereof—that may impede the career advancement of women leaders. For example, only 27 percent of female executives reported that their organization employs succession planning to help promote the careers of women leaders. Similarly, leadership development best practices such as job rotations (13 percent), formal mentoring programs (19 percent), and setting formal targets for promoting women managers and executives (4 percent), are greatly underutilized, according to women executive respondents. Overall, the report concludes that "few organizations have established pro-diversity practices intended to advance the careers of women healthcare managers."

In what has been a glaring and persistent challenge for many healthcare organizations, racial and ethnic minorities are also underrepresented on the executive teams of hospitals and health systems. Conducted by the AHA's Institute for Diversity in Health Management,⁵¹ the results of a 2013 survey of the CEOs of all 5,922 US registered hospitals illustrate the depth of healthcare's diversity challenges. The survey findings show that 31 percent of patients represent a racial or ethnic minority group while only 14 percent of board members and 12 percent of executive leaders are also non-white minorities (figure 1.4).

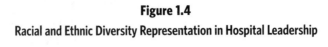

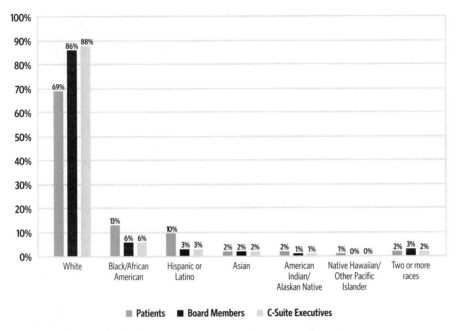

Notes: Survey of the CEOs of the 5,922 US registered hospitals. The response rate was 19 percent (1,109 hospitals), and the survey participants were generally representations of all types of hospitals.

Source: Institute for Diversity in Health Management, Health Research & Education Trust (HRET), and the American Hospital Association (2014)

Furthermore, only 9 percent of CEOs represent a racial or ethnic minority group, which is unchanged from the 2011 survey results. With the notable exception of the chief diversity officer (58 percent), the representation of racial and ethnic minorities across all executive leadership positions (chief operating officer, chief financial officer, chief medical officer, chief nursing officer, and chief HR officer) ranges from 6 to 17 percent. These results are far below the percentage of minority patients and virtually unchanged from the 2011 survey findings. Specific to succession management capabilities, only 27 percent of survey respondents report that their 'hospital has a plan to increase the number of ethnically, culturally, and racially diverse executives serving on the senior executive team.' Along a similar vein, a 2015 ACHE survey examining the career attainments of healthcare executives across racial and ethnic backgrounds revealed that relatively few healthcare organizations are implementing succession management practices to promote executive team diversity.[52] For example, only 47 percent implement formal mentoring programs while just 26 percent have a plan to enhance the ethnic, racial, and cultural diversity of the senior executive team. When asked to list suggestions for best practices that will promote diversity in healthcare management, the executive respondents recommended "ensuring diversity representation on boards and among leadership teams, ensuring succession planning, and having a commitment to develop and promote staff from within."

Leveraging Succession Management Best Practices

While the preceding discussion of healthcare industry trends is alarming, there is now strong evidence that hospitals and health systems can successfully overcome these challenges by implementing best practices in succession planning and talent development. The following chapters provide healthcare executive teams and boards with compelling evidence illustrating the impact of succession management capabilities on hospital performance outcomes, including value-based purchasing metrics (patient satisfaction, Medicare spending per beneficiary episode, etc.), workforce performance (annual turnover for nursing staff, executives, etc.), leadership development (percentage of key leadership roles with at least one 'ready now' candidate, internal/external hiring ratio for executive positions, etc.), and executive team diversity (gender and ethnicity diversity of C-suite and executive positions). In order to provide healthcare practitioners with an accessible, practical, and evidence-based resource, the following chapters illustrate succession management best practices across a diverse mix of organizations. This practical discussion of succession management capabilities includes numerous policies, practices, and programs across a range of healthcare delivery organizations, including public, investor-owned health systems (e.g., Hospital Corporation of America), faith-based health systems (e.g., Trinity Health, Providence St. Joseph Health), private regional health systems (e.g., Intermountain Healthcare, Novant Health), academic health systems (Cleveland Clinic), and government organizations (Parkland Health & Hospital System). Furthermore, the following case study chapters showcase how several health systems are leveraging specific succession management and talent development capabilities to drive a range of strategically-aligned performance outcomes.

Conclusion

Overall, compelling research evidence and several crucial industry trends greatly intensify the business case for succession management capabilities in healthcare organizations. Although healthcare has historically lagged most other industries in terms of making sound talent management investments, the staggering costs and unmitigated risks associated with underdeveloped or nonexistent succession management practices warrant the full attention of executive teams and boards. While the current healthcare environment poses many formidable challenges, succession management and talent development capabilities provide healthcare executives with invaluable tools for overcoming the industry's historic strategic and workforce changes.

CHAPTER 2

Evidence-Based Model of Succession Management & Talent Development Best Practices: Talent Management Capabilities (TMCs)

> *Effective talent management starts at the top, with an engaged, educated, and forward-thinking CEO and board of directors, as well as, an explicit connection between the organization's business strategy and an enabling talent strategy. Once that connection to strategy is established, it becomes clear to senior leaders that an investment in talent is necessary and critical to achieving organizational goals.*
>
> Debra A. Canales
> Executive Vice President and Chief Administrative Officer
> Providence St. Joseph Health

Healthcare executives must address the accelerating transition from volume- to value-based medical care, increasing intensity of hospital mergers and acquisitions, reimbursement degradation, and massive workforce demographic shifts, such as the looming retirement wave across key talent pools. Escalating healthcare reform efforts and evolving incentive structures place healthcare providers under even greater pressure to demonstrate the value of their services via clinical quality performance metrics. Healthcare organizations with best-in-class talent management capabilities report that the most important step in developing exemplary practices is establishing a strong business case for senior leadership teams and the governing board.[53] Given the myriad challenges facing executive teams in the current healthcare environment, the business case for developing talent management capabilities must be clear, compelling, and evidence-based.

To compel healthcare executive teams and board members to view talent development and succession management practices as strategic capabilities, human resources executives must clearly articulate the business case for such investments. The talent management approach—defined as the integrated system of strategies, policies, and programs designed to identify, develop, deploy, and retain leadership talent to achieve strategic objectives and meet future business needs[54]—seeks to ensure healthcare organizations have a sufficient supply of capable leaders to achieve strategic objectives. Research across industry sectors clearly demonstrates that investment in talent management practices yields impressive gains in business performance outcomes, including market value, return on capital, employee productivity, and net income.[55] Regrettably, senior leadership teams and governing boards of healthcare organizations often lack a compelling, data-driven case for talent development and succession management practices which represents a fundamental obstacle for healthcare executives, as the business case for such investments must be communicated to a diverse set of stakeholders—health system management team, regional executives, board members, clinical leaders, medical group and foundation leaders, and others.

Supported by years of qualitative, quantitative, and case-based empirical studies of hospitals and health systems, the talent development and succession management model presented in this chapter comprises eight critical sets of capabilities that distinguish high-performing healthcare organizations. In addition to highlighting key research findings from the development and validation of the best-practices model, dubbed **Talent Management Capabilities (TMC)**, data on the ROI of talent management for healthcare organizations is presented. Specifically, the **TMCs** impact on a range of hospital performance outcomes, including value-based purchasing metrics, annual turnover metrics, executive team diversity, leadership bench strength, and other key performance measures are discussed. Finally, the chapter lays out a set of recommendations for how healthcare executives can leverage the best-practices model to establish the business case for senior leadership teams and board members in your organization.

Talent Management Capabilities (TMC) Model

The **Talent Management Capabilities (TMC)** model, developed on the basis of hundreds of interviews, annual benchmarking surveys, quantitative analyses of hospital performance data, and case studies of hospitals and health systems with exemplary performance outcomes, outlines eight success factors that distinguish succession management best practices in healthcare organizations. While there are many published and commercial talent management models widely available to healthcare organizations,[56] the **TMC** model is distinctive in its focus on provider organizations and the unique contextual challenges faced by hospitals and health systems. Although there is currently scant empirical, evidence-based research on talent management practices in healthcare settings, the **TMC** model has been validated through numerous qualitative, quantitative, and case studies of hundreds of hospitals and health systems across the country.[57] The development and validation of the **TMC** model, supported by research findings, and its eight distinct sets of succession management and talent development practices are described below.

Developing the TMC Model

As the central focus of a multi-year, longitudinal research project, the development of the **TMC** model began with a series of qualitative studies examining succession planning and talent management best practices across national health systems.[58] During the project's early phases, the research focus was learning from those health systems that had recently executed very successful executive transitions (CEO and other senior leadership roles) and/or had achieved stellar reputations for exemplary succession management practices and succession outcomes. These qualitative studies consisted of dozens of semi-structured interviews with hospital and health system CEOs, presidents, chief human resources officers (CHROs), organization development executives, and other seasoned healthcare professionals. Healthcare executives were asked to describe their critical succession management challenges and the primary strategies, practices, and policies that comprise their respective talent management systems. Presented in table 2.1, hundreds of hospitals and health systems from across the spectrum—academic medical centers, faith-based health systems, investor-owned healthcare companies, and community-based hospitals—participated in development of the TMC model.

Based on a comprehensive analysis of the executive interviews and the talent management materials submitted by the participating organizations, a best-practices model of talent development and succession management was developed. Illustrated in figure 2.1, the model includes eight talent management capabilities and their associated best practices.

Table 2.1
Sample of Healthcare Organizations Participating in Research Projects on the Talent Management Capabilities Model*

• Advocate Health Care	• Intermountain Healthcare	• Reading Health System
• Banner Health	• John C. Lincoln Health Network	• SCL Health System
• Beaumont Hospitals	• Kadlec Regional Medical Center	• Scripps Health
• Blanchard Valley Health System	• Kaiser Permanente	• Sentara Healthcare
• Catholic Health Initiatives	• Keck Medicine of USC	• St. Charles Health System
• Centura Health	• Lee Memorial Health System	• St. Joseph Health
• The Children's Hospital of Colorado	• Massachusetts General Hospital	• Sutter Health
• Clarian Health Partners, Inc.	• MedStar Health, Inc.	• Tenet Healthcare
• Cleveland Clinic Health System	• MemorialCare Health System	• Trinity Health
• Covenant Health	• Mountain States Health Alliance	• UCLA Health System
• Dartmouth-Hitchcock	• Novant Health, Inc.	• Univ. of New Mexico Hospitals
• Dignity Health	• Ochsner Health System	• Univ. of Utah Hospitals & Clinics
• Eastern Main Healthcare Systems	• Parkland Health & Hospital System	• Univ. of Washington Medicine
• Geisinger Health System	• Providence St. Joseph Health	• ValleyCare Health System
• Hospital Corporation of America (HCA)		• Vanguard Health
• Indiana University Health		• Yale New Haven Health

*Listed alphabetically.

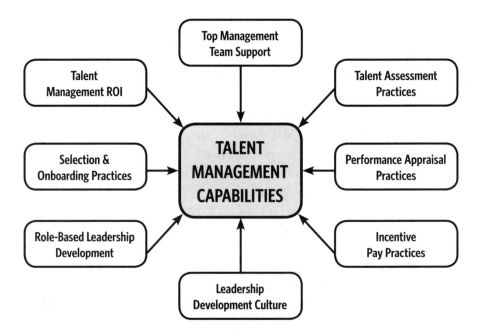

Figure 2.1
Talent Management Capabilities Model

Top Management Team Support: A foundational element of the **TMC** model, **Top Management Team Support**, is the extent to which the senior leadership team formally describes talent management as a strategic priority, actively participates in the talent management process, and communicates a sense of urgency for investing in talent management practices. Healthcare organizations with strong senior leadership support utilize multi-level executives (system, region, facility) in numerous capacities, including formal mentors, advisors, project sponsors, guest speakers, and core faculty for executive development programs. A critical driver of strong senior team support is the organization's ability to clearly articulate the 'business case' for talent management and its role in executing major strategic initiatives. Victor Buzachero, Scripps Health's senior vice president for Innovation, Human Resources, and Performance Management, explains, "We've worked extremely hard to refocus HR around our organization's strategic plans. We've done a good job of communicating and reminding the board that talent management is a part of our strategy, and detailing the leadership that's required for strategic initiatives. From the CEO and board perspectives, when we say we're going to buy a hospital or start a medical school, they're looking at HR and asking 'What's our talent plan for this? How are you going to staff support and lead these strategic initiatives?' It's building the talent to support that part of our strategy." The upcoming case studies of Hospital Corporation of America and Kaiser Permanente both illustrate examples of national health systems that leverage strong top management team support in the development of best-in-class executive development programs for healthcare leaders. The **Top Management Team Support** best practices are listed in table 2.2.

Table 2.2
Talent Management Capabilities (TMC) Model: Top Management Team Support

The Senior Leadership Team:
1. Describes talent management as a strategic priority.
2. Actively participates in the talent review process.
3. Communicates a sense of urgency for investing in talent management practices.
4. Supports the integration of talent management practices into our operations.
5. Teaches in our leadership development programs several times per year.
6. Spends at least 20 percent of its time on mentoring and developing other leaders in our organization.

Talent Assessment Practices: At the core of exemplary succession management capabilities is a rigorous talent review process or set of **Talent Assessment Practices**. These practices include the formal processes through which high-potential leaders and successors to critical leadership roles are identified via standardized assessment instruments, nine-box grids, and other tools. For best-practice healthcare organizations, talent assessment practices are not merely extensions of the annual performance review process. Exemplary talent review practices require targeted time and resources to assessing leadership talent across levels (system, region, and facility), identifying strategically critical positions, and developing succession profiles. Best-practice organizations establish annual talent review processes that are executed across organizational levels and utilize formal assessment tools, including validated assessments of high-potential leadership competencies and nine-box grids, which plot leaders at a given level (system, region, facility) across quadrants according to job performance (y-axis) and leadership potential (x-axis). Central to the process, talent assessment best practices must clearly link assessment results and leadership developmental experiences. Overall, effective talent review processes should balance discussion of high-potential assessment results with thoughtful examination of leadership development opportunities.

Healthcare organizations with exemplary talent assessment practices clearly identify the strategic talent pools for which talent review processes are conducted. For many hospitals and health systems, these positions often include hospital or facility C-suite roles—CEO, COO, CFO, and CNO. For hospitals seeking greater alignment with clinical quality initiatives, as well as physician alignment, CMO and clinical integration positions are also assessed as strategic talent pools. Critically, the board must be fully engaged in the talent review process for the CEO's direct reports and other system or enterprise-wide executives. Mike Helm, former chief human resources officer at Sutter Health, underscores the importance of the board's role in effective succession management. "The Sutter Health board's insights and feedback to me and Pat Fry (former CEO) were very helpful in the development of senior leaders and our leadership development programs, especially for physician leaders," says Helm. "They held us accountable to ensure we were developing successors for the system CEO, a key responsibility for the CEO and the board. There were a few years of planning and work with the board chair and the compensation committee to evaluate successors and ensure that development opportunities were created, ultimately resulting in a smooth transition of leadership." Indeed, Sutter Health's COO Sarah Krevans assumed the CEO role in January 2016, punctuating the conclusion of a very smooth and highly successful CEO succession process. The **Talent Assessment Practices** are listed in table 2.3.

Table 2.3

Talent Management Capabilities (TMC) Model: Talent Assessment Practices

---

1. Formal assessments (e.g., nine-box tools) are utilized to plot employees in key positions according to job performance and leadership potential.
2. Talent review sessions consist of cooperative and collaborative decision-making.
3. Talent review sessions are characterized by authentic, non-politicized dialogue.
4. High-potential employees are identified in the context of our organization's strategic priorities.
5. High-potential employees are formally assessed at front-line levels of management (e.g., supervisor, shift leader, etc.).

Performance Appraisal Practices: Given the critical role of accurate assessment of job performance as part of an effective talent review process, **Performance Appraisal Practices** are the third set of the talent management capabilities. The essence of this capability is a credible and data-driven performance appraisal process that is deemed objective and defensible by managers across levels—as they are most often the leaders who propose talent in their respective region, function, or facility as worthy of high-potential designations—and includes the utilization of objective job performance outcomes in performance appraisal processes. Scripps Health's Victor Buzachero describes the importance of a robust, objective performance appraisal process that contributes to credible high-potential designations. "Our set of high-potential definitions came from an assessment of management performance outcomes around the financial metrics that an individual produces, including patient satisfaction scores, turnover, and employee satisfaction," says Buzachero. "Four years ago, [the high-potential assessment process] was purely a subjective process of a manager's perspective of his or her direct reports' performance and their potential." A system-wide, standardized performance management system that is trusted by managers across levels is a critical success factor for driving effective talent review sessions. "Having credible performance appraisal data completely changes the conversation around the table during talent review sessions," says Herb Vallier, executive vice president and chief human resources officer at Ascension Health, "It's awfully difficult to not see differentiation of talent when you begin to look at job performance measures that are fairly standard across the system. It really changes the conversation about why a given leader is producing these kinds of results." The **Performance Appraisal Practices** are listed in table 2.4.

Table 2.4

Talent Management Capabilities (TMC) Model: Performance Appraisal Practices

1. The performance management system is deemed credible by managers across our organization.
2. The performance management system is deemed credible by employees in key positions.
3. Managers annually receive 360-degree feedback that is development based (not part of their formal performance appraisal).
4. Managers meet with their superiors at least twice per year for a formal discussion of their performance.
5. High-potential employees meet with their superiors at least twice per year for a formal discussion of their performance.

Incentive Pay Practices: This dimension of the **TMC** model consists of pay policies and incentive pay programs for boards, executive teams, and CEOs to incentivize strong support for talent management practices. In addition, this capability includes the organization's efforts to align goal-setting and annual performance review practices with talent management activities. Debra Canales, executive vice president and chief administrative officer at Providence St. Joseph Health and a veteran of the healthcare industry, describes the importance of linking talent objectives directly to an organization's strategic objectives, and of using pay practices and incentives to sustain focus. "It starts with a CEO and board of directors who understand that having a supply of talent leaders and clinicians is fundamental to delivering the organization's strategy and goals," says Canales, "once that connection is established, supporting talent management practices and initiatives can be developed along with quantitative and qualitative measures. Organizational or individual incentives can be designed to support and sustain desired talent outcomes. In the end, it all gets back to the notion that 'you get what you measure.'" Ascension Health's Herb Vallier also notes the importance of leveraging incentive goals for driving the attention and focus of management teams on succession management outcomes. "We've made succession planning activities part of the incentive goals that get the process put in place. We've had our first outcome goals that have paid out for having accomplished these activities as well. There's been a little bit of skin in the game and the expectation that folks will deliver on these activities," says Vallier. The **Incentive Pay Practices** are listed in table 2.5.

Leadership Development Culture: An unmistakable characteristic of organizations with highly effective succession management practices is the establishment of a culture that values fairness, enforces process transparency, and seeks to maximize employees' leadership potential. **The Leadership**

Table 2.5
Talent Management Capabilities (TMC) Model: Incentive Pay Practices

---

1. Performance appraisal practices incentivize managers to support talent management practices.
2. The incentive pay structure for our senior leadership team incentivizes support for talent management practices.
3. The board of directors advocates an incentive pay structure that incentivizes CEO support of talent management practices.

Development Culture best practices consist of formal programs and policies that ensure employees and their managers view the high-potential designation and talent review processes as fair, equitable, and transparent. Practically, these best practices emphasize the consistency of communication to business units and employees regarding the outcomes of the talent review process. The predominant best practice of leading health systems is an *implicit* designation whereby managers communicate high-potential status to candidates via advanced development plans comprised of exclusive learning and development opportunities, including invitations to leadership academies, stretch assignments, cross-divisional assignments, and other high-profile development opportunities. Emphasizing the importance of continuing development and enhancement of key leadership competencies and deemphasizing high-potential status is an approach sharply in contrast with organizations that either explicitly tell high-potential leaders of their status or those that adopt a 'black box' approach whereby high-potential designations and related successor profiles are cloaked in secrecy. Robert Sachs, former vice president of Learning and Development at Kaiser Permanente,[*] describes the delicate balance of achieving transparency and consistent communication of high-potential designations across a national hospital network. "We don't give [our high potentials] the grid. We don't tell them 'you're in box number six or nine.' We give our managers scripts that outline having a conversation…'we see value and potential in what we've witnessed in your contributions and where we see your skill set,'" says Sachs.

Strongly related to the policy of implicitly communicating the results of talent review processes is the best practice of providing managers with targeted training to properly discuss talent review outcomes with their direct reports.

---

*Robert Sachs retired from Kaiser Permanente on January 1, 2016.

For highly effective healthcare organizations, this training consists of arming managers with scripts or discussion protocols that guide the post-talent review discussions with direct reports. Deanna Kenard, former senior vice president and chief human resources officer at Methodist Health System, underscores the importance of ensuring a strong leadership development culture through targeting management training on talent conversations. "We provide our executives with scripts to follow whether they're having a conversation with a high potential or a limited performer or a solid performer," says Kenard. "The protocols require that there is some feedback and communication back to individuals with regard to their level assessment." The Leadership Development Culture practices are listed in table 2.6.

Table 2.6
Talent Management Capabilities (TMC) Model: Leadership Development Culture

1. Employees view the process for designating high potentials as fair and equitable.
2. Managers across our organization view the process for designating high potentials as fair and equitable.
3. Our organization seeks to achieve transparency with the high-potential designation process.
4. Our organizational culture de-emphasizes the status associated with high-potential designations.
5. Managers are trained to formally communicate high-potential designations to employees.

Role-Based Leadership Development: A hallmark of exemplary talent management systems is the range and quality of leadership development experiences that are assigned to high-potential leaders across management levels. The leadership development strategy focuses on identifying role-based job experiences in which high-potential leaders complete assignments in new functions, business units, or regions. Highly effective role-based leadership development experiences include job rotation assignments and new roles or major projects that require high-potential leaders to adopt a broader perspective on the health system by serving in a different function, region, or business unit. Debbie Kiser, vice president of Learning and Development at Novant Health, notes the importance of linking talent review discussions with stretch assignments that place high-potential leaders in unfamiliar roles. "We sit down and look at the projects and we try to move people as far away from their day-to-day work as we can so that they are put on project teams that they may never have even been exposed before," says Kiser. "Those are indeed stretch-work assignments. I think the difference with high potentials for us is trying to find specific assignments to help that leader grow, change, and develop. More frequently now than our system has ever seen, it's taking them out of their role and placing them somewhere else, even if it's in a temporary assignment. The talent review process is forcing that development conversation to happen."

Summarizing Kaiser Permanente's broader leadership development philosophy, former vice president of Learning and Development Robert Sachs states, "Our belief is that an awful lot of leadership development happens as a result of experiences. We try to develop job rotations and identify experiences that will give people an opportunity to broaden their perspectives, develop new skills, and get some different insights. It could be doing work on a national initiative or project if you're a regional person. If you're a national person, it could be trying to do some more intensive work in a region. We've had a high-potential leader who was in healthcare delivery operations and was seen as someone who could potentially become a regional president, but didn't have any sales and marketing background. So that person began to attend some of the regular meetings with our sales and marketing teams in order to understand some of the issues of pricing, underwriting, and distribution. We try to create those sorts of development opportunities and experiences for people." Kaiser Permanente's Strategic Leadership Program, described in chapter 6, expertly leverages 'strategic projects' as role-based development experiences by requiring high-potential leaders to design and execute a project that addresses one or more pillars of the health system's national strategy.

As part of a Role-Based Leadership Development strategy, leading healthcare organizations develop internal leadership academies that require participants to complete team-based, action learning projects. For many leading healthcare systems, including Sutter Health, Henry Ford Health System, Cleveland Clinic, and Trinity Health, participation in an internally developed healthcare leadership academy is an ideal development opportunity for high-potential leaders.[59] Leadership academy cohorts are assembled to reflect multiple forms of diversity, including gender, ethnicity, management level, and both clinical and administrative backgrounds. Consisting of approximately thirty-five professionals, the cohorts are organized into teams and assigned action learning projects that address critical, organization-wide challenges or opportunities. Each project is sponsored by an executive team member whose operational focus is closest to the project topic. In some cases, board members also get involved in the sponsorship of action learning projects. The results and recommendations of the action learning teams are presented directly to the top management team for review and potential implementation. The focused attention from the top management team sends a clear message to high-potential leaders about the importance of the action learning projects to the health system and to their careers. The Role-Based Leadership Development best practices are listed in table 2.7.

Table 2.7
Talent Management Capabilities (TMC) Model: Role-Based Leadership Development

1. Our organizational culture encourages managers to 'release' high-potential employees for developmental assignments elsewhere in the hospital or across our health system.
2. Our organization employs job rotations whereby leaders are re-assigned on at least a half-time basis to temporary roles for skill development.
3. Our organization employs an action learning program in which high-potential employees learn new skills by completing team projects that address critical, organization-wide problems and reflecting on their experiences in a facilitated session.
4. Our organizational culture discourages talent hoarding—managers keeping high-potential employees from leaving their current positions.

Selection & Onboarding Practices: This element of the **TMC** model includes practices aimed at selecting and socializing leaders into critical leadership roles. **Selection & Onboarding Practices** include the quality and frequency with which managers and executives who are selected into key leadership roles, both internal and external candidates, complete a formal onboarding program. These practices also include selection processes for key leadership positions that consist of behaviorally based interviews that are aligned with key leadership competencies. This practice is critical in healthcare organizations given the importance of affirming a candidate's readiness for advancement and interest in leadership roles, particularly for clinical leadership positions. Best practices include the development of formal onboarding programs for new leaders that target a range of leadership transition challenges across levels (employees, leaders, and executives). Exemplary onboarding programs for leaders consist of activities designed to facilitate clear successes or 'early wins' in the first year, including a comprehensive stakeholder analysis, 90-day transition plan with clear milestones and performance outcomes, and new leader assimilation programs that provide newly placed executives and their direct reports with a facilitated team-building and agenda-setting experience in the first three months. Jim Dunn, executive vice president and chief talent officer at Parkland Health & Hospital System, affirms the central role of onboarding practices for contributing to 'early wins' and preventing executive derailment. "We invest a lot to give our leaders what they need to do the job effectively by providing them the necessary tools to assess and develop their teams from all viewpoints," says Dunn. "Onboarding has a huge payoff for us as it directly impacts first year productivity and reduces turnover." Chapter 3 offers a detailed case study of Cleveland Clinic's multi-phased executive onboarding program and its impact on newly placed executives' job performance, productivity, and engagement. The **Selection & Onboarding Practices** are listed in table 2.8.

Table 2.8
Talent Management Capabilities (TMC) Model: Selection & Onboarding Practices

1. Managers hired from outside our organization complete a formal onboarding program (a systematic learning and socialization process lasting at least three months).
2. Employees promoted into managerial positions or roles that are new to our organization complete a formal onboarding program.
3. The distinctiveness of our organization is made clear to external candidates for key positions.
4. The selection process for managerial positions involves behaviorally based interviews linked to leadership competencies.

Talent Management ROI: The final element of the **TMC** model, **Talent Management ROI**, consists of capabilities for utilizing clear metrics and ROI analyses to evaluate talent management practices and ensure that such data are reviewed by the governing board, leadership teams across the health system, and other key stakeholders. Best practices include the development of a talent management scorecard that comprises several critical metrics, including the ratio of internal/external hires for executive-level (VP and above) roles; percentage of key leadership roles with at least one 'ready now' internal candidate; turnover of high-potential leaders; and executive team gender and ethnic diversity. For example, Intermountain Healthcare's dashboard for assessing talent management practices across their twenty-two hospitals includes leadership development metrics (talent pool depth for directors, executives, and physician leaders; and Gallup's 'Change Leadership Index' as part of the annual employee engagement survey); succession management metrics (internal/external placement executive rate; leadership bench strength; high-performer/high-potential leader turnover; movement of high-performer/high-potential leaders across the system); and employee engagement metrics (annual employee engagement score for leadership development program alumni compared to all managers). Illustrated by Intermountain Healthcare's scorecard, the alignment of talent management metrics with the health system's leadership development strategy and consistent communication of these metrics to leadership teams and the board represents a critical capability.

Central to the overarching theme of this book—healthcare organizations transitioning toward greater evidence-based decisions with respect to investment in succession management capabilities—each of the health systems showcased in the following chapters adopts a rigorous approach to evaluating the impact of talent management practices. Cleveland Clinic evaluates the impact of its executive onboarding program across multiple job performance and leadership development metrics. The effectiveness of Sutter Health's succession management practices is illustrated by several core metrics, including internal/external executive placement rate, leadership bench strength, and executive team diversity. The strategic impact of Hospital Corporation of America's (HCA) Executive Development Program is measured by analysis of the company's hospital C-suite turnover, internal/external placement rate, and executive team diversity. Finally, an evaluation of Kaiser Permanente's Strategic Leadership Program is evaluated by assessing annual turnover, promotions, and performance reviews of program alumni. The **Talent Management ROI** best practices are listed in table 2.9.

Table 2.9

Talent Management Capabilities (TMC) Model: Talent Management ROI

1. Our organization utilizes metrics and ROI analyses to evaluate the effectiveness of our talent management practices.
2. Our organization's talent management metrics are reviewed by the governing board.
3. Our organization's talent management metrics are clearly communicated to management teams across the hospital or health system.

Validating the TMC Model

The next phase of the longitudinal research project consisted of refining the **TMC** model through quantitative, survey-based studies that establish the impact of talent management capabilities on a range of workforce and hospital performance metrics. The process of validating the **TMC** model involved surveying national samples of hospitals and health systems to assess the extent to which succession management and talent development capabilities drive business outcomes. The first step in this project phase was developing a survey instrument to assess the **TMC** best practices and also collect relevant workforce and hospital performance metrics. The following sections describe the **TMC** validation survey, the sample of participating healthcare organizations, and key survey findings.

Healthcare Talent Management Survey

Designed to measure the talent development and succession management best practices that comprise the **TMC** model and a series of hospital and workforce performance metrics, the **Healthcare Talent Management Survey** was administered to a large national sample of hospital and health system executives in 2013 and 2015.[60] The survey's purpose was to understand the degree to which **TMCs** are practiced in healthcare organizations and the impact of these practices across a range of critical performance outcomes. Healthcare executives rated how often the **TMCs** are practiced at their respective organization on a Likert-type scale consisting of (1) not at all, (2) rarely, (3) sometimes, (4) usually, and (5) always. Statistical tests for the reliability of each dimension of the **TMC** model (Cronbach alpha results) and the factor structure of the overall instrument (factor analysis results) demonstrated strong support for the stability and construct validity of the survey.[†] Next, the executives provided a series of hospital performance metrics and workforce outcomes. The hospital performance data were cross-referenced with publicly available sources, including the websites and most recent annual reports of the participating organizations.

Performance Metrics

The selection of performance metrics for the **Healthcare Talent Management Survey** was based on two key criteria. First, the key findings from the preceding qualitative phase of the research project were considered. Specifically, the workforce and hospital performance metrics that leading health systems utilize to evaluate the efficacy of their talent management practices were included in the survey. Second, a review of the existing research on evaluation metrics for talent management programs identified a set of key metrics for the survey.[61] The following summarizes the four final sets of performance metrics in the survey:

1. *Value-Based Purchasing Metrics:* These hospital performance metrics include the four domain scores (Clinical Process of Care, Patient Experience of Care, Outcome, and Efficiency) as reported by the Centers for Medicare and Medicaid Services (CMS). The Patient Experience of Care domain score is comprised of the Hospital Consumer Assessment of

---

[†] *The 2015 survey's factor analysis results and Cronbach alpha reliability analyses are available in the full report of survey findings at http://www.grovesconsultinggroup.com/wp-content/uploads/2015/07/ResearchReport.TalentMgmtPractices.20151.pdf.*

Healthcare Providers and Systems Survey (HCAHPS) results. A full description of all four domain scores is provided on the CMS website.[‡]

2. *Workforce Performance Metrics:* These metrics include Employee Productivity (net patient revenue/FTEs); and Annual Turnover rates for executives (VP and above), nursing staff, and high-potential employees.

3. *Leadership Development Metrics:* These metrics include Leadership Bench Strength; Internal/External Executive Placement (percentage of open executive, VP level and above positions filled by internal candidates); Annual Executive Searches (total number of executive searches per medical center); and Annual Executive Search Costs (total estimated fees for executive searches per medical center).

4. *Leadership Diversity Metrics:* The final set of metrics include Executive Gender Diversity (percentage of all executive, VP-level and above positions occupied by women); C-Suite Gender Diversity (percentage of all C-suite positions occupied by women); Executive Ethnicity Diversity (percentage of all executive, VP-level and above positions occupied by ethnic minorities); and C-Suite Ethnicity Diversity (percentage of C-suite positions occupied by ethnic minorities).

Sample Characteristics

The 2015 **Healthcare Talent Management Survey** was administered to a diverse, national sample of executives at hospitals and health systems. The sample was specified according to *Modern Healthcare*'s list of the 200 Largest Healthcare Systems by annual revenue, the Top 100 Integrated Health Networks, and the 100 Top Hospitals. In partnership with the American Hospital Association (AHA) and Witt/Kieffer, Inc., the names and e-mail addresses of the top HR officer at each organization were collected. Due to invalid e-mail addresses and outdated records (e.g., retirements), the final sample size for survey administration was 376. In response to an e-mail invitation with a link to the survey, 142 executives participated in the study on behalf of their respective organization for a response rate of 38.8 percent.

Overall, the survey participants comprised large hospitals and health systems with an average of 16,741 full-time employees, $2.58 billion in net patient

---

[‡] *Value-based purchasing metrics for the survey participants were obtained at the Centers for Medicare and Medicaid website: https://data.medicare.gov/data/hospital-compare.*

revenue, twenty medical centers, and 2,410 licensed beds for Fiscal Year 2015. Community and independent medical centers (30 percent) and multi-hospital health systems (32 percent) represented the most common types of healthcare delivery organizations in the sample, while academic medical centers or health systems (19 percent) and specialty hospitals (10 percent) were also represented. The ownership status of the survey participants included 64 percent not-for-profit (non-governmental), 19.5 percent for-profit (investor/privately owned), and 16.5 percent public (federal, state, or local government or institution). As illustrated in figure 2.2, the majority of survey respondents consisted of chief HR officers (29 percent), vice presidents of HR (20 percent), and chief administrative officers (16 percent).

Figure 2.2
Position Title of Executive Participants in Healthcare Talent Management Survey 2015

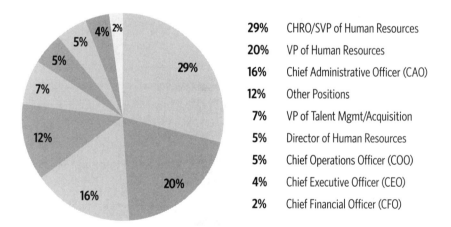

%	Position
29%	CHRO/SVP of Human Resources
20%	VP of Human Resources
16%	Chief Administrative Officer (CAO)
12%	Other Positions
7%	VP of Talent Mgmt/Acquisition
5%	Director of Human Resources
5%	Chief Operations Officer (COO)
4%	Chief Executive Officer (CEO)
2%	Chief Financial Officer (CFO)

Survey Results: Utilization of TMCs in Healthcare Organizations

To what extent do hospitals and health systems utilize the **Talent Management Capabilities (TMCs)**? Illustrated in figure 2.3, the survey results demonstrate that **Top Management Team Support** and **Selection & Onboarding** were the most frequently utilized **TMCs** as measured by the summed percentage of 'always' or 'usually' responses. By comparison, **Incentive Pay Practices**, **Leadership Development Culture**, and **Role-Based Leadership Development** were the least frequently utilized **TMCs** as measured by summed percentage of 'rarely' or 'not at all' responses. The remaining **TMCs—Performance Appraisal Practices**, **Talent Assessment Practices**, and **Talent Management ROI**—were inconsistently utilized with the 'sometimes' rating garnering the highest percentage response. The utilization of talent management practices in healthcare organizations can be grouped according to high-, moderate-, and low-utilization, as described below.

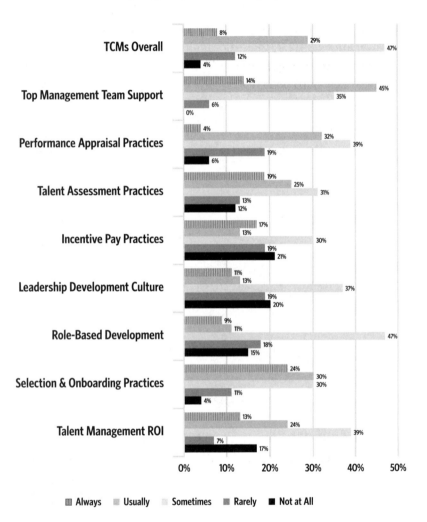

Figure 2.3
Utilization of Talent Management Capabilities (TMCs) for Participating Hospitals & Health Systems

High-Utilization TMCs: Overall, the executives reported high utilization of **Top Management Team Support** practices. Displayed in table 2.10, the vast majority of survey respondents reported that their senior leadership team 'always' or 'usually' describes talent management as a strategic priority for their organization. Similarly, 74 percent of respondents stated that their senior leadership team actively participates in their organization's talent management process. By contrast, only 35 percent of healthcare organizations reported that their senior leadership team 'always' or 'usually' spends at least 20 percent of its time on mentoring and developing other leaders. The survey results also demonstrated that healthcare organizations prioritize **Selection & Onboarding Practices**. Overall, 81 percent of respondents reported that the selection process for managerial positions 'always' or 'usually' involves behaviorally-based interviews linked to leadership competencies. Finally, just over half (52 percent) of organizations require employees promoted into managerial positions to complete a formal onboarding program while only 47 percent 'always' or 'usually' have externally hired leaders complete a formal onboarding program.

Table 2.10
Talent Management Capabilities Highly Utilized by Healthcare Organizations

Talent Management Capability	Utilization Frequency		
	Always or Usually	Sometimes	Rarely or Not at All
Top Management Team Support			
The senior leadership team describes talent management as a strategic priority.	90%	6%	4%
The senior leadership team actively participates in the talent review process.	74%	22%	4%
The senior leadership team communicates a sense of urgency for investing in talent management practices.	67%	27%	6%
The senior leadership team supports the integration of talent management practices into our operations.	65%	31%	4%
The senior leadership team teaches in our leadership development programs several times per year.	53%	14%	33%
The senior leadership team spends at least 20 percent of its time on mentoring and developing other leaders in our organization.	35%	36%	29%
Selection & Onboarding Practices			
The selection process for managerial positions involves behaviorally based interviews linked to leadership competencies.	81%	15%	4%
The distinctiveness of our organization is made clear to external candidates for key positions.	73%	18%	9%
Employees promoted into managerial positions or roles that are new to our organization complete a formal onboarding program.	52%	24%	24%
Managers hired from outside our organization complete a formal onboarding program.	47%	20%	33%

Moderate-Utilization TMCs: Healthcare organizations reported inconsistent utilization of **Talent Assessment Practices, Performance Appraisal Practices**, and **Talent Management ROI**. Presented in table 2.11, most respondents described talent review sessions as characterized by authentic, non-politicized dialogue and as consisting of cooperative and collaborative decision-making. By a wide margin, the least utilized talent assessment practices were the utilization of formal assessments to plot employees according to job performance and leadership potential and the formal assessment of high-potential employees at front-line management levels. Executives also reported inconsistent utilization of **Performance Appraisal Practices** for managing leadership talent. Sixty-four percent of executives reported that their organization's managers do not receive 360-degree feedback that is development based while 34 percent stated that their high-potential employees do not regularly meet with their supervisors for a formal discussion of their performance. Similarly, only 46 percent of executives reported that their organization's talent management metrics are reviewed by the governing board. Finally, just 35 percent of respondents stated that their organizations 'rarely' or 'never' utilize metrics and ROI analyses to evaluation the efficacy of talent management practices.

Low-Utilization TMCs: The **TMCs** with the lowest utilization rates across the participating hospitals and health systems included **Incentive Pay Practices, Leadership Development Culture**, and **Role-Based Leadership Development**. Displayed in table 2.12, half of the executives reported that their boards 'rarely' or 'never' advocate an incentive pay structure that incentivizes CEO support of talent management practices. Similarly, 45 percent of executives stated that their senior leadership team's incentive pay structure does not incentivize support for talent management practices. Across all **TMCs**, **Leadership Development Culture** practices were utilized the least frequently. Only 28 percent of executives described their employees as viewing the process for designating high potentials as 'always' or 'usually' fair and equitable, while 43 percent reported their organization 'rarely' or 'never' seeks to achieve transparency with the high-potential designation process. Finally, executives reported a mix of utilizing **Role-Based Development Practices**. Close to one-third of executives stated that their organizations 'rarely' or 'never' utilize action learning programs to development high-potential employees and other critical talent pools. While 44 percent of respondents described their organization as generally supportive of allowing their high-potential employees to seek developmental assignments elsewhere across the organization, a strong majority reported that they 'rarely' or 'never' use job rotations for skill development.

Table 2.11
Talent Management Capabilities Moderately Utilized by Healthcare Organizations

Talent Management Capability	Utilization Frequency		
	Always or Usually	Sometimes	Rarely or Not at All
Talent Assessment Practices			
Talent review sessions are characterized by authentic, non-politicized dialogue.	66%	21%	13%
Talent review sessions consist of cooperative and collaborative decision-making.	63%	19%	18%
High-potential employees are identified in the context of our organization's strategic priorities.	54%	22%	24%
Formal assessments (e.g., nine-box tools) are utilized to plot employees in key positions according to job performance and leadership potential.	46%	8%	46%
High-potential employees are formally assessed at front-line levels of management (e.g., supervisor, shift leader, etc.).	36%	21%	43%
Performance Appraisal Practices			
The performance management system is deemed credible by managers across our organization.	65%	20%	15%
The performance management system is deemed credible by employees in key positions.	62%	23%	15%
Managers meet with their superiors at least twice per year for a formal discussion of their performance.	45%	34%	21%
High-potential employees meet with their superiors at least twice per year for a formal discussion of their performance.	41%	25%	33%
Managers annually receive 360-degree feedback that is development based (not part of their formal performance appraisal).	17%	19%	64%
Talent Management ROI			
Our organization's talent management metrics are reviewed by the governing board.	46%	28%	26%
Our organization utilizes metrics and ROI analyses to evaluate the effectiveness of our talent management practices.	37%	28%	35%
Our organization's talent management metrics are clearly communicated to management teams across the hospital or health system.	32%	35%	33%

Table 2.12

Talent Management Capabilities Minimally Utilized by Healthcare Organizations

Talent Management Capability	Utilization Frequency		
	Always or Usually	Sometimes	Rarely or Not at All
Role-Based Leadership Development			
Our organizational culture discourages talent hoarding—managers keeping high-potential employees from leaving their current positions.	48%	33%	19%
Our organizational culture encourages managers to 'release' high-potential employees for developmental assignments elsewhere in the hospital or across our health system.	43%	25%	31%
Our organization employs an action learning program in which high-potential employees learn new skills by completing team projects that address critical, organization-wide problems and reflecting on their experiences in a facilitated session.	41%	28%	31%
Our organization employs job rotations whereby leaders are re-assigned on at least a half-time basis to temporary roles for skill development.	13%	20%	67%
Leadership Development Culture			
Managers across our organization view the process for designating high potentials as fair and equitable.	41%	24%	35%
Our organization seeks to achieve transparency with the high-potential designation process.	37%	20%	43%
Our organizational culture de-emphasizes the status associated with high-potential designations.	30%	28%	42%
Employees view the process for designating high potentials as fair and equitable.	28%	24%	35%
Managers are trained to formally communicate high-potential designations to employees.	26%	20%	54%
Incentive Pay Practices			
The incentive pay structure for our senior leadership team incentivizes support for talent management practices.	44%	11%	45%
Performance appraisal practices incentivize managers to support talent management practices.	41%	38%	21%
The board of directors advocates an incentive pay structure that incentivizes CEO support of talent management practices.	35%	15%	50%

Survey Results: Impact of TMCs on Performance Metrics

What do healthcare organizations gain by executing talent development and succession management best practices? The survey findings indicate that **TMCs** strongly impact numerous hospital and workforce performance metrics. Correlational and hierarchical regression analyses demonstrate that **TMCs** are significantly associated with both hospital and workforce performance outcomes.§ To illustrate these results, the following section presents a series of bar graphs comparing the performance metrics of healthcare organizations with high **TMC** utilization (survey respondents scoring at least one standard deviation above the mean **TMC** score for all organizations), to those with low **TMC** utilization (survey respondents scoring at least one standard deviation below the mean **TMC** score for all organizations). These illustrations allow for a more direct comparison of the business performance metrics for healthcare organizations with exemplary talent management practices (high) versus those with less-developed practices (low). The impact of the **TMCs** across each set of hospital and workforce performance metrics is presented below.

Value-Based Purchasing Metrics: Overall, the **TMCs** are strongly associated with the value-based purchasing performance metrics reported by the Centers for Medicare and Medicaid Services (CMS). Illustrated in figure 2.4, hospitals and health systems with high **TMC** utilization reported significantly stronger outcomes across the value-based purchasing performance domains. The **TMCs** demonstrated the strongest relationship with the Efficiency Domain, which assesses Medicare Spending-per-Beneficiary (MSPB-1). This important hospital efficiency metric assesses payments for services provided to a beneficiary during a spending-per-beneficiary episode in which the payments are standardized and adjusted to account for variation in geographic costs and variation in patient health status. Higher scores on this standardized metric indicate greater Medicare spending per patient or beneficiary. Likewise, the Medicare Spending-per-Episode metric assesses the mean payment for services or claims during the hospital's Medicare Spending-per-Beneficiary (MSPB) episodes. These mean Medicare payment amounts are price-standardized to remove the effect of geographic differences and add-on payments for indirect medical education (IME) and disproportionate share hospitals (DSH).

---

§ *The results from correlational and hierarchical regression analyses are available at http://www.grovesconsultinggroup.com/wp-content/uploads/2015/07/ResearchReport.TalentMgmtPractices.20151.pdf.*

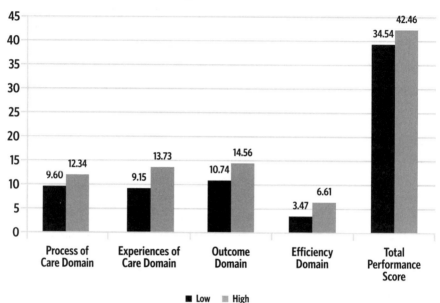

Figure 2.4
Impact of Talent Management Capabilities (TMCs) on Value-Based Purchasing Performance Domains

Presented in figure 2.5, hospital organizations with high utilization of **TMCs** overall reported overall spending of $17,493 per Medicare episode compared to $20,706 for those organizations with low TMC utilization.

Further analysis of the Experience of Care domain, and specifically HCAHPS survey scores, indicate that several **TMCs** are critical for driving patient satisfaction. Figure 2.6 illustrates the impact of each **TMC** on the overall HCAHPS score. Hospital organizations with high **TMC** utilization reported a 71 percent overall HCAHPS score compared to 64 percent for those organizations with low TMC utilization. **Performance Appraisal Practices**, **Talent Assessment Practices**, and **Selection & Onboarding Practices** were the most important drivers of higher patient satisfaction scores.

Workforce Metrics: Summarized in table 2.13, healthcare organizations with high **TMC** utilization reported an employee productivity ratio of $173,484 (net patient revenue per FTE) compared to $110,748 for survey participants with low **TMC** utilization. The $62,736 difference in net patient revenue per FTE represents a 56.6 percent improvement that is associated with consistent utilization of talent development and succession management best practices. The survey results were similarly salient for annual executive and nursing turnover. Hospitals and health systems with high **TMC** utilization reported an

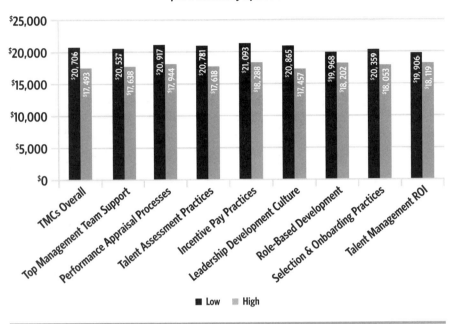

Figure 2.5
Impact of Talent Management Capabilities (TMCs) on Mean Medicare Spending per Beneficiary Episode

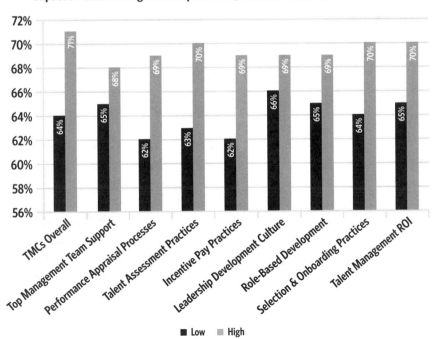

Figure 2.6
Impact of Talent Management Capabilities (TMCs) on Overall HCAHPS Score

average 3.33 percent turnover for executive-level positions (VP or higher), which sharply contrasted with a 19.95 percent turnover rate for organizations with inconsistent talent management practices. **Importantly, Talent Assessment Practices** was the most significant driver of the sharply lower annual executive turnover rates.

Table 2.13
Impact of Talent Management Capabilities (TMC) on Workforce, Leadership Development & Leadership Diversity Metrics

Performance Metrics	High TMC Utilization	Low TMC Utilization	Primary TMC Drivers
Workforce Metrics			
Nursing Turnover	8.74%	13.61%	▪ Selection & Onboarding Practices
Executive Turnover	3.33%	19.95%	▪ Talent Assessment Practices
Employee Productivity	$173,484/FTE	$110,748/FTE	▪ Incentive Pay Practices
Leadership Development Metrics			
Leadership Bench Strength	52%	7%	▪ Selection & Onboarding Practices
Internal/External Executive Placement Rate	68%	21%	▪ Talent Assessment Practices
Annual Executive Search Costs/ Medical Center	$13,696	$129,333	▪ Selection & Onboarding Practices
Leadership Diversity Metrics			
C-Suite Gender Diversity	52%	24%	▪ Selection & Onboarding Practices
C-Suite Ethnic Diversity	43%	12%	▪ Top Management Team Support
Executive Gender Diversity	54%	43%	▪ Top Management Team Support
Executive Ethnic Diversity	32%	17%	▪ Top Management Team Support

Healthcare organizations with high **TMC** utilization reported an average 8.74 percent annual nursing turnover rate compared to 13.61 percent for hospitals and health systems with low **TMC** utilization. Overall, this difference represents a 36 percent lower annual nurse turnover rate for healthcare organizations with advanced succession management capabilities. Across all **TMCs, Selection & Onboarding Practices** was the most significant driver of lower annual nursing turnover. Research indicates that the total estimated cost of nursing turnover, including hiring costs, training costs, and lost productivity, is *conservatively* $31,486 per nurse.[62] When applied to the survey's sample of healthcare organizations (mean FTEs = 16,741) and assuming that nurses comprise 20 percent of all employees, the 36 percent reduction in annual nursing turnover for high-performing hospital systems represents a total annual cost savings of $5.13 million. The annual nursing turnover costs for healthcare organizations with high **TMC** utilization was $9.21 million (293 new nurses) compared to $14.35 million for organizations with low **TMC** utilization (456 new nurses).

Leadership Development Metrics: Presented previously in table 2.13, healthcare organizations with highly developed **TMCs** reported a mean leadership bench strength metric of 52 percent compared to only 7 percent for hospitals and health systems with weak or inconsistent **TMCs**. Leadership bench strength is a critical performance outcome for assessing the health and long-term viability of leadership teams.[63] Across all **TMCs**, **Selection & Onboarding Practices** were the most important drivers of high leadership bench strength for the participating hospitals and health systems. For internal/external executive placement rate, which assesses the percentage of executive positions (VP and above) staffed by internal candidates, organizations with high **TMC** utilization reported an average of 68 percent compared to just 21 percent for survey participants with low **TMC** utilization. Consistent with the survey results for executive turnover, **Talent Assessment Practices** was the strongest driver of high internal/external executive placement rates. Finally, the overall number and costs of executive searches were driven by high utilization of **TMCs**. Survey participants with highly developed **TMCs** realized only $13,696 in annual executive search costs per medical center, while organizations with weak or inconsistent **TMCs** reported $129,333 in such costs.

Leadership Diversity Metrics: Summarized above in table 2.13, survey participants with high **TMC** utilization reported that 54 percent of all executive positions (VPs and above) were occupied by women while 32 percent of such positions were occupied by ethnic minorities. In sharp contrast, hospitals and health systems with inconsistent **TMCs** reported that women occupied only 43 percent of executive positions while ethnic minorities occupied just 17 percent of such positions. For C-suite positions, these differences were even more pronounced. Organizations with high **TMC** utilization reported that 52 percent of C-suite executives were women while 43 percent were ethnic minorities. These leadership diversity metrics were much worse for organizations with low **TMC** utilization—only 24 percent of C-suite positions were held by women and just 12 percent by ethnic minorities. The **TMCs** that demonstrated the greatest impact on enhancing gender and ethnic diversity amongst C-suite and executive staff were **Top Management Team Support** and **Selection & Onboarding Practices**.

Conclusion

The general lack of compelling research supporting the business case for succession management capabilities—particularly in the current era of healthcare reform and increasing focus on value-oriented performance metrics—remains a critical obstacle to sustained investment in such practices. Nonetheless, healthcare organizations must demonstrate far greater accuracy in identifying and developing emerging leadership talent much earlier in their careers due to rapidly aging senior management teams, increasing executive turnover, and limited leadership bench strength to replace the coming retirement wave.

This chapter presented a model of talent management best practices derived from years of qualitative, quantitative, and case-based studies of hospitals and health systems. The **Talent Management Capabilities** model, distinctive in its focus on healthcare organizations and the unique contextual challenges faced by healthcare executives, outlined eight sets of practices that distinguish high-performing hospitals and health systems. National benchmarking studies offer strong empirical evidence for the impact of the **TMCs** across a series of hospital and workforce performance outcomes, including value-based purchasing, workforce, leadership development, and leadership diversity metrics. By leveraging the research findings presented in this chapter, healthcare executives may benchmark and enhance their organization's succession management capabilities while ensuring strong alignment with system-wide strategic initiatives.

CHAPTER 3

Assimilating New Leaders in an Era of Unprecedented Change: Executive Onboarding at Cleveland Clinic

> *In healthcare today, the environment isn't just changing—it's transforming at a rapid pace. We need leaders, whether internal promotes, transfers, or external hires, to quickly master their new roles. The cost of a delayed onboarding, or worst yet, failure of a new executive hire, can be crippling to an organization's success. Our executive onboarding process is key to us continuing to meet our growth needs and exceed our goals.*
>
> Joseph Cabral
> Chief Human Resource Officer (CHRO)[**]
> Cleveland Clinic

Cleveland Clinic

Cleveland Clinic is an internationally renowned, 7.9 billion-dollar healthcare system comprised of the Cleveland Clinic, nine regional hospitals, eighteen family health and ambulatory surgery centers, and facilities in Ohio, Florida, Nevada,

---

[**] *Joseph Cabral served as Cleveland Clinic's CHRO at the time of the case study. He is currently employed in the same role at Partners HealthCare in the Greater Boston Area.*

Canada, and Abu Dhabi, United Arab Emirates. Recipient of numerous distinctions and awards, including the number two overall ranking by *U.S. News & World Report*'s 2016-17 Best Hospitals, number one ranking for cardiology, and top five rankings for urology, orthopedics, gastroenterology and GI surgery, rheumatology, pulmonology, and other specialties,[64] Cleveland Clinic delivers healthcare services through patient-centered, integrated practice units or institutes. With each institute focusing on a specific disease or organ system, teams of medical and surgical specialists emphasize collaboration and open sharing of knowledge, data, and resources to coordinate care for over 6.62 million patient visits, 164,704 admissions, and 208,807 surgical cases in 2015. These patients are served in local, regional, and international facilities by over 49,000 employees who are called 'caregivers,' including administrative and non-clinical professionals, to reflect the organization's deep commitment to patient-centered care.

Cleveland Clinic operates as a physician-led, multispecialty group practice that integrates clinic and hospital healthcare services with research and education missions, including seventy-four accredited residence training programs and over $166 million in total grant and contract revenue. Consistent with the clinical model of medicine and the organization's core values emphasizing quality, innovation, teamwork, service, compassion, and integrity, Cleveland Clinic physicians are salaried via renewable annual contracts that do not offer incentives for additional tests or procedures. Central to the organization's talent management and succession planning practices is the administrative structure—the Board of Governors (BOG) and Medical Executive Committee (MEC). The BOG and MEC, which comprises physicians elected by staff and selected administrators, report to the board of directors and are charged with all professional and policy issues across the health system.

To support the identification and development of talent to serve in administrative roles across the system, Cleveland Clinic has established a well-earned reputation as an industry leader for talent management and executive development. The organization's Education Institute and human resources teams offer numerous training and development programs for current and aspiring healthcare leaders, including the Samson Global Leadership Academy and Executive Visitors' program 'Leading in Healthcare,' an integrated leadership development program that includes administrators, nurses, and staff physicians. The health system's steadfast commitment to these talent development programs and others has earned numerous awards for leadership development and workforce engagement, including the prestigious designation as a 'Best Organizations for Leadership Development (BOLD)' in 2016 by the National Center for Healthcare Leadership.[65] Awarded to only nineteen healthcare organizations, the BOLD designation recognizes hospitals and health systems that utilize evidence-based leadership development practices to enhance both health and healthcare in their respective communities.

Given the incredible frequency and intensity of changes in the healthcare industry, as well as the massive workforce demographic shifts, Cleveland Clinic places strong emphasis on driving high employee engagement through numerous talent management best capabilities, including its executive onboarding program. "Cleveland Clinic is growing its global footprint during a time when patient demographics and our workforce are rapidly changing," explains Joseph Cabral, CHRO. In recognition of the robust link between caregiver engagement, patient satisfaction, and hospital safety outcomes—specifically the role of leaders in driving caregiver engagement outcomes, Cleveland Clinic embarked on a journey to redesign its executive onboarding program. The increasing complexity of leader roles across the health system coupled with the organization's renewed focus on employee engagement during a period of unprecedented industry change demanded new strategies for assimilating internal and external candidates into new leadership roles.

The following case study describes how Cleveland Clinic implemented the redesigned executive onboarding program that addresses the transition needs of internal caregivers promoted into leadership roles and external candidates placed into executive positions. First, I describe the primary strategies and practices of the executive onboarding program (EOP), including firsthand experiences of new Cleveland Clinic leaders who completed the program and their respective hiring executives. Second, a series of critical success factors for implementing executive onboarding are discussed in the context of evidence-based best practices supported by case study findings. Next, multiple performance metrics are presented as evidence of the EOP's effectiveness, including the program's impact on newly placed executives' engagement, productivity, and job performance. The chapter concludes with a discussion of key lessons learned and a series of practice recommendations for developing exemplary onboarding practices for healthcare leaders.

Cleveland Clinic's Onboarding Framework

Recognizing the numerous changes taking place in the broader healthcare industry and the increasing complexities of leadership roles across the organization, including the challenges inherent in driving employee engagement during a period of large-scale organizational change, Cleveland Clinic embarked on a strategic initiative in 2015 to redesign its onboarding program for all caregivers. In an effort to transform the onboarding experience for new employees and particularly those in leadership roles, the redesigned onboarding program consists of three primary phases or distinct sets of activities. Illustrated in figure 3.1, the onboarding phases consist of Pre-boarding, Orientations, and Onboarding.

Figure 3.1

Cleveland Clinic Onboarding Phases

TIMELINE	Pre-boarding	RESPONSIBILITY
Pre-Day 1	• Includes all activities from acceptance of offer to Day 1 (welcome letter, forms, benefits package, company info, etc.).	Human Resources
	Orientations	
1st Week	• Program designed to provide all new caregivers with standard information about the organization (strategy, history, operations, culture, etc.).	Human Resources
	Onboarding	
1st 90 Days	• Long-term process to transition new caregivers into the organization. • Includes welcome and integration (introductions, lunch, building tour, etc.), detailed work plan (job responsibilities, initial assignments, etc.), and peer sponsor.	Hiring Manager

- **Pre-boarding:** This phase includes all activities from the moment an offer is accepted by a new caregiver through the first day on the job, including welcome letters, personal meetings and calls with the hiring executive, a thumb drive containing benefits materials, and archival information describing the organization's history and administrative practices. Although this phase is the responsibility of human resources, and specifically the Office of Learning and Performance Development (OLPD), hiring managers and executives are often engaged in private meetings and discussions with new leaders and executives during this period.

- **Orientations:** During a caregiver's first week on the job, a series of orientation programs accelerate the new hire's assimilation to the organization and leadership role. The distinct yet coordinated orientation programs consist of an overall Cleveland Clinic orientation, named **New Caregiver Orientation**, which is completed by all new caregivers irrespective of job role or management level. This orientation includes an executive welcome, review of Cleveland Clinic history, quality and safety overview, and discussion of the **Cleveland Clinic Patient Experience**, which is an enterprise-wide initiative that integrates exceptional employee and patient experiences. The various administrative units, institutes, and other departments conduct separate orientations that offer specialized topical and cultural content to help new leaders quickly assimilate into their work unit and roles. For those new caregivers in leadership roles, including internal promotions and external hires in supervisor, manager, director, and executive roles, the **New Leader Orientation** offers a one-day program that highlights key organization-wide initiatives (e.g., employee engagement), systems (e.g., KRONOS), and processes (e.g., performance management) to help new leaders 'get up to speed' quickly. As part of the orientation, executive speakers from various functions, including finance, supply chain, quality & patient safety, patient experience, information technology, and human resources, deliver presentations and network with the new leaders.

- **Onboarding:** While the Pre-boarding and Orientation phases are designed and delivered by OLPD, the hiring manager or hiring executive is responsible for conducting the third phase of the onboarding process. To help support effective execution of this final phase, which generally consists of the first ninety days of the caregiver's employment, the OLPD team developed a comprehensive online Onboarding Toolkit consisting of numerous forms, best practices, tools, and other materials utilized by hiring managers and executives to accelerate the onboarding process. The toolkit includes templates, unit/department checklists that meet regulatory requirements, peer sponsor or preceptor instructions, and other materials. For all caregivers, the Onboarding phase consists of several assimilation activities, including colleague introductions, building and facility tours, peer sponsor or preceptor assignments, and 90-day work plans.

Summarized in figure 3.2, the Cleveland Clinic Onboarding Framework outlines the variety of assimilation activities that are customized to the needs of three primary groups of onboarding participants: new caregivers (staff), new leaders (supervisors, managers, and directors), and new executives (executive directors, vice presidents, and other executive roles). While all new Cleveland Clinic employees complete the **New Caregiver Orientation** and COMET Compliance Modules, new leaders and executives are afforded specialized socialization and assimilation activities.

Executive Onboarding Program

Critical to the success of Cleveland Clinic's comprehensive executive onboarding program (EOP)—modeled after industry best practices both within and outside of healthcare—is the inclusion of both caregivers who have been promoted into senior leadership roles and those executives hired from outside of the

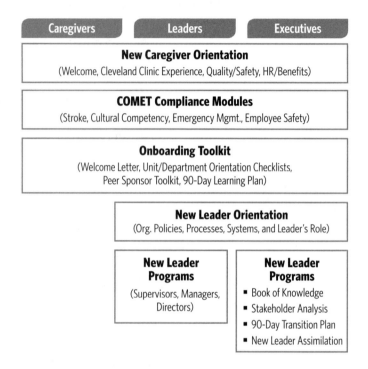

Figure 3.2

Cleveland Clinic Onboarding Framework

organization. A central EOP design feature is customizing onboarding practices to the unique needs of each new executive, which requires careful assessment of his or her new leadership role and work context to determine the ideal mix of onboarding activities. This customization demands strong collaboration and trust between the hiring executive and OLPD professionals. While OLPD maintains the lead in developing onboarding tools and facilitating various assimilation processes for new executives, hiring executives play a principal role throughout the process. Below are the four primary executive onboarding practices and the respective roles of the hiring executive and OLPD:

1. *Executive Book of Knowledge:* As part of the pre-boarding process, new executives receive a welcome letter from Cleveland Clinic's president and CEO and the *Executive Book of Knowledge*. Delivered in a USB thumb drive, the *Executive Book of Knowledge* includes a comprehensive menu of files that address the following leadership-oriented topics: Cleveland Clinic mission, vision, and values; enterprise-level strategic direction, goals, and targets; business plans and budgeting processes; organization chart; key leadership initiatives (e.g., employee engagement, HCAHPS,

diversity, etc.); talent development resources (e.g., OLPD courses and employee onboarding resources); performance management processes, forms, and guides; overview of the executive's institute or department, including résumés of direct reports, key initiatives and status, and workforce analytics scorecard; and many other basic informational resources (e.g., first 90-days best practices, leader contact sheet, maps, etc.). New executives are given several weeks prior to their start date to read through the materials to ensure a comprehensive grounding in the history, strategic orientation, and administrative processes and systems across the organization.

2. *Stakeholder Analysis:* Prior to the new executive's arrival, the hiring executive and an OLPD professional meet to discuss the many internal and external stakeholders with whom the interviews should be conducted. Given the highly complex nature of Cleveland Clinic and its matrix organizational structure, selection of the right set of stakeholders is critical for driving rapid assimilation into the leadership role. Cleveland Clinic's highly collaborative and consensus-driven culture demands that leaders operate from an expansive network of colleagues across divisions, institutes, and work units. As such, the list of stakeholder interviews includes colleagues from within new executive's work unit, internal stakeholders from other work units and management levels, and external stakeholders. The OLPD professional asks each stakeholder to offer his or her perspectives and feedback on a range of transition issues facing the new executive, including the following questions: *What are your expectations for the role? What should the new leader focus on in the first thirty, sixty, and ninety days? What relationships must the new leader develop to be successful? What will be the key measures of success for the new leader?* and *What support will you give to the new leader?* After completion of the stakeholder interviews, the OLPD professional prepares a comprehensive report that includes confidential summaries of the perspectives shared by the new executive's key stakeholders. For most new executives, an average of six interviews are conducted to complete the stakeholder analysis and report. However, it is not uncommon for stakeholder interviews to include up to twelve internal and external stakeholders, including city mayors and C-suite executives. The new executive and OLPD professional meet to review the stakeholder analysis report in detail and discuss recommendations for accelerating learning and transition into the leadership role. Reflecting the strong partnership between hiring executives and OLPD professionals, the stakeholder analysis process is flexibly deployed such that some hiring executives prefer to have their new leaders conduct

the stakeholder interviews during their first four to six weeks on the job.

3. *90-Day Transition Plan:* Developed by OLPD with input from hiring executives across the organization, the transition plan allows new executives to chart several sets of learning activities and deliverables for the first ninety days. The plan requires new executives to formally state the key stakeholders they will meet to conduct interviews; their learning priorities across Cleveland Clinic's processes, systems, training opportunities, and culture; and the primary work activities and deliverables that will lay the groundwork for an 'early win' or significant contribution to their respective division or institute. Hiring executives meet with their new leaders to approve the plan and agree on a date to review after three months. To assist new executives with developing their 90-day plans, OLPD offers numerous strategies and best practices of leaders who have successfully transitioned into significantly larger roles. Based on Michael Watkins' influential research[66] that details these key strategies and best practices, new executives formulate their 90-day plans with a focus on securing early wins, accelerating learning opportunities, developing strong relationships with their new bosses, creating coalitions across the organization, and maintain work/life balance.

4. *New Leader Assimilation:* Adapted from General Electric's new manager assimilation program and best practices supported by research findings,[67] the new leader assimilation (NLA) process facilitates rapid development of strong relationships between the new executive and his or her direct reports. NLA consists of a series of facilitated sessions to foster clear communication and develop strong team relationships. For the first session, an OLPD facilitator meets with the incoming executive's direct reports and captures their responses to a series of questions about the new executive's leadership style, key challenges that the work unit will face in the coming year, and what they want most from the new executive. This initial session is conducted without the presence of the new executive. Next, the OLPD facilitator meets with the new executive to review the responses from the first session and discuss a strategy for feeding this information back to the direct reports. Finally, the new executive meets with his or her direct reports in a second session to present the aggregate responses from the initial session, address any additional questions or concerns from the direct reports, seek clarification where needed, and develop an action plan that adopts suggestions from the direct reports. Approximately six months following these initial sessions, the OLPD facilitator again meets with the new executive's direct reports

to discuss his or her strengths, development areas, and suggestions for actions or behaviors that staff would like to see from the new executive. The follow-up process is repeated whereby an OLPD facilitator meets with the new executive to review the responses and subsequently meets with the entire team to discuss feedback and action plans moving forward.

Evidence-Based Success Factors

While Cleveland Clinic's executive onboarding program (EOP) consists of several best practices supported by research on employee socialization[68] and leader assimilation,[69] the ultimate questions concerning the program's efficacy remain: What makes Cleveland Clinic's EOP best-in-class for healthcare executives? What is the EOP's impact on key performance metrics? What are the EOP's execution best practices? To address these fundamental questions and also identify improvement opportunities, OLPD initiated an independent and comprehensive assessment (see About the Research at the end of the chapter for a summary of assessment methodology) of the executive onboarding program. The assessment findings revealed a set of seven critical execution drivers or 'success factors' that distinguish the EOP as best in class for healthcare executives. Initiated after completion of the EOP's redesign in 2014-2015, the assessment identified the success factors through analysis of multiple data sources, including archival data (onboarding tools, materials, performance metrics) and dozens of interviews with hiring executives, recently hired executives, new caregivers, and OLPD professionals. Summarized in table 3.1, the success factors offer practical insights into how the various executive onboarding components drive strong performance outcomes, including high engagement, productivity, and job performance for first-year executives. For each success factor, representative executive excerpts and the corresponding onboarding phase are listed.

Strong Hiring Executive-OLPD Alliance

The EOP's success begins with a strong alliance and mutually-beneficial partnership between Cleveland Clinic hiring executives and the OLPD. As the process and content experts, OLPD professionals work diligently to understand the unique needs of each hiring executive with regards to the new executive and his or her assimilation needs. The foundation of this partnership is customized onboarding tools and activities to meet the needs of the new executive and his or her work unit. While some onboarding activities are standardized across all new hires irrespective of management level or work unit, such as the **New Caregiver Orientation**, many executive onboarding activities require thoughtful

Table 3.1
Executive Onboarding Success Factors

Phase	Success Factor	Executive Excerpts
PRE-BOARDING	Strong Hiring Executive-OLPD Alliance	▪ I've worked very closely with my HR business partner to think strategically about what programs make the most sense for our new leaders as they come onboard. We offer them an array of opportunities, and [we are] proactive in getting those things scheduled so that [the new executives] feel they've got some significant planning already underway when they get here and that it's going to help them get acclimated. ▪ In onboarding these new leaders, my HR business partner has brought me things that I didn't know existed. Having that partnership with her is so critical to our success and she has really helped think about how to customize and to make sure it's meaningful for each leader.
PRE-BOARDING	Comprehensive and Personalized Integration Activities	▪ I don't think it can be underestimated as to [the importance of] listening to what that new leader needs. You're going to have this investment for every new caregiver that comes onboard, but from a leader's perspective, I think that being proactive to what the new leader needs prior to joining is really critical. I spent a lot of time with all of my new leaders before they even set foot in the clinic, but it was based on what they wanted. ▪ My onboarding started well before my start date. It wasn't just the packets I got in the mail or the benefits and even the 'Book of Knowledge.' [My new boss] was sending me goals and objectives historical for 2013, information about the problems they had…work structures of my own team at the detailed level in addition to her team's processes.
PRE-BOARDING	Hiring Executive Prioritization of Onboarding	▪ The most important component of [the onboarding program] is a personal commitment to making it a priority and doing a lot of planning and considerate thought around what I need to do to make sure that this process is successful for my new leaders. I want this to be a very successful hire. That means my personal investment in making it a good thing. I put the personal investment of getting to know the leader as a person and making sure that I'm addressing their questions and being accessible. ▪ It's that personal commitment of taking a lot of time to really make sure that these leaders are getting well acclimated at their colleague level outside of [our business division] as well as that executive level outside of [our business division], because it's those relationships that are going to be so critical to our success. Then it's being in meetings together, taking time to make sure that they're introduced to everyone.
ORIENTATION	Socialization to Culture and Leadership Role	▪ The biggest challenge for me is just understanding the formal and informal way that things happen around here—how things get done. The New Leader Orientation was very helpful. I liked the idea that it was designed for everybody. There's a core indoctrination embedded within that and it covered a lot of helpful material. ▪ [The New Leader Orientation] was incredibly helpful because this is such a big and complex place that just understanding the core basics is really important. A lot of getting up to speed in an organization is simply knowing how to do basic stuff. This is a unique environment from the sense of it's a matrix organization with dozens of leaders spread throughout the organization. Finding ways to navigate the leadership structure is critical.

Table 3.1 contd.

Executive Onboarding Success Factors

Phase	Success Factor	Executive Excerpts
ONBOARDING	Rapid Assimilation to New Team	▪ I found [the New Leader Assimilation] to be incredibly valuable to break down barriers with my new team so that they understood that I was human; I wanted to know about them; I wanted them to feel comfortable bringing things to me; and I wanted to be approachable. It was a very meaningful exercise to break the ice with them and help me start to form relationships with them. Of the different things I've done during my onboarding, I think [the new leader assimilation] may have been the most meaningful for me and hopefully for [my new team]. ▪ The New Leader Assimilation—phenomenal experience, absolutely phenomenal. It was very insightful for everyone involved in the process. I would say managing expectations [is a primary benefit]. People come into things with different perceptions. As a new leader, I may look at things differently than my direct reports or line staff, and [the process] gave me some insight of what challenges they think that I may incur or may not have thought of. I was able to take the time to listen and hear some of the history before jumping to conclusions.
	Opportunities for Early Wins	▪ My supervisor gave me a tremendous amount of support. It was never formally outlined as: "Well, the first ninety days I expect this stuff to happen." I got involved right away with our leadership team and started driving forward with new ideas and approaches. It was very readily accepted and my supervisor gave me a lot of guidance around how to pitch ideas to different people. So because [my job duties] are new and because I was the reigning expert, they were looking to see what I would recommend. ▪ What my supervisor did extremely well was getting me involved with all of her other direct reports any time the word 'pricing' was mentioned. I was included in those discussions and meetings at high levels. There was research done that was presented to our CFO, and I was invited to that meeting. That was the second week I was here. Instead of being locked away and just reading materials, her approach was to get me actively engaged with the organization. I could say I think that is the single best orientation approach that somebody can take.
	Cross-Level and Cross-Unit Relationship Building	▪ [The interviews] are important because it's so much about relationship-building as a leader at the clinic that I want to make sure that I give them an opportunity to start building those relationships. They will be able to help form who their go-to people are going to be. Because they'll have lots of support within finance and within revenue cycle management, but they're about to go so far outside of [those functions] that I think their mentor is going to [help build relationships] outside of our direct team. ▪ In many situations, those folks outside of my direct team were involved in the [new executive] interview process. We had delegates right from the start say, "I'm bringing on a new leader. You are an important customer for us or an important relationship; I would like you to be a part of the interview process." They were engaged from day one.

consideration to meet individual needs. Hiring executives' awareness of the menu of executive onboarding tools and resources provided by OLPD is a critical factor in the pre-boarding process. Furthermore, hiring executives recognize the value of early partnership and collaboration with OLPD professionals to create meaningful socialization and integration activities for each new executive. Karen Mihalik, executive director of Revenue Cycle Management, onboarded several new executives in 2014 and 2015 as part of Cleveland Clinic's strategic initiative around cost repositioning. Describing the importance of the strong OLPD partnership and its impact on new executives' assimilation to Cleveland Clinic, she remarked:

> I am so impressed by the [onboarding] tools that are there. It's been really nice to share with all of our new leaders and say, "This is something that the organization has invested heavily in recent years. I'm really proud to be able to share this information with you because I think we do a great job at this." Maybe that's part of why they're coming back and saying, "You know, this is really good." They recognized that it's good, and I am proud of it. I have been at the clinic for almost twenty years. It's been a real investment by HR to help us as leaders build consistent messaging for all caregivers, but especially in that new leader onboarding process.

Comprehensive and Personalized Pre-Boarding Activities

The second key EOP success factor is the comprehensive menu of pre-boarding activities that are personalized for each onboarding executive. Hiring executives and their OLPD partners work diligently to ensure that new executives receive key materials well before their start date and also a personalized experience. Joe Cabral, Cleveland Clinic's chief human resource officer and a participant in the executive onboarding process, remarked, "I was amazed by the *Book of Knowledge*. It was unique to my role, and I appreciated the amount of work that went into ensuring that I had the right information, feedback, and support to excel at Cleveland Clinic." Executive participants in the onboarding process are impressed by both the comprehensive nature of the *Book of Knowledge* as well as the informal meetings and conversations with their respective hiring executive weeks or months prior to their start date. Many hiring executives emphasize the importance of these informal meetings to establish rapport with their new team member. One hiring executive stated, "The [new executive] was so inquisitive yet so busy wrapping up his old job but he really wanted to know more about his new position, so we spent two hours on a Sunday morning before his start date. I got more out of the two hours because he felt comfortable and committed to the clinic than just about anything else that I could have done." New executives emphasize the importance of these materials and discussions with their new bosses as a means of easing the transition into their new roles. One new executive described the importance of a comprehensive, personalized pre-boarding process as follows:

> I told my new boss, "I'd love to start meeting ahead of my start date." It wasn't a requirement, and it allowed us to get to know each other more outside of the interview setting and think about our styles. On Saturdays, I would volunteer time because I was personally interested, and it was in response to some of the things [my new boss] was already sending. We already started to talk about the 30/60/90-day plans and I started capturing those things in the templates that were provided for the onboarding goals.

Hiring Executive Prioritization of Onboarding Activities

An obvious but nonetheless critical EOP success factor and driver of the program's success is the tremendous commitment of time and energy—the high level of engagement—that hiring executives devote to participating in onboarding activities. Recently onboarded executives have expressed strong appreciation for the time and careful attention devoted to their integration into the organization and their new role. OLPD professionals present a clear and compelling business case for the value of executive onboarding activities to hiring executives, such as citing research evidence of the performance outcomes of best-in-class onboarding programs, thereby strengthening their commitment to the process. Noting the temptation to allow other pressing issues to take priority over his onboarding experience, a new operations executive noted, "My supervisor set up pretty extensive weekly meetings with her and that was very helpful. She was able to stick to it, which is another thing. It's easy to schedule and then skip it when something else takes precedence over [our meetings]. She was very diligent about following through with it and I thought that was really helpful for me." Karen Mihalik, executive director of Revenue Cycle Management, emphasized the importance of hiring executives' commitment to the onboarding process:

> The most important component of the executive onboarding program is a personal commitment [by hiring executives] to making it a priority and doing a lot of planning and considerate thought around what we need to do to make sure that it is successful for our new leaders. That means my personal investment in getting to know the leader as a person and making sure that we're addressing their questions and being

accessible to them, which is really the most critical part. One of the nicest things that I've heard from each of [my newly hired executives] individually is that our program "has been the best onboarding experience I've ever had in my career." That means so much to me because we're starting off on the right foot and they feel that we're investing in them. Of course, I want to invest them. I need to invest in them because they're a big part of our future.

Socialization to Culture and Leadership Role

Fast socialization into the organizational culture and their respective leadership role via the **New Leader Orientation** (NLO) is the fourth EOP success factor. The ability to learn from functional experts across Cleveland Clinic and meet with new leaders from other work units is critical to the socialization process. Numerous recently onboarded executives referenced the importance of learning about Cleveland Clinic's core values, informal operating norms and assumptions, and other cultural knowledge as part of the one-day NLO. An outcome commonly referenced by the new executives was the NLO's immediate impact on helping 'get up to speed' in their role and positioning them to make an immediate impact. Similarly, many executives noted that due to the immense complexity of the organization and changes to the healthcare landscape, the NLO provides an important primer on "the formal and informal way that things happen around here" and how to "navigate the leadership structure" within a matrix design and culture of collaboration. An institute administrator noted, "I thought [the NLO] was a really excellent program. It was only a day long but it was a really good cross section of different areas of Cleveland Clinic and it was presented by people who were functional experts in their area. We had finance people. We had HR people. We had training. It was really a nice way of introducing you to those areas." Coupled with the series of materials that new executives received prior to their start date, a well-designed NLO is a critical element of the socialization process into leadership roles across the organization.

Rapid Assimilation to the New Team

Of the many activities that comprise Cleveland Clinic's EOP, the **New Leader Assimilation** (NLA) is universally lauded by new executives as providing rapid and highly effective assimilation onto their respective teams. Across all elements and phases of executive onboarding, the NLA is most frequently referenced for its high quality and impact on new executives' overall onboarding experience.

Many noted that the NLA was incredibly beneficial to their teams and work units to 'break down barriers' with their new direct reports and help jump-start relationship-building with numerous stakeholders. Many new executives described the NLA as the most important part of their entire onboarding experience, as one executive noted, "I think [the NLA] may have been the most meaningful for me and hopefully for [my new team]." The new executives described several common explanations for the NLA's effectiveness, including setting clear expectations for the new executive and his/her team members, quickly building relationships and establishing mutual trust, getting to know one another on a personal level, developing a collective team vision, and managing expectations for all team members such that poor experiences and other obstacles with prior leaders are addressed openly. Executives also emphasized that the NLA process allows for multiple stakeholders to participate in the facilitated feedback process, including those outside of the executive's team. Given the organization's highly collaborative culture and matrix design that places a premium on leadership influence outside of one's immediate team, the NLA offers new Cleveland Clinic leaders a solid foundation for developing strong relationships across the organization. Referencing the NLA's importance to her onboarding experience, a new finance executive noted:

> It was very, very well received. I enjoyed it myself but the new leaders on my team were fearful [of the new leadership assimilation process] because this area had a history of issues. The feedback we received from the leaders on my team was more beneficial for them than even for me because it really eased their mind. It let them get to know me and learn a lot of things about me and my style. [The feedback session] was with all of my directors and my managers at the next layer because I invited them. I also requested that some key peer stakeholders that are in IT organizations be invited to those feedback sessions with HR and the follow-up sessions where I basically looked at their feedback and questions and responded.

Opportunities for Early Wins

A sixth important EOP success factor is the program's ability to provide new executives with early opportunities to make making meaningful contributions in their work units and across Cleveland Clinic. Long cited as a best practice for onboarding executives,[70] positioning new executives to secure 'early wins' is a critical EOP success factor. In addition to the 90-day transition plan and stakeholder interviews, hiring executives play an integral role in facilitating opportunities for new executives to make meaningful contributions in their first year, including demonstrating a high tolerance for innovation and arranging meetings and other networking experiences with influential executives across Cleveland Clinic. This success factor reflects a leadership philosophy amongst hiring executives that challenges the status quo, and indeed, their own viewpoints on key issues is a valued part of the onboarding process. A new patient financial services executive remarked, "My boss is incredibly open to my new ideas. She said, 'We want your fresh set of eyes on this…give us your ideas…if you've seen it done better somewhere else, or if you have a new way of doing it, we are open to it. They may question and challenge and want to understand, but that's what I expect out of them.' She's incredibly open to my new ideas and suggestions." Finally, hiring executives are very savvy about strategically networking their new executives with stakeholders across the organization, recognizing the complex and heavily matrixed nature of the leadership structure and culture of collaborative decision-making.

Cross-Level and Cross-Unit Relationship-Building

The seventh and final success factor that drives EOP's performance outcomes is heavy emphasis on developing stakeholder relationships across management levels and business units. The organization's matrix design places a premium on the ability of new executives to quickly establish rapport with influential leaders across Cleveland Clinic. As part of the stakeholder interviews conducted during the first ninety days, new executives described the importance of meeting with key stakeholders outside of their respective work units to obtain important perspectives from an enterprise level. As with several other themes, an integral component of building relationships with influential stakeholders across the organization was the hiring executive's ability to identify and schedule interviews as part of the new executive's first three months. Another best practice identified by new executives was the inclusion of external stakeholders as participants in the interviews, which reinforces the value placed on gaining independent views of the respective executive's new work unit. An institute administrator described the importance of the stakeholder interviews and working with his bosses to develop critical relationships across the organization:

> My boss and I met every other week, so before my 90-day transition plan, she and I had already discussed the things that I need to do in the first ninety days and so we monitored it from that standpoint. I actually have another boss, my department chairman. So going back between those two bosses, making sure that I understood what's important to both of them, and getting to know the right people and building relationships,

that was really the expectation that was on me for the first 120 days—build relationships and build relationships and build relationships. If you're not comfortable with a matrix environment, healthcare is not the place for you.

Evidence-Based Evaluation: Executive Onboarding Performance Metrics

Ultimately, the long-term success of Cleveland Clinic's EOP is dictated by its impact on key performance metrics, particularly those that resonate most with hiring executives across the organization. In an effort to rigorously assess the impact of the redesigned EOP, and thereby further establish the business case for the program, OLPD identified three primary performance metrics: executive job performance, executive engagement, and executive productivity. While each of these metrics is strongly associated with high-performance onboarding programs,[71] they are also aligned with Cleveland Clinic's strategic initiative concerning employee engagement and its link to both the patient care experience and hospital safety outcomes. The EOP evaluation strategy and key results across each performance metric are described below:

1. *Executive Job Performance:* To assess the EOP's impact on first year executive job performance, the *Annual Performance Review* ratings for executives who participated in the EOP activities (New Leader Orientation, Stakeholder Analysis, etc.) were compared to executives who did not complete these activities. To estimate the impact of the redesigned EOP on first-year job performance, only executives who began their tenure at Cleveland Clinic in 2014 were included in this analysis. Illustrated in figure 3.3, EOP participants (n = 194) were rated significantly higher on their first-year job performance ratings for the top-box score *(exceptional performance)* compared to those executives who did not participant in the EOP. By comparison, close to three times fewer EOP participants scored in the lowest category *(meets most expectations)* compared to executives who did not complete the EOP.

2. *Executive Engagement:* The 2015 annual employee engagement survey also demonstrated the EOP's positive impact on executive's assimilation to Cleveland Clinic and their leadership role. Overall, EOP participants (n = 124) reported a mean 4.44 employee engagement survey rating while executives who did not complete EOP activities (n = 16) reported an overall engagement rating of 4.31 (see figure 3.4). The aspect of

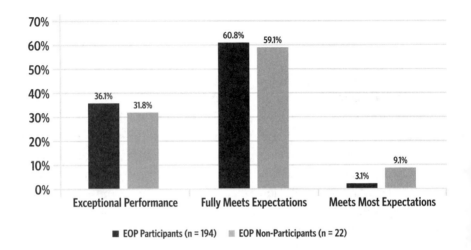

Figure 3.3

First Year Performance Review Ratings for Participants and Non-Participants of Cleveland Clinic's Executive Onboarding Program (EOP)

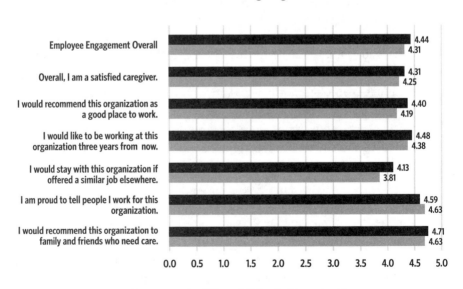

Figure 3.4

First Year Employee Engagement Ratings for Participants and Non-Participants of Cleveland Clinic's Executive Onboarding Program (EOP)

employee engagement that clearly distinguished EOP participants (mean = 4.13) versus non-participants (mean = 3.81) was concerning their intent to "stay with this organization if offered a similar job elsewhere." As part of the annual employee engagement survey administered by Press-Ganey, executives also rated the degree of leadership support they received during their first year at Cleveland Clinic.

Depicted in figure 3.5, EOP participants reported significantly higher leadership support overall (mean = 4.52) compared to non-EOP participants (mean = 4.32). Notably, the leadership support survey items capture new executives' evaluation of their bosses, their work, and the degree to which they are engaged in meaningful decision-making processes. Given the EOP's emphasis on hiring executives' central role in the new executive onboarding process, the significant differences between EOP participants and non-participants across these survey items offer strong support for the program's impact on executive assimilation. New executives who complete the EOP are significantly more likely to feel strongly supported by their boss via consist performance feedback, job design that affords meaningful work, and collaborative decision-making in their business unit.

Figure 3.5
First Year Leadership Support Ratings for Participants and Non-Participants of Cleveland Clinic's Executive Onboarding Program (EOP)

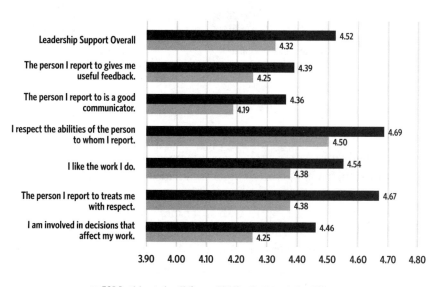

3. *Executive Productivity:* To assess the EOP's impact on first year executive job productivity, OLPD collected baseline data via a *New Leader Survey* in 2013 and again in 2015. For both years, the survey was administered to new executives who completed the EOP with the intent of identifying performance improvements that may be attributed to the EOP redesign. The survey asked new executives to evaluate the EOP across several criteria, including effectiveness ratings of the program's various elements and self-assessments of executives' preparedness and productivity in their leadership roles. Illustrated in figure 3.6, comparison of the 2013 and 2015 survey results demonstrate that the number of new executives sourced from external talent pools increased in 2015 while executives sourced from internal transfers or promotions decreased in 2015. In addition to the challenge of integrating significantly greater numbers of new leaders who were entirely new to Cleveland Clinic and its unique culture, OLPD was also faced with a group of new leaders with sharply less experience.

Figure 3.6

New Cleveland Clinic Executives Sourced from External and Internal Talent Pools for 2013 and 2015

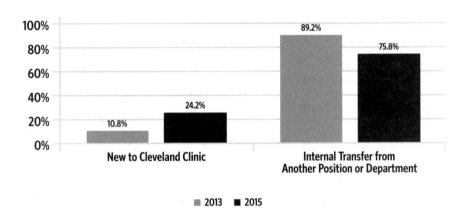

Figure 3.7 shows the number of years of Cleveland Clinic tenure for newly hired executives precipitously decreasing at higher levels of tenure. There were significantly greater numbers of new executives hired in 2015 with five or fewer years of Cleveland Clinic tenure and sharply lower numbers of new executives in 2015 with six or more years of experience, demonstrating the remarkable challenge that faced OLPD and its efforts to redesign the EOP. Without exception, executives who completed the EOP in 2015 provided distinctly higher evaluations of the program elements and their productivity compared to the 2013 EOP participants.

Figure 3.7

Years of Cleveland Clinic Tenure for New Executives Hired for 2013 and 2015

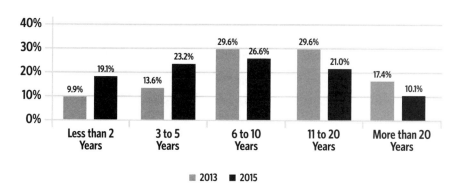

Figure 3.8 presents survey results illustrating that 60 percent of executives in 2015 (n = 134) 'strongly agreed' or 'agreed' that they were provided the necessary training on key policies and processes to fully execute their leader job duties. This represents a marked increase from the 46 percent of executives in 2013 (n = 98) who agreed with this statement.

Figure 3.8

New Cleveland Clinic Executives' Evaluation of the Executive Onboarding Program (EOP) for 2013 and 2015

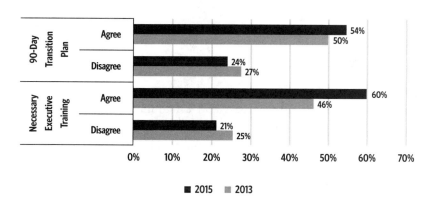

New executives in 2015 were also far more likely to assess higher preparedness and productivity in their job role compared to new executives in 2013 (see figure 3.9). When asked to identify the point during their onboarding experience in which they were confident that they had the skills, knowledge, and abilities to fully executive their leadership role, 46.9 percent of executives in 2013 (n = 99) responded that they were 'still discovering areas that I need to understand' compared to 37.2 percent of executives (n = 99) in 2015. Taken together, these survey findings offer strong support for the redesigned EOP's impact on executive job productivity during a challenging period of notably greater volume of leaders who were new to Cleveland Clinic and possessed significantly fewer years of experience.

Figure 3.9

New Cleveland Clinic Executives' Evaluation of Preparedness and Productivity in their Leadership Role for 2013 and 2015

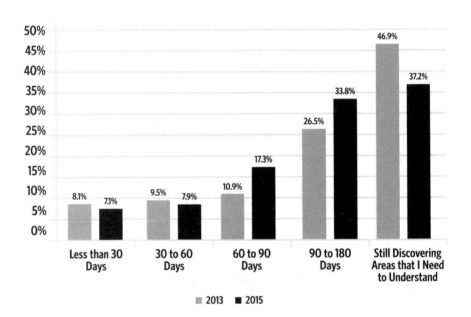

Lessons Learned

This case study described how Cleveland Clinic implemented a redesigned executive onboarding program that effectively addresses the leader transition needs of both internal caregivers and external candidates placed into executive positions. The evidence-based success factors for implementing a best-in-class executive onboarding program for healthcare leaders offer several important lessons learned for hospital organizations.

1. *Develop a clear and compelling onboarding framework that is standardized across hospitals and business units.* A key factor in establishing the business case for onboarding activities is to clearly and articulately present a comprehensive framework of onboarding processes, practices, and tools to a broad mix of stakeholders, including hospital management teams, clinical leaders, board members, and HR professionals. Stakeholders across

the health system must not only be conversant with the organization's philosophy and approach to executive onboarding, but also able to articulate the value and impact of onboarding on key performance metrics.

2. *Establish clear areas of ownership and responsibility for onboarding activities across key stakeholders.* The central role of hiring executives in the execution of onboarding activities cannot be overstated. Very early in the program development process, HR teams must partner with hiring executives across the health system to solicit their input on program design and also their commitment to performing a central role in the execution of key onboarding activities. While HR teams can develop exemplary pre-boarding materials, orientations, tools, and processes, the impact of these practices will be muted without careful nurturing of relationships with hiring executives and clearly designating their central role in program execution.

3. *Customize onboarding activities to meet the unique needs of the new executive and his or her work unit and hiring executive.* As part of the overarching onboarding framework, delineate activities and practices that are requisite and those that are customizable to fit each new executive's needs. Organization and business unit orientations and compliance modules are mandatory activities for integrating new executives into the health system's culture. The customization of various new leader and executive onboarding activities, both in terms of content and timing, strengthens HR's relationship with hiring executives in meeting the unique needs of the business unit and the new executive. Customize program elements and processes to meet individual executive needs, such as extending the length and intensity of transition plans as needed, designing new leader assimilation activities to include stakeholders from outside of the executive's immediate team, and establishing formal mentoring relationships when the former job incumbent remains with the organization.

4. *Adopt an evidence-based evaluation strategy to establish the business case.* Garnering strong support from hiring executives and stakeholders across the organization demands presenting a data-driven case for the positive impact of executive onboarding on key performance metrics. While new executive evaluations of onboarding activities after program completion are an important element of an evaluation plan, they fall far short of clearly establishing and reinforcing the business case. The collection of baseline (pre-program) data and post-program outcomes across a series of performance metrics identified by HR leaders and hiring executives,

including executive productivity, engagement, job performance, and retention, provides a powerful means to identify opportunities to improve the program and conduct ROI analyses that enhance the program's reputation amongst key stakeholders across the organization.

5. *Establish a culture of strong personal commitment from hiring executives.* Critical to any successful executive onboarding process is the deep personal commitment of time and energy by hiring executives throughout the program. As part of the executive onboarding program design or redesign process, establish clear norms concerning the role of hiring executives and the level of personal commitment that is requisite for a best-in-class program. For organizations developing an entirely new onboarding program, conduct pilot programs with hiring executives who have had positive experiences with onboarding, mentoring, and other assimilation activities in other roles and organizations.

6. *Align onboarding activities with leadership expectations driven by business strategy and organizational culture.* Given the healthcare industry's unprecedented evolution and the corresponding changes to leadership expectations in hospital organizations, executive onboarding activities must be sharply aligned with current strategic initiatives and highly sensitive to organizational culture. Leading in a highly complex environment that demands strong collaboration across a matrixed structure places a premium on executive onboarding activities that facilitate immediate relationship-building with direct reports and stakeholders from multiple management levels and business units. As such, comprehensive stakeholder analysis and new leader assimilation activities are invaluable onboarding practices that are strongly aligned with organizational strategy, structure, and culture.

Conclusion

Cleveland Clinic embarked on an ambitious journey to redesign its onboarding program during a period of unprecedented industry change that demanded new approaches to assimilating leaders into executive roles. Consistent with its well-earned reputation for exemplary leadership development in healthcare organizations, Cleveland Clinic implemented a series of executive onboarding best practices that are strongly aligned with the organization's strategic commitment to caregiver engagement, patient satisfaction, and hospital safety outcomes. As described in this case, and as applied at Cleveland Clinic, an evidence-based executive onboarding program performs an indispensable function in developing talent to effectively serve in complex healthcare leadership roles.

About the Research

The research to support this case study was conducted by Kevin S. Groves, PhD, and Groves Consulting Group during an 18-month period in 2014 and 2015. Cleveland Clinic's Office of Learning and Performance Development (OLPD) initiated an independent and comprehensive assessment of the newly redesigned executive onboarding program to evaluate its strengths, development areas, and impact on key performance metrics. The assessment was designed to accomplish the following objectives:

- Evaluate the key program phases of the executive onboarding process, including pre-boarding, orientation, and onboarding practices;

- Conduct semi-structured interviews with program stakeholders across levels and functions, including hiring executives, new executives who recently completed the EOP, and OLPD professionals, to identify best practices and development opportunities; and

- Assess the program's impact on key performance metrics, including executive engagement, executive job performance, and executive productivity.

The OLPD assessment strategy consisted of collecting data from the following sources:

1. *OLPD Professionals:* A series of open-ended interviews were conducted with OLPD professionals to review and discuss all extant materials for the caregiver and executive onboarding programs. The interviews were aimed at discussing the design and execution of all caregiver and executive onboarding practices.

2. *Hiring Executives:* A sample of hiring executives across the organization was selected for participation in one-hour, semi-structured interviews. The sample included the Cleveland Clinic executives who were the highest utilizers of OLPD's onboarding programs and tools in 2014 and 2015. The interviews were conducted by phone with each executive and transcribed by an electronic recording service for subsequent analysis.

3. *Executive Participants:* A sample of executives who completed the onboarding program in 2014 and 2015 participated in one-hour, semi-structured

interviews. The interviews were conducted by phone with each manager and transcribed by an electronic recording service for subsequent analysis.

4. *Archival Data:* Archival data and information, including caregiver and executive onboarding materials and tools, performance metrics, and other extant materials were obtained for review and analysis.

CHAPTER 4

Executing a Best-in-Class Succession Management System: Talent Review and Succession Planning Practices at Sutter Health

> *Our nationally recognized talent review and succession planning program allows us to cultivate leaders from within, and the Sutter Health Board and I identified [Sarah Krevans, Chief Operating Officer] early on to one day assume my role. It's part of the transition planning we do within the organization [to maintain top executive talent]. Given Sarah's background, it's the perfect time to transition. I encourage other organizations to invest in their teams and to take time to mentor and plan for succession, so they experience smooth transitions in leadership.*
>
> Pat Fry
> Chief Executive Officer (2005-2016)
> Sutter Health

Sutter Health

Spanning a network of twenty-four hospitals, thirty-four outpatient surgery centers, numerous cardiac, cancer, trauma, and behavioral health centers, and home health and hospice facilities, Sutter Health is a $10.2 billion not-for-profit health system that provides award-winning, personalized health services in more than twenty counties across Northern California, Hawaii, and Southern California. Its affiliated physicians and hospitals serve more than one hundred communities in Northern California, including the Greater Sacramento Valley,

San Francisco Bay Area, Central Valley, and Sierra Foothills. With more than five thousand affiliated physicians from the Sutter Medical Network and fifty thousand employees, Sutter Health provided patients with compassionate and personalized medical care for eleven million-plus outpatient visits and eight hundred thousand emergency room visits in 2016. In recognition of advancing its mission to serve communities through compassion and excellence in healthcare services, Sutter Health has received numerous awards for quality of medical care, safety and patient experience, innovation, and workforce development. For 2016, Sutter Health was recognized by Truven Health Analytics, The Joint Commission, The Leapfrog Group, American Heart Association, and HomeCare Elite amongst other distinctions. Furthermore, four Sutter Health hospitals—California Pacific Medical Center, Mills-Peninsula Health Services, Sutter Medical Center-Sacramento, and Sutter Roseville Medical Center—were rated among the best hospitals in California by *U.S. News & World Report*.[72]

Sutter Health operates as a fully integrated health system comprised of its hospital network, award-winning affiliated medical groups and medical foundations, and the Sutter Health Plus health plan. In a 2014 restructuring initiative intended to speed decision-making and create a more nimble and responsive health system, Sutter Health reorganized from five regions into two primary divisions—Valley Division and Bay Area Division. The Valley Division now includes the Sacramento and Central Valley regions while the Bay Area Division is formed by the West Bay, East Bay, and Peninsula Coastal regions. The primary administrative structure consists of hospital or affiliate CEOs reporting to their respective service area president, who are direct reports of the system CEO. In addition to clinic and hospital healthcare services, Sutter Health is committed to medical research conducted across several affiliated research institutes, including California Pacific Medical Center Research Institute, The Jordan Research and Education Institute, Palo Alto Medical Foundation Research Institute, and Sutter Institute for Medical Research. Among the notable medical innovations stemming from Sutter-affiliated research institutes was the world's first heart-lung machine developed by clinicians at California Pacific Medical Center. Strongly committed to medical education and training, Sutter Health operates several residency training programs, including the Family Residency Program at Sutter Medical Center of Santa Rosa that was recognized by *U.S. News & World Report* as among the country's top ten postgraduate programs for family medicine.[73]

With respect to its commitment to leadership development, workforce engagement, and succession planning, Sutter Health received top-ten scoring and won a 2014 BOLD (Best Organizations for Leadership Development) award from the National Center for Healthcare Leadership.[74] This award recognizes the health system's long-standing commitment to nurturing physicians and employees across levels through customized development opportunities, including academic and experiential learning, coaching, networking and relationship-building, and an array of leadership development programs. While Sutter Health has developed deep capabilities across several talent management practices, its signature succession management system stands out as a cornerstone, best-in-class practice that consistently drives critical performance outcomes and distinguishes the health system as an industry leader. Throughout a challenging period between 2013 and 2016, its succession management capabilities were tested with a reorganization from five regions into two divisions, the vacancies of seven hospital CEO positions in 2014, and several transitions in critical leadership roles on the system management team including the chief medical, chief nursing, and chief human resource officer positions. In perhaps the greatest test of the succession management system's efficacy, president and CEO Pat Fry announced in May 2015 that he would retire in January 2016.

The following case study describes how Sutter Health's succession management system was executed during this critical period of rapid organizational change and leadership transitions. First, I will discuss Sutter Health's talent strategy and succession management framework, including key talent assessment practices, talent review sessions, and succession planning processes. Based on a comprehensive study of Sutter Health's succession management practices during this challenging period, a series of evidence-based success factors for implementing a best-in-class succession management system are presented. This discussion of succession management best practices includes firsthand experiences and viewpoints of HR executives and senior leadership teams across levels (hospital, region/division, and system) who are responsible for executing talent assessment practices and succession planning processes. Next, several critical performance metrics are presented as evidence of the effectiveness of Sutter Health's succession management system, including leadership development metrics (e.g., internal/external hiring ratio for executive positions, leadership bench strength) and leadership diversity metrics (e.g., percentage of female successors to executive positions). Finally, this chapter concludes with a discussion of lessons learned and best-practice recommendations for developing a best-in-class succession management system.

Sutter Health's Talent Strategy

Across Sutter Health's many talent management practices, the succession management system remains the organization's signature human resource capability after maturing and evolving over the last eight years. The foundation for the succession management system is Sutter Health's **Talent Strategy**, which is illustrated in figure 4.1. The **Talent Strategy** outlines the basic philosophy and values associated with Sutter Health's people strategy and emphasizes the importance of strong alignment with the business strategy, which is critical given the unprecedented industry changes and ongoing transition from a volume- to value-based business model. The key elements of the **Talent Strategy**, and the powerful role of a mature succession management system, are outlined below.

Figure 4.1
Sutter Health Talent Strategy

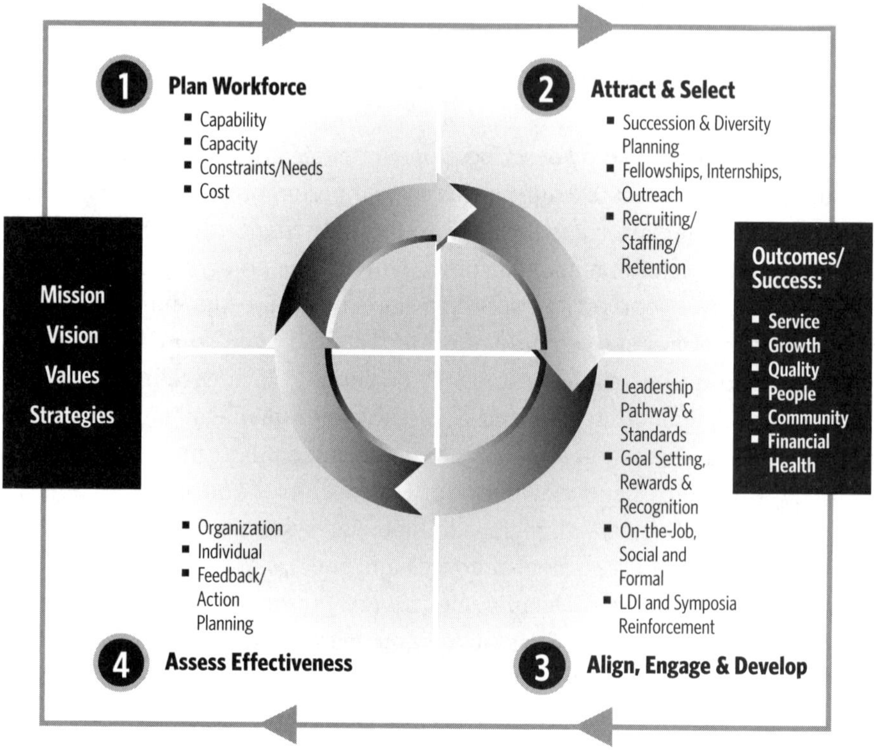

Mission
Vision
Values
Strategies

① Plan Workforce
- Capability
- Capacity
- Constraints/Needs
- Cost

② Attract & Select
- Succession & Diversity Planning
- Fellowships, Internships, Outreach
- Recruiting/Staffing/Retention

③ Align, Engage & Develop
- Leadership Pathway & Standards
- Goal Setting, Rewards & Recognition
- On-the-Job, Social and Formal
- LDI and Symposia Reinforcement

④ Assess Effectiveness
- Organization
- Individual
- Feedback/Action Planning

Outcomes/Success:
- Service
- Growth
- Quality
- People
- Community
- Financial Health

Plan Workforce

Sutter Health's workforce planning practices anticipate the talent pools that are strategically aligned with the health system in terms of capabilities, capacity, cost, and various constraints or needs (e.g., location, unions, executive diversity, etc.). For example, Sutter Health conducts annual retirement forecasts for employees in management roles, including supervisors, managers, directors, and executives. Presented to management teams and the board each year, the forecasted 'retirement wave' anticipates those management levels, functional areas, hospitals, and service areas that are most vulnerable to talent attrition. Similar to many hospitals and health systems, Sutter Health anticipates significant retirements in senior leadership roles as 72 percent of all Sutter Health executives are at least fifty years of age while close to one third (32 percent) are greater than sixty years of age.

Attract & Select

Talent attraction and selection practices include the succession management system, diversity planning, administrative fellowships, internships, and other talent outreach efforts, and the entire recruiting, staffing, and retention system. Importantly, this element of the **Talent Strategy** includes onboarding programs and practices for employees and those promoted into leadership roles or placed into such positions from external sources. Given the unique challenges associated with attracting talent into leadership roles, specifically the reticence of many skilled clinicians to transition into management and administrative positions, Sutter Health leverages its performance management and succession management systems to identify key talent pools—particularly high-potential leaders—and foster their ongoing development to cultivate a rich pipeline of internal talent.

Align, Engage, and Develop

Sutter Health aligns, engages, and develops talent through numerous programs and practices, including the creation of Leadership Pathways for nurses, physicians, and administrative leaders, on-the-job development opportunities, and both formal and informal networks (e.g., affinity groups, development program alumni groups) that allow employees across business units, hospitals, foundations, and service areas to engage with one another. Critical to the ongoing assessment and development of leadership talent, Sutter Health offers an impressive range of multi-level development programs for nurses (Sutter Certified Nurse Leader, Sutter Health Signature Series) and physicians (Introduction to Physician Leadership, LeaderLab, Executive Development for Physicians), as well as programs that integrate clinical and administrative leaders (Management & Clinical Excellence, Accelerated Change Excellence). Sutter Health's **Leadership Academy** is the signature leadership development program for senior-level leaders across the system and a critical element of the succession management system. The year-long program consists of a diverse cohort of executive participants, typically twenty-five to thirty directors and vice presidents from across functions and clinical roles who have been identified as high-potential leaders, who complete a range of experiential, didactic, and team-based action learning activities. Each participant is sponsored by an executive at the affiliate, service area, or system level to ensure an impactful developmental experience throughout the program. The **Leadership Academy**'s core learning and development experiences include 360-degree leadership assessment and executive coaching, classroom learning sessions facilitated by external experts and senior executives across the system, interviews with senior executives, live case studies addressing Sutter Health's challenges and priorities, and team-based action learning projects that allow diverse groups of high-potential leaders to address system-wide challenges and present their findings directly to the executive sponsors. The focus and intended outcomes of the **Leadership Academy** are both ambitious and critical to the effectiveness of the succession management system:

- *Focus:* Identify and develop leadership talent to drive critical innovation and change for the health system; prepare and develop executive leadership bench strength; and create a leadership team to drive Sutter Health's system-wide strategic priorities—affordability, quality, and access.

- *Outcomes:* Number of graduates from the program who are appointed to critical system-wide projects, selected for critical affiliate or hospital projects, assigned greater roles/responsibilities, and promoted into new positions.

Assess Effectiveness

Assessing the effectiveness of Sutter Health's talent strategy centers on directing changes across all talent management activities based on performance assessment at both the organization and individual levels. The impact of talent management activities on organizational performance is assessed via a dashboard of metrics that includes workforce potential and readiness for higher roles, workforce diversity, employee engagement, turnover and retention rates, and succession planning metrics. Equally important is assessing effectiveness at the individual level through self- and manager-evaluations, and how performance feedback is translated into a development plan. The results of assessment activities for organizational effectiveness and individual effectiveness are utilized to align reward and recognition programs, which are primary drivers of engagement. The formal assessment and system-wide communication of the impact of talent management practices on key performance metrics is a critical element of executing a best-in-class succession management system.

Sutter Health's Succession Management System

Succession Planning Objectives

Designed and executed by Sutter Health University's (SHU)[75] human resource and organization development professionals, the succession management system has evolved over the last eight years as part of Sutter Health's talent management strategy. Formally defined as "a process to identify, assess, develop, source, and deploy leadership resources," the succession management system is designed to accomplish two overarching goals:

1. Build bench strength and succession depth in critical leadership positions throughout the Sutter Health System.

2. Ensure the right talent, in the right location, and at the right time, effectively meets Sutter Health's strategic goals.

To accomplish these, SHU professionals work collaboratively with executive teams across the health system (affiliate, division, and system levels) to establish succession management objectives that are aligned with Sutter Health's strategic initiatives. These strategic priorities include developing a diverse talent pool across management levels, implementing a uniform, standardized approach to managing leadership talent across all affiliates and divisions, and cultivating a system-wide culture of career growth and development that enhances employee engagement and patient care. Importantly, effective execution of the succession management system that ensures strong alignment with Sutter Health's strategic initiatives is driven by SHU's efforts to implement the following strategies:

- *Cultivate Strong Succession Plans for Critical Leadership Positions:* A key principle for SHU and executive teams across Sutter Health is the identification of critical leadership positions for which comprehensive succession plans are developed. These positions include chief executive officer (CEO) or chief administrative officer (CAO), chief operating officer (COO), and chief nursing officer (CNO) at the affiliate (hospital) level, in addition to divisional and system-level executive roles. However, the succession planning process is adaptable to other talent pools as required by executive teams across levels (affiliate, service area, system, or department). For example, chief finance officer (CFO), chief medical officer (CMO), clinical integration positions, and numerous other clinical and administrative leadership roles are also targeted talent pools for succession plans.

- *Create a central, searchable repository of leadership talent:* A critical success factor for system-wide execution of talent management and succession planning practices is the adoption and utilization of a software platform to codify leadership talent across the organization. For Sutter Health, SHU professionals and leadership teams across levels populate Sutter Health's Performance Success and Development Process (PSDP) platform (a technology solution powered by Oracle Taleo) with performance management and succession management data. A best-in-class succession management system is successfully driven by developing and maintaining a comprehensive repository of leadership talent that allows the board and executive teams to adopt a system-wide perspective on leadership talent. The disciplined development and updating of the PSDP system allows Sutter Health to avoid the outdated and ineffective 'replacement planning' approach that limits the pool of critical positions' potential successors to the direct reports of those vacating such roles. A centralized, searchable, and fully populated PSDP system allows Sutter Health to adopt a system-wide view of talent management, including much wider and deeper talent pools for succession decisions, development opportunities that exist outside of a given leader's affiliate or division, and the ability to assess system-wide talent gaps given retirement forecasts, health system growth, new positions, and other key factors.

- *Foster a culture of career growth and development:* As part of Sutter Health's strategic initiative to excel as an employer of choice in the healthcare industry, the health system cultivates a work environment in which employees across functions and levels are offered clear career paths and associated development opportunities. This strategy is critical given the reticence of many talented clinicians to transition into administrative roles across healthcare delivery organizations. Employees across levels, functions, and clinical roles, particularly nurses and physicians, are afforded career paths that include professional development courses via SHU's many course offerings, comprehensive leadership development programs, job rotations and other role-based assignments, mentor and preceptor programs, and roles on division- and system-wide initiatives or task forces.

- *Develop a system-wide approach to talent management and succession planning:* Finally, a critical strategy associated with driving the 'One Sutter' initiative is aligning all of the health system's affiliates, foundations, and other entities around a single, uniform process for performance management, career development, succession planning, and other key talent management practices. Given Sutter Health's growth over the last decade and the diversity of hospitals and geographies comprising the health system, and the corresponding disparity of talent management approaches and supporting practices across some entities, the adoption of a single system and vocabulary to identify, assess, develop, and place leadership talent is a critical success factor.

Leadership Assessment: Talent Profiles and Potential Metrics

The succession management system is executed through two complementary processes: the completion of a series of leadership assessment data and talent profiles that are captured in PSDP; and annual talent review meetings across levels (affiliate, service area, and system) in which the talent profiles and critical leadership positions are discussed, calibrated, and translated into development plans.

High Potential Assessment: Sutter Health assesses high-potential leadership with a concise, validated tool based on research by the Corporate Leadership Council, Lominger (Korn Ferry), Bersin by Deloitte, and DDI.[76] A critical starting point for creating a robust leadership assessment process is developing common language around key terminology, including the term 'high potential.' For Sutter Health, a high-potential employee is defined as "someone who is capable of rising to and succeeding at a more senior, critical role. An employee's potential is defined in terms of their personal aspirations, functional ability, and engagement." As part of the annual talent review process, executive teams across levels (affiliate, service area, system) complete a ten-item assessment of their direct reports across the following dimensions:

- *Personal Aspirations:* An individual's interest in leadership opportunities and further advancement at Sutter Health.

- *Functional Abilities:* An individual's cognitive and behavioral abilities, including change agility, creative and critical thinking, and communication skills.

- *Engagement:* An individual's commitment to continuous learning, results orientation, political savvy, and overall presence facing adversity.

Talent Profiles: Sutter Health's annual talent review process asks executive teams across levels to complete comprehensive talent profiles that include much more than high potential assessments of their direct reports. Fully integrated into the PSDP system, talent profiles require executives to provide a series of key data points for each of their direct reports. Illustrated in figure 4.2, the talent profile is a comprehensive assessment of both the individual and the position across several critical dimensions. After completing the leadership potential assessment and providing ratings for 'risk of loss,' 'impact of loss,' and 'promotability range,' the executive describes the employee's 'best next move' including the functional area (nursing, operations, IT, finance, HR, etc.), management level (grow in current role, promote to director, etc.), and type of business (transition to larger hospital, region, or system office). The executive also describes each direct report in terms of his or her readiness to succeed one or more specific roles or persons across the health system. This data point represents an important metric for evaluating the efficacy of the succession management system—leadership bench strength. Most importantly, executives work with their direct reports to complete the development planning section of the talent profile, which details development needs, potential development programs (Leadership Academy, Management and Clinical Excellence, Accelerated Change Excellence, Sutter Certified Leadership for nurse leaders, etc.), and specific development activities based on Sutter's 4 E Model: explore, experience, exposure, and education. This discussion between the executive and each direct report is critical for gauging his or her aspirations for future leadership positions and gaining buy-in for potential leadership development experiences.

Annual Talent Review Process

Armed with the leadership potential and development planning data provided by the **Talent Profiles**, executive teams across Sutter Health participate in annual talent review meetings. Illustrated in figure 4.3, the annual talent review process begins with talent review meetings at the affiliate (hospital) level in March and April, and rolls up to the divisional level in May, and culminates at the system level in July. Following the system-level talent review meeting, the chief human resources officer (CHRO) engages Sutter Health's board chair and executive compensation committee in talent reviews of the system CEO's direct reports (executive leadership team) and emerging system-level executives. At this final stage of the annual process, the CHRO and Sutter Health board play key roles in providing insights and feedback to SHU professionals in the targeted development of senior leaders and SHU's executive development programs. This critical element of the annual talent review process holds SHU accountable for developing successors to the system CEO, a key responsibility of the board and the system CEO. With support from the CHRO, the board chair and executive compensation committee evaluate potential successors to the system CEO and create relevant development opportunities for potential successors. As demonstrated by the promotion of Sutter Health's COO Sarah Krevans to the CEO position in January 2016, a smooth system

Figure 4.2
Sutter Health's PSDP Succession Planning: Manager Assessment and Talent Review Worksheet

Employee Name: _____

Manager Name: _____

	High	Medium	Low
1. Potential	☐	☐	☐
2. Risk of Loss	☐	☐	☐
3. Impact of Loss	☐	☐	☐

4. Promotability Range _____ to _____ months Examples: 6mo., 12 – 24 mo., 36 + mo., etc.

5. Next Best Move
  Potential job role employee could fill
    Function: _____ Examples: Nursing, Operations, IT
    Level: _____ Examples: Grow in current role, Director
    Business Type: _____ Examples: Large Hospital, Region, Division

6. Successor To
  Specific Role/Person: _____
    Readiness: ☐ Ready Now ☐ 1 to 2 Years ☐ 3+ Years

7. Development Planning (to be discussed with employee)
  Development Needs: _____
Potential Development Programs: _____
                  Examples: Leadership Academy, ACE, MCE
Potential Development Activities
Based on 4E Model: _____
      Explore: _____
      Experience: _____
      Exposure: _____
      Education: _____

8. Identify Successors
  Successor Name: _____
  Rank (circle one):   1   2   3
  Readiness: ☐ Ready Now ☐ 1 to 2 Years ☐ 3+ Years
  Interim Replacement: ☐ Yes ☐ No

CEO transition is ultimately the result of several years of planning and collaborative work amongst SHU, the board chair, and the executive compensation committee.

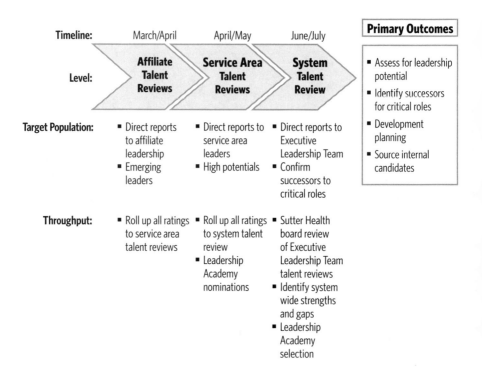

Figure 4.3
Sutter Health's Annual Talent Review Process

Consistent with best practices for minimizing rater errors and biases associated with conflating ratings of high potential versus high performance,[77] talent review meetings are conducted months after completion of the annual performance review period. The time lag between annual performance reviews and the start of the talent review process is not trivial, as maintaining the focus of talent review meetings on discussion of leadership potential and development experiences—and not confusing performance with potential—is critical to effective talent review discussions. At the affiliate and service area talent review meetings, leaders collectively discuss in their respective organizations with a focus on the following key outcomes:

1. Identify successors for the system CEO and other members of the executive leadership team (ELT).

2. Identify successors for critical leadership roles (CEO, CAO, COO, and CNO) and emerging leaders, including overall readiness level and possible next step roles; validate manager assessment data.

3. Determine development needs and next steps for creating development plans for high potentials, successors to critical roles, and emerging leaders.

4. Nominate candidates for the **Leadership Academy** and/or other development programs (e.g., Executive Development for Physicians, Management and Clinical Excellence Program (MCE), Accelerating Change Excellence (ACE), Physicians' LeaderLab, etc.).

For the system-level executive leadership team (ELT), the talent review meeting is the culminating activity of the entire talent review process. The ELT is charged with providing the highlights of leadership talent in their respective divisions and functions with a particular focus on successors to the CEO and COO roles across the system. Consistent with the overall philosophy of balancing the discussion around both assessment and development, ELT members also assess these successors' development needs, elements of their development plans, and selection of candidates for the **Leadership Academy**. Peter Anderson, an ELT member and senior vice president of Strategy and Business Development, remarked, "In addition to the traditional talent review, system executives are involved in reviewing three hundred evaluations on a number of characteristics, including overall potential for advancement for next immediate term. It's very effective and time consuming, but also appropriate to identify leaders, their development needs, and a career path for them–there is not an easy way to do it fast. I feel it is very well orchestrated."

An invaluable element of the talent review process is the facilitator's role, which is performed by an SHU professional. All talent review meetings are facilitated by an internal consultant from SHU's HR and Organizational Development (OD) professionals or by a trained HR leader. The facilitator plays multiple roles throughout the talent review process:

- *Pre-Talent Review Meeting:* The talent review meeting facilitator meets with the senior leader (CEO, service area president, system CEO) of the executive team to determine the target population for the talent review. This discussion is critical given the necessary time for executive teams to effectively accomplish the multiple goals of the talent review meeting—calibrate ratings for leadership potential, 9-box grid placements (see figure 4.4), and development planning. Executive teams are encouraged to allocate a half day for assessing twenty to thirty people/roles during a talent review meeting. The target populations for review include critical leadership positions (CEO, CAO, COO, and CNO), successors to these roles, and emerging leaders. Prior to the talent review meeting, the talent review facilitator ensures that both employees and managers input the necessary talent profile data (leadership potential ratings, risk of loss, impact of loss, etc.) into the PSDP system.

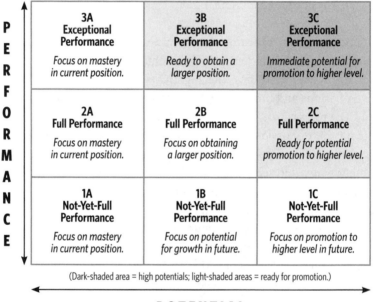

Figure 4.4
Sutter Health's Performance and Potential 9-Box Grid

(Dark-shaded area = high potentials; light-shaded areas = ready for promotion.)

- *Talent Review Meeting:* During the talent review meeting, the talent review facilitator invites the executives to discuss their direct reports and emerging leaders in their respective department or work unit in an effort to calibrate the leadership potential ratings and placement of individuals across the 9-box grid. A critical responsibility of the facilitator is to ensure that the executive team remains focused on discussing each individual's potential for future leadership roles and not performance in the current role. The facilitator also works to ensure that the placement of individuals across the 9-box grid reflects the sentiments of the executive team and the data presented at the meeting, not exclusively the perspective of the individual's direct manager. The broader discussion of an individual's leadership potential, successors, and development needs across the entire executive team provides necessary calibration and validation of the direct manager's assessment data. Finally, the facilitator anchors the discussion of leadership development planning and potential educational or role-based opportunities around a system-wide perspective that avoids 'talent hoarding'—managers keeping high-potential employees from leaving current positions or pursuing role-based developmental assignments elsewhere across Sutter Health. Finally, this discussion is aided by summary descriptions of each talent profile and the corresponding leadership development guide that comprises the 9-box grid. The facilitator and executive team jointly determine the relevant leadership development focus for individuals who are rated as 'potential for higher level' (table 4.1), 'focus on current position' (table 4.2), and 'growth to larger position' (table 4.3).

Table 4.1

Sutter Health Talent Profiles and Developmental Guide for Talent Rated as 'Potential for Higher Level'

9-Box Grid Dimension	Talent Profile	Developmental Guide
3C Exceptional Performance Immediate Potential for Higher Level	• Exceptional performer, exceeds dynamic goals • Gets all the important things done, plus • Demonstrates many competencies beyond current position • Ready to assume higher thought leadership role in area of expertise • Ready to add new functions to current position	*Ready for two-level promotion within next thirty-six months.*
3B Exceptional Performance Growth to Bigger Position	• Exceptional performer, exceeds dynamic goals • Gets all the important things done, plus • Demonstrates many competencies beyond current position • Shows ability to assume higher thought leadership role in area of expertise • Shows ability to add new functions to current position	*Ready for one-level promotion in functional area of expertise with broader responsibility.*
2C Full Performance Immediate Potential for Higher Level	• Solid performer, meets dynamic goals • Gets all or most of the important things done • Demonstrates many competencies beyond current level or role • Acknowledged leadership ability and impact outside area of responsibility	*Ready for potential one-level promotion in functional area of expertise, or with broader/new areas of responsibility.*

Table 4.2

Sutter Health Talent Profiles and Developmental Guide for Talent Rated as 'Focus on Current Position'

9-Box Grid Dimension	Talent Profile	Developmental Guide
3A **Exceptional Performance** *Focus on Current Position*	▪ Exceptional performer, exceeds dynamic goals ▪ Gets all the important things done, plus ▪ Demonstrates role model competencies for current position ▪ Seen as thought leader in area of expertise ▪ Has achieved potential or reached desired position	*Continue developing in current position; tap for coaching, special assignment, or task force.*
2A **Full Performance** *Focus on Current Position*	▪ Solid performer, meets dynamic goals ▪ Gets all or most of the important things done ▪ Demonstrates essential competencies for current position ▪ Seen as proficient in area of expertise and position ▪ Leadership skills are commensurate with position	*Target ways to achieve greater results and improve competencies for growth position; consider lateral move.*
1A **Not-Yet-Full Performance** *Focus on Current Position*	▪ Low performer, falls behind in meeting dynamic goals ▪ Is not getting most of the important things done ▪ Lacks essential competencies in one or more of these areas: professional knowledge, relationships, management or leadership ▪ Seen as ineffective in area of expertise and position	*Target key areas for improvement or re-assign to lower level of organization.*

- *Post-Talent Review Meeting:* After completion of the talent review meetings, an SHU professional or HR leader updates the PSDP system with the final leadership potential ratings, successors, and development planning action items. All changes and updates to the leadership potential metrics and successor information stemming from the talent review discussions are captured in PSDP. Finally, the executives schedule 'development discussions' with their respective high potentials, identified successors, and emerging leaders to create development plans.

Evidence-Based Success Factors

Without question, Sutter Health's talent review and succession management practices are consistent with research on succession planning and leadership

Table 4.3

Sutter Health Talent Profiles and Developmental Guide for Talent Rated as 'Growth to Larger Position'

9-Box Grid Dimension	Talent Profile	Developmental Guide
2B Full Performance *Growth to Larger Position*	• Solid performer, meets dynamic goals • Gets all or most of the important things done • Demonstrates some competencies beyond current level or role • Strong leader in area of expertise and shows ability/interest in new areas	*Preparing for potential one-level promotion in functional area of expertise or for broader responsibility in current position.*
1B Not-Yet-Full Performance *Potential for Growth in Future*	• Inconsistent performer • Is not getting many noticeably important things done • Needs improvement in essential competencies • Follows work directions, when given them • Demonstrates strengths in leadership, results or other key areas	*Check for appropriate job match or other problems; may be new to position.*
1C Not-Yet-Full Performance *Potential for Higher Level in Future*	• Needs to improve several areas of performance • Is not getting some of the important things done • Contribution in some areas is very good • Recognized as team player, informal leader, or role model in one or more of essential competencies • Demonstrates strengths in leadership, results, or other key areas	*Target key areas for improvement and reinforce strengths; may be new to position.*

development best practices.[78] However, an evidence-based approach for evaluating the efficacy of these practices demands answers to the following questions: What makes Sutter Health's talent review and succession management practices best-in-class for healthcare organizations? What is the impact of these practices on key performance metrics? What are the critical *execution* best practices for designing and implementing talent review and succession management practices? To address these key questions and identify potential improvement opportunities, SHU initiated an independent and comprehensive assessment (see About the Research for a summary of assessment methodology) of its talent review and succession management practices. Summarized in table 4.4, the assessment identified six primary success factors that establish Sutter Health's talent review and succession management process as a best-in-class system. The success factors were revealed through analysis of multiple data sources, including archival data (leadership assessment tools, talent review materials, performance metrics, etc.) and dozens of interviews with executives across levels and SHU professionals. Overall, the success factors offer insights into how the various talent assessment and succession management elements drive strong performance outcomes. Each success factor is discussed below and illustrated by excerpts from executives across Sutter Health.

Table 4.4
Sutter Health's Talent Review & Succession Management Success Factors

Success Factor	Execution Principles
Executive Team Commitment	▪ Describe talent assessment as a strategic priority ▪ Fully engage in talent assessment process and talent review meetings ▪ Participate in a range of leadership development programs and activities as project sponsors, mentors, speakers, advisors, and other roles
Strategic Talent Pool Designation	▪ Adopt clear definition of high-potential leadership that is consistently applied across executive teams ▪ Clearly designate those positions or roles that are strategically critical ▪ Align talent review session agenda according to the strategically critical positions or roles
Strong Assessment-Development Link	▪ Ensure talent review agenda balances the calibration of leadership potential ratings with discussion of development opportunities ▪ Partner with executive teams to identify range of development activities aligned with strategic initiatives
Performance and Potential Assessment Lag	▪ Conduct annual job performance reviews and talent reviews in distinct sessions separated by several weeks or months ▪ Focus talent review discussions on potential for succeeding in more senior, critical roles and redirect when dialogue diverts to current job performance
System-Wide View of Leadership Talent	▪ Cultivate an executive team culture that adopts an organization-wide lens for assessing and developing talent ▪ Encourage and reward the 'release' of talent for developmental roles across regions, divisions, and hospitals
Open, Honest Dialogue & Transparency	▪ Facilitate rich dialogue across talent review sessions that encourages executives to challenge one another's views ▪ Ensure open and honest calibration of leadership potential ratings and 9-box grid placements across executive teams ▪ Cultivate transparency by ensuring executives hold development sessions with direct reports to discuss talent review outcomes and development opportunities

Executive Team Commitment

The first success factor is the outstanding level of commitment to succession management from Sutter Health's executive teams. Executives across the Sutter Health board, system-level ELT, service areas, and affiliate hospitals consistently demonstrate a strong commitment to supporting the talent review and succession management process, as well as describing talent management as a strategic priority for the health system. In addition to maintaining sustained participation and engagement in many aspects of the talent review process, including formal (talent review sessions and sponsoring **Leadership Academy** projects) and informal (mentoring high potentials and emerging leaders) activities, executive teams strongly demonstrate their personal beliefs in the value of identifying and nurturing future Sutter Health leaders. Dr. Richard Slavin, CEO of Sutter Health's preeminent Palo Alto Medical Foundation, remarked, "managing talent is my job—I consider most of what I do is managing the talent, which includes supporting the senior leadership team and mentoring future physician and non-physician leaders." Similarly, many executives described succession management as a central value of their respective system, division, and affiliate leadership team. The following excerpts underscore the executive team's deep commitment to the succession management process:

> *I think of succession management as one of the most important things we are doing in our role, among a number of things we manage at the system executive level. Succession planning discussions and talent review sessions for senior leaders in the organization, and emerging leaders like the fellowship program, are driven by system executives. There is a high level of engagement and common understanding of the importance of the topic. (Jeff Gerard, president, Bay Area Service Area)*

> *Our executive team members are very highly engaged with the [**Leadership Academy**] sessions–they make time on their calendar for any one of them—they sponsor the work teams and projects and they are very passionate about it. It's a statement of value, attendance, and almost unanimous participation in making it a priority. (Mike Helm, senior vice president & chief human resources officer, 2004-2015)*

> *I am one who has a special affection for succession planning–for the elements of growth and development. My personal belief is there are few things more rewarding than identifying someone with drive, motivation, and talent, and giving them the opportunity to grow and perform and achieve their personal goals. And to see individuals promoted in*

the company—that you had some small piece of helping with their growth and development. (David Bradley, East Bay Region president, 2012-2015)

Strategic Talent Pool Designation

A second key success factor is the execution of a consistent process for identifying high-potential leaders and targeting strategic talent pools. The facilitated talent review sessions adopt a clear and consistent definition of high-potential leadership that is reinforced across the system, service area, and affiliate executive teams. By working directly with the senior leader of each executive team to clearly identify the target talent pools, talent review facilitators ensure greater depth and quality of the talent review discussions for the strategically critical roles. Marcia Reissig, CEO of Sutter Health's home care division (Sutter Care at Home), stated, "historically in healthcare, you were promoted if you've been a good clinician. Someone who is a really good nurse becomes a front-line manager but does not know anything about being a good manager. To have a lasting impact on the big picture, we've identified the critical positions where we need to focus our attention. This is one of the key parts of our talent review process—that more intense focus on the key people we are trying to develop." This practice is consistent with leading companies across industries for aligning human capital practices with business strategy.[79] In short, the resources devoted to talent management activities are strongly aligned with talent pools that have the greatest strategic impact. The skilled facilitation of review sessions enforces discipline across executive teams with regard to not conflating performance with potential, as well as maintaining collaborative and non-politicized dialogue.

Strong Assessment-Development Link

A third success factor is the balanced focus on both assessment of leadership potential and the requisite development opportunities for individuals across the 9-box grid. Supported by the PSDP Management Assessment and Talent Review Worksheet (figure 4.2), talent review discussions are characterized by clear and consistent links between the assessment results and developmental action items. Multiple developmental experiences are discussed and debated by executive teams, including Lean projects (project-based efforts to eliminate waste and inefficiencies in a given process or practice to enhance quality outcomes[80]), **Leadership Academy** participation, division/system projects, and the creation of new positions. Consistent with Sutter Health's strategic initiatives, individuals assessed as 'high-potential/high-performance leaders' (figure 4.4) are immediately assigned to Lean projects to develop expertise in driving out inefficiencies and lowering costs associated with a business process in their respective department. Employees placed in the upper-right box of the 9-box grid are deemed exceptional performers with immediate potential for higher levels. Therefore, for these employees, the developmental focus centers on accelerated leadership development activities (**Leadership Academy** participation, Lean projects, addition of new functions to current position) that will facilitate a two-level promotion within two to three years. Emphasizing the importance of ensuring a robust set of potential development opportunities for high-potential leaders, Dr. Jeffrey Burnich, an ELT member and senior vice president of Medical & Market Networks, remarked, "I think we have a really strong **Leadership Academy**, Leadership Development Institute, ACE, MCE, and all different [leadership development programs]—we sit down with the 9-box grid and we go through those routinely. I have been very impressed [that our succession management process] brings different executives together across the organization to sponsor initiatives and projects that are elements of these development programs, such as attending the **Leadership Academy** team project presentations. We can see how emerging leaders really perform. We can see up-and-coming talent like a farm league for baseball–it's a super way to do it."

Performance- and Potential-Assessment Lag

Another key successor factor that is more technical in nature but is nonetheless an important driver of effective outcomes in the time lag between performance and potential assessments. Affiliate executive teams allow sufficient time to elapse between the conclusion of the annual performance review period and commencement of the talent review process, including leadership potential ratings and the talent profile. Completion of performance reviews and leadership potential ratings in distinct sessions that are separated by several weeks or months helps cultivate an executive team culture that allows for calibration and challenging of one another's ratings and contributes to greater consistency of talent review outcomes. Summarizing his executive team's views on the importance of the lag between the performance review period and the talent review process, the CEO of a prominent Sutter Health medical center stated, "The leadership potential assessment process that we go through allows for the opportunity to challenge those ratings, and as a result there is much more consistency in terms of our outcomes. As the hospital's executive team, we go through the process of evaluating one another's direct reports—it's a very similar pushback. We have the same discussions regarding performance evaluation ratings. We made a conscious decision not to do leadership potential ratings at the same time as the performance evaluation—to separate them and do performance evaluations, then six months later we do potential assessments." This technical aspect of the talent review process is consistent with research on talent assessment best practices concerning how to best reduce rater errors and biases associated with conflating ratings of job performance and leadership potential.[81]

System-Wide View of Leadership Talent

The fifth success factor driving Sutter Health's strong succession management outcomes is the cultivation of an executive team culture that views leadership talent from a health system perspective. Executive teams across Sutter Health view the process for assessing leadership talent using a system-wide lens and not a silo-driven perspective that seeks to retain high-potential leaders in their respective hospitals or service areas. The executive teams express a strong value in discouraging talent hoarding and supporting the release of their talented associates to other affiliates, service areas, or divisions across Sutter Health. Sutter Health's former chief medical officer and ELT member Dr. Gordon Hunt remarked, "I want to bring up another best practice of our talent review process—to release the best and brightest to other parts of the organization. I see it on a regular basis, one person in one region is moved to another. This approach is a model for the organization as a whole. I find it extremely helpful in recruiting. People figure out that you're not going to drive them into the ground—you are going to help them grow, and when it's time to move, you help them move." Referencing the personal pride associated with contributing to the success of another service area or affiliate in the system, Bay Area Service Area president Jeff Gerard stated, "there's much less discussion of poaching talent, and part of that is working so closely together as an executive team. It now feels like a badge of honor to add value to another part of the system, and the better you feel about development opportunities regarding to your best people." Finally, Sutter Care at Home's CEO Marcia Reissig poignantly described the delicate balance between advocating for her affiliate while also adopting a system-wide view of leadership talent:

> One of our acute care regional CIO positions became available but our high potential did not get the job because he did not have acute care experience. It was a big disappointment and we did not want him to leave the system. We identified him as a candidate for the **Leadership Academy**—but he was hesitant to attend due to the time commitment. I told him, "you want to do all these big things–look who gets promoted." He agreed to go. The **Leadership Academy** was a great experience for him. This, along with other aspects of our talent management pro-

gram, helped him reconsider his areas of interest. Today, he is a system executive in the strategy area. This is a good example [of our succession management process]; we talked to him constantly to get to know his aspirations. He is a high potential and we did not want to lose him. It always made me feel good about myself–that I was brave enough to talk with him about leaving [our affiliate]—if it was best for him.

Open, Honest Dialogue & Transparency

A final success factor associated with the succession management process is the depth and honesty of the dialogue that characterizes the talent review discussions across executive teams, and the resulting impact on employee perceptions of transparency. Many executives across levels highlight the rich dialogue that takes place as part of talent review meetings and the cultural tolerance to challenge one another's views. James Conforti, Valley Service Area president and ELT member, remarked, "the part I like the most [about the talent review process] is where I have rich dialogue with my team and discussions about people, their current performance, readiness, and potential. We have to complete the 9-box grid and it adds rigor to the process. But from my perspective, I like the dialogue about their true performance, and true potential moving forward. I think that the more honesty and more discussion in those conversations, the more effective our process is." The importance of calibrating leadership potential and 9-box grid placements through integration of multiple perspectives—not solely the candidate's immediate manager—is lauded by executives as a critical best practice. Conforti continued, "One critical thing that happens when we do it as a team is that other people's perceptions of that person come into play—it's not just one person's view. Someone may have worked with that individual in a cross-functional capacity; they worked with that person on the project and you don't get that type of rich dialogue if you are doing it just one on one."

A related outcome associated with a highly effective talent review process is the extent to which employees view the process as fair and transparent. An often-cited dilemma associated with succession management is whether or not to inform candidates of their status as it relates to talent review outcomes.[82] At Sutter Health, the focus is on cultivating system transparency by ensuring executives conduct individual development sessions with their direct reports following the talent review process. Rather than emphasize the categories in which direct reports are slotted across the 9-box grid, executives focus the discussion on the relevant developmental opportunities. By avoiding explicit terminology around being designated as a high potential, and instead, discussing the range of accelerated development opportunities afforded employees who demonstrate leadership potential and strong job performance, executives minimize the risks of alienating employees who are not rated as high potential. Furthermore, executive teams guard against the risk of any complacency amongst high-potential leaders by explaining that the talent review system is a dynamic process—potential ratings, 9-box grid placements, and development opportunities will change each year. Echoing the importance of maintaining a transparent talent review process, an ELT member explained, "I think the talent review process is very transparent—people throughout the company know how people are nominated and selected. How succession planning works across Sutter Health, and particularly **Leadership Academy** selections, is a very transparent process." Similarly, a hospital CEO described the importance of maintaining transparency and openness to challenge one another as central tenets of the talent review process. She asserted, "Our [talent review process] is a very transparent process. We have very open discussions and allow people to challenge each other, talk about managers and nursing staff. For example, the ACU manager indicates that someone is a high potential but someone in Ancillary Services might say, 'I've seen [this person in a less favorable light].' It's a good process that is transparent and honest. I have worked in organizations where managers are very protective of their own folks so we might not be able to get to the truth like we have with open transparency and the opportunity to challenge each other."

Evidence-Based Evaluation: Succession Management Performance Metrics

For the ultimate stakeholders of Sutter Health's succession management practices, particularly the board and system, service area, and affiliate executive teams, efficacy is determined by the impact of these practices on key performance metrics. The long-term success of the talent review process and continuing support from senior leadership across the health system depends upon a clear, evidence-based approach that clearly demonstrates the succession management system's strategic impact. In an effort to regularly assess the succession management system's impact on key performance metrics, and subsequently communicate these findings to the board and executive teams across the system, SHU focuses its evaluation strategy on four primary metrics. They are part of the annual succession management scorecard that is presented to the board. The following section describes the evaluation strategy and presents key results across each performance metric:

1. *Internal/External Executive Placement Rate:* Illustrated in figure 4.5, Sutter Health's internal/external executive placement rate offers clear evidence

of sustained excellence between 2011 and 2015. Assessed as the percentage of open executive positions (VP and above) filled by internal candidates, SHU establishes an annual goal of 70 percent. Remarkably, Sutter Health's internal executive replacement rate for this five-year period was 71 percent. In 2015, the internal executive placement rate achieved a high of 80 percent while 50 percent of all internal executive placements were graduates of the **Leadership Academy**. In 2014, six of the seven open affiliate CEO positions were filled by internal candidates who were assessed via the talent review process. These results offer clear evidence of the succession management system's sustained excellence relative to both its stated goal of 70 percent as well as the national average for comparable hospitals and health systems. According to the **Healthcare Talent Management Survey**,[83] the national benchmark mean score for internal/external executive placement rate is 51 percent.

Figure 4.5
Sutter Health's Internal/External Executive Placement Rate (2011-2015)*

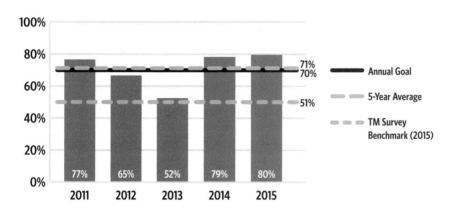

Notes: *Percentage of open executive positions (vice presidents and above) filled by internal candidates. The TM Survey Benchmark (2015) is the average internal/external executive placement rate across a national sample of hospitals and health systems from Healthcare Talent Management Survey 2015.

2. *Leadership Bench Strength:* Presented in figure 4.6, Sutter Health's executive leadership bench strength offers clear evidence of leadership depth for critical roles across the health system with the average being 47 percent between 2011 and 2015. Critical leadership roles at Sutter Health include hospital or affiliate CEO or CAO, COO, and CNO. By comparison, results of the **Healthcare Talent Management Survey**[84] report a 31 percent

leadership bench strength score for a national sample of hospitals and health systems. Notably, Sutter's Health's leadership bench strength, which essentially assesses the depth of Sutter Health's leadership pipeline, significantly improved over the five-year period.

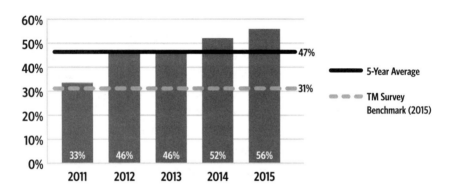

Figure 4.6
Sutter Health's Executive Leadership Bench Strength (2011-2015)

Notes: The TM Survey Benchmark (2015) is the average executive leadership bench strength across a national sample of hospitals and health systems from Healthcare Talent Management Survey 2015.

3. *Succession Management Depth:* In effort to assess the depth and broad utilization of the succession management process across Sutter Health's service areas and affiliates, SHU tracks the volume of critical positions assessed, successors identified, and high-performing/high-potential leaders identified throughout the system. Figure 4.7 presents clear evidence of the increasing utilization of the succession management system across Sutter Health. During a four-year period (2011-2014), the system-wide number of successors identified and high-performing/high-potential leaders has precipitously increased annually. Similarly, the overall percentage of critical positions assessed throughout the health system has increased each year. Overall, these metrics offer strong evidence of the depth and utilization of succession management across Sutter Health.

4. *Executive Gender and Ethnic Diversity:* The final set of key metrics for evaluating the succession management system's efficacy is executive team diversity. Sutter Health has consistently targeted executive team gender and ethnic diversity as important outcomes of an effective talent review and succession management process. From 2011 through 2015,

Figure 4.7

Sutter Health's Succession Management Depth: Assessment of Critical Positions, Successors, and High-Performing/High-Potential Leaders (2011-2014)*

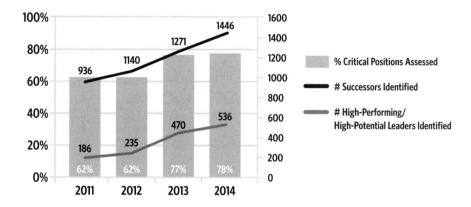

Notes: *Percentage of Critical Positions Assessed is the overall percentage of critical roles (CEO, CAO, COO, and CNO) across the health system that have been assessed via the annual talent review process. Number of Successors Identified is the overall number of successors identified via the annual talent review process across the health system, including multiple successors and/or external successors for some positions. Number of High-Performing/High-Potential Leaders Identified is the overall number of leaders assessed in the top right box of the 9-box grid.

the percentage of executive roles (VP and above) occupied by women has remained between 43 percent and 46 percent (figure 4.8). By comparison, the national benchmark score for executive gender diversity according to the **Healthcare Talent Management Survey**[85] is 42 percent. Impressively, the percentage of female successors to executive roles has ranged between 62 and 69 percent from 2011 to 2015. Considering the executive gender diversity results in tandem with the leadership bench strength metric, Sutter Health's pipeline for critical leadership roles is loaded with many talented, high-performing, high-potential women.

Similarly, Sutter Health actively tracks and seeks to enhance the ethnic diversity of executive teams. Across a five-year period (2011-2015), the percentage of executive roles (VP and above) occupied by ethnic minorities has remained between 10 and 11 percent (figure 4.9). Although these metrics are just below a national benchmark score of 14 percent for executive ethnic diversity, according to a national sample of hospitals and health systems, the percentage of successors to executive positions has shown an upward trend between 2011 and 2015. Overall, these

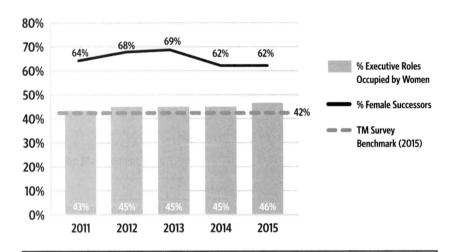

Figure 4.8
Sutter Health's Executive Gender Diversity (2011-2015)*

Notes: *Percentage of executive positions (VP and above) occupied by women. The TM Survey Benchmark (2015) is the average executive gender diversity across a national sample of hospitals and health systems from Healthcare Talent Management Survey 2015.

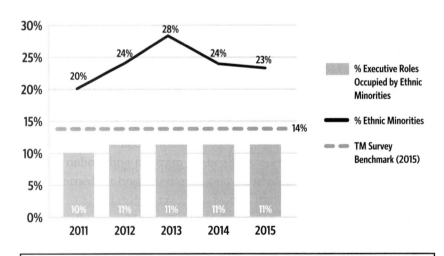

Figure 4.9
Sutter Health's Executive Ethnic Diversity (2011-2015)*

Notes: *Percentage of executive positions (VP and above) occupied by ethnic minorities. The TM Survey Benchmark (2015) is the average executive ethnicity diversity across a national sample of hospitals and health systems from Healthcare Talent Management Survey 2015.

metrics offer clear evidence of the ongoing improvement of gender and ethnic diversity across Sutter Health's executive teams.

Lessons Learned

This case study illustrated the primary elements of Sutter Health's talent review and succession management system, and its impact on key performance outcomes that are valued by the board and executive teams across the health system. The evidence-based success factors that explain the efficacy of Sutter Health's exemplary talent review and succession management system highlight a series of important lessons for hospital organizations.

1. *Identify Strategic Talent Pools:* In an environment of limited resources—notably time and attention from hospital executive teams and boards charged with executing succession management processes—a critical best practice is to clearly identify the talent pools that are strategically aligned with the organization. For many hospitals and health systems, these positions include hospital or facility C-suite roles—CEO, CAO, COO, CFO, and CNO. For hospitals seeking greater alignment with clinical quality initiatives, as well as physician alignment, CMO and Clinical Integration positions are also assessed as strategic talent pools.

2. *Conduct Rigorous Talent Reviews:* For best-practice hospital organizations, annual talent review sessions are executed with the same rigor and discipline as the annual performance review process. Importantly, the goal of the talent review process is not replacement planning—the identification of the most likely direct report to replace an incumbent leader—but to cultivate talent profiles and succession plans for strategically critical positions and create a central, searchable repository of leadership talent. Highly effective talent reviews are full-day sessions facilitated by HR professionals in which executive teams assess their direct reports, calibrate ratings across team members, and discuss development plans for employees rated as high potentials and high performers.

3. *Engage the Board in Talent Reviews for the System Leadership Team:* Exemplary succession management systems meaningfully engage key board members, including the board chair and the HR or compensation committee, in the annual talent review process for the CEO's direct reports and emerging system-level executives. A critical lesson learned is the importance of ensuring that the annual talent review process provides the board chair and other key board members or committees with the

opportunity to assess the talent reviews for the CEO's direct reports, identify developmental needs, and craft development opportunities for potential successors.

4. *Utilize Formal Assessment Tools:* Another lesson learned for many hospitals that have initiated annual talent review processes, and subsequently seen them resisted by top management teams, is the importance of using formal assessment tools. Failure to use validated, formal assessment tools when assessing leadership talent can inadvertently contribute to talent review discussions that become politicized and characterized by talent hoarding. While best-practice organizations utilize a range of formal assessment tools to support the review process, two such instruments are central for the process: a validated high-potential leadership assessment and 9-box grid. HR professionals work diligently with top management teams to clearly define each dimension of the 9-box grid and the career development implications for employees falling within each box. For best-practice organizations, a robust 9-box grid is supported by utilizing a validated assessment of leadership potential. Rather than assessing potential with simple categories (e.g., high potential, solid performer, etc.) and the rater errors and biases that accompany such approaches, highly effective talent reviews utilize validated leadership potential assessments that measure the traits (e.g., aspiration to be in a leadership role) and leadership competencies (e.g., learning agility) aligned with performance in future leadership roles.[86]

5. *Link Potential Assessment Results and Developmental Experiences:* Hospital organizations with highly effective succession management practices ensure that the annual talent review session balances the discussion of assessment results with thoughtful examination of development opportunities for employees moving forward. The facilitated debate that calibrates high-potential ratings across the 9-box grid and the corresponding discussion of accelerated job assignments, training, and other development experiences are both invaluable. In partnership with HR professionals, management teams must arm themselves with a range of development opportunities that are strongly aligned with the strategic initiatives of the hospital or health system. For many best-practice health systems, including Sutter Health, Henry Ford Health System, Cleveland Clinic, and Trinity Health, participation in an internally developed healthcare leadership academy represents an ideal development opportunity for high-potential employees.[87] Job rotations or temporary job transfers, Lean

projects, system-wide task forces, and specialized courses or training programs represent additional developmental experiences that should be strongly connected to talent assessment discussions.

6. *Stagger Annual Performance Review and Talent Review Processes:* A more subtle but nonetheless impactful lesson learned is the timing of talent review processes. Hospital organizations with exemplary talent assessment practices avoid the challenges associated with asking management teams to simultaneously assess job performance and leadership potential. Not only does this practice risk diluting the talent assessment discussion given time pressures, but the incidence of rater errors and cognitive biases is much greater. The key lesson learned is to conduct talent assessment activities several months after completing annual performance reviews so that talent review sessions remain focused on discussion of the skills, capabilities, and experiences demanded by future roles.

7. *Disciplined Utilization of Performance Management Platform:* The final lesson learned from this case study is the disciplined use of a performance management platform or comprehensive software solution that seamlessly engages both employees and supervisors in the completion of talent profiles. The platform provides a central, searchable repository of leadership talent that includes data on high potential assessment results, risk and impact of loss, potential future positions or job roles, development planning, and potential successors. As with many talent management processes, a critical best practice is using the talent profile as a dynamic tool that must be updated by both employees and their managers throughout the year. To support the disciplined use of the software system, offer training modules for managers to support their work in updating talent profiles and talking with employees about their high-potential status.

Conclusion

For more than eight years, Sutter Health has invested in the development and ongoing improvement of its talent review and succession management system. As a cornerstone talent management capability, the quality and consistency of the succession management process drives critical performance metrics across the health system. As detailed in this case, Sutter Health's exemplary talent review and succession management system has developed strong bench strength and succession depth in critical leadership positions that will continue to effectively advance the organization's strategic goals.

About the Research

The research to support this case study was conducted by Kevin S. Groves, PhD, and Groves Consulting Group during the 18-month period between July 2014 and January 2016. Sutter Health University (SHU) initiated an independent and comprehensive assessment of the Sutter Health's talent development and succession management practices to accomplish the following objectives:

- Evaluate the multi-level processes and practices of the succession management system, including leadership assessment, talent review meetings, and leadership development practices;

- Conduct semi-structured interviews with executive stakeholders across levels (ELT members, executive leaders, service area presidents, and affiliate CEOs) and functions (Strategy, Human Resources, Legal Counsel, Clinical Integration, Finance, etc.) and SHU professionals, to identify best practices and development opportunities; and

- Assess the impact of talent review and succession management practices on key performance metrics, including internal/external executive placement rate, leadership bench strength, and executive team gender and ethnic diversity.

The assessment strategy consisted of collected data from the following sources:

1. **SHU Professionals:** A series of open-ended interviews were conducted with SHU professionals to review and discuss all extant materials for talent review, leadership assessment, and succession management practices. The interviews were aimed at discussing the design and execution of all talent review and succession management practices.

2. **Sutter Health Executives:** The organization's system executive team, service area presidents, and a sample of affiliate (hospital or medical foundation) CEOs participated in semi-structured interviews. The purpose of the interviews was to assess the composition, efficacy, and consistency of Sutter Health's talent review and succession management practices across three levels: system, service area, and affiliate (hospital or medical foundation). The individual interviews were conducted in

person or by phone, and transcribed by an electronic recording service for the purpose of subsequent analysis.

3. ***Observation:*** Several critical talent development and succession management practices and programs were observed for data collection, specifically annual talent review meetings conducted by an affiliate organization and a region, and several Leadership Academy sessions.

4. ***Archival Data:*** Archival data and information, including talent review, leadership assessment, and succession management materials and tools, performance metrics, and other extant materials were obtained for review and analysis.

CHAPTER 5

Accelerated Executive Development at HCA: Just-in-Time Development and Placement of Hospital C-Suite Leaders

> When you think about executive development, this program is phenomenal in terms of jumpstarting one's career. I'm not aware of anything in the industry that can take a budding healthcare executive and get him or her into the executive offices at as accelerated a pace as this program does. I think that's exactly the reason for its popularity. I think the real attractive aspect of this program is less the focus on training but more the focus on career acceleration. Think about the [EDP candidate] who completed his/her master's degree at age twenty-five, and then has to complete one to two years of experience in a healthcare setting. At age twenty-seven, they are an associate COO and within twenty-four months a good number will be COO of an HCA hospital—that simply is not likely to happen with any other career path to the executive offices in the healthcare business.
>
> Peter Marmerstein
West Florida Division President
HCA

Hospital Corporation of America (HCA)

One of the nation's leading providers of healthcare services, Hospital Corporation of America (HCA) comprises 170 locally managed hospitals and 118 freestanding surgery centers across twenty states and six hospitals in England. Based in Nashville, Tennessee, HCA is responsible for approximately 5 percent of all US hospital services that are delivered by 233,000 employees and thirty-seven thousand active physicians. Ranked 63rd on the *Fortune 100* list of America's largest companies,[88] HCA is the largest for-profit operator of healthcare facilities in the world with $41.5 billion in 2016 revenue. HCA is recipient of numerous awards and recognitions for the quality of care delivered across its vast network, including 106 of its hospitals on The Joint Commission's list of Top Performers on Key Quality Measures[89]—the independent accrediting organization for assessing quality outcomes at hospitals and health systems. Thomson Reuters and Truven Health Analytics rated eight HCA hospitals among its list of 100 Top Hospitals.[90] HCA was also acknowledged in 2016 as a 'World's Most Ethical Company' by the Ethisphere Institute for the seventh consecutive year.[91] While HCA's affiliated physicians and hospitals serve hundreds of diverse communities across the US, the company's largest footprint of facilities is in Florida, Texas, Tennessee, and Virginia.

HCA operates as a federation of healthcare facilities managed by a divisional structure that is comprised of multiple groups of hospitals and healthcare services. The company's two primary hospital groups include the National Group and American Group, which each comprise seven divisions and their respective hospitals and surgery centers in geographic areas. For example, the American Group includes the Gulf Coast Division and its sixteen hospitals located in the Houston metropolitan area. The North Florida Division, a member of the National Group, comprises twelve hospitals across Orlando, Tallahassee, and Pensacola. HCA's divisional structure also includes an Operations & Service Lines Group, Physician Services Group, and HCA International, which includes the company's London hospitals. While HCA's vast network includes general, acute care, psychiatric, and rehabilitation hospitals, the company's facilities do not typically engage in extensive medical research and education programs. HCA's administrative structure consists of the hospital or surgery center CEOs reporting to their respective division president, who reports to their corresponding group president. The group presidents are members of HCA's Nashville-based senior leadership team currently headed by chairman and CEO Milton Johnson.

Throughout its rich history and rapid growth over the last two decades, HCA has sustained a strong commitment to attracting and developing executive leadership talent. Former HCA chairman and CEO Jack Bovender, who was elected into *Modern Healthcare*'s 'Health Care Hall of Fame'[92] in 2015, launched several workforce development, patient safety, and administrative efficiency initiatives. Shortly after being named CEO in 2001, Bovender initiated the creation of HCA's COO Development Program to address the challenges of an increasing number of division presidents and hospital executives reaching retirement and an overall lack of ethnic and gender diversity across HCA's hospital C-suites. After becoming CEO, Bovender realized that HCA needed to develop the capability to more swiftly identify and develop emerging leadership talent. In an interview with *Modern Healthcare*,[93] Bovender remarked, "We were very committed at HCA—and continue to be committed—to promoting from within. We see it as somewhat of a problem when we have to go outside of the company" for executive leadership talent. Importantly, Bovender signaled the importance of leadership diversity by naming himself HCA's chief diversity officer and publicly announcing the program's focus on increasing the number of women and ethnic minorities in HCA's leadership pipeline. Bovender's COO Development Program has since evolved into an integrated Executive Development Program (EDP) that develops leadership talent for multiple hospital C-suite roles, including COO, CNO, and CFO.

HCA's unwavering support for executive development has continued with chairman and CEO Milton Johnson. In his first year at the helm in 2014, Johnson established the company's executive development capability as one of HCA's strategic initiatives. Specifically, Johnson committed to further cultivating HCA's executive development practices as unparalleled in the healthcare industry by spearheading the launch of the **HCA Leadership Institute**. The **Leadership Institute** is charged with advancing HCA's vision by building strategic and operational capabilities through multiple executive development programs, including the company's signature Executive Development Program (EDP). In addition to developing deep and diverse leadership bench strength across HCA executive teams, Johnson cites the pace of industry change as a critical driver of the EDP's importance to the company. "Our expectations of our leaders are expanding to keep pace with the changes in healthcare, and the challenges to attract and retain the best individuals in our industry is greater than ever before," said Johnson. Consistent with HCA's values and history as an industry leader in executive development, Johnson nurtures a culture of leadership development amongst his Nashville-based executive team. Bill Rutherford, HCA's CFO and executive VP, states that "through our Executive Development Program, our future CNOs, COOs, and CFOs are becoming HCA leaders through hands-on experience, extensive healthcare management training, and one-on-one mentorship by HCA executives."

The following case study describes HCA's Executive Development Program (EDP) and its prominent role in supporting the company's strategic agenda during a time of unprecedented industry and workforce changes. This case study highlights a best-in-class executive development program for healthcare organizations seeking accelerated development and placement of leadership talent into executive roles. First, the primary EDP objectives and program phases are described, including the program's targeted talent pools, learning model and core curriculum, mentoring activities, and on-the-job learning. Based on a comprehensive assessment of the EDP program, this chapter presents a set of evidence-based best practices for designing an executive development program aimed at accelerated placement of high-potential talent into C-suite roles. These best practices are supported by the personal experiences of HCA's talent management and executive development executives, EDP alumni working in hospital CEO, CFO, COO, and CNO roles, division presidents, group presidents, and members of the Nashville-based corporate leadership team. Next, several performance metrics are presented as evidence of the EDP's impact on HCA's business outcomes, including annual turnover of C-suite executives, placement rates of EDP alumni into C-suite roles, and the gender and ethnic diversity of HCA's executive teams. Finally, there is a discussion of lessons learned and best-practice recommendations for developing a best-in-class executive development program for healthcare leaders.

Executive Development Program

Mission & Goals

The EDP serves an important role as part of HCA's broader talent management strategy and efforts to develop a strong pipeline of leadership talent for executive roles across its facilities. Designed to support one of HCA's critical strategic initiatives—cultivating an unparalleled executive development capability—the EDP's specific objectives[94] include:

- Attract top talent by offering a highly respected, selective, and best-in-class Executive Development Program;

- Provide associates with hands-on administrative exposure and experience in order to prepare for success as HCA's future executive leadership team;

- Provide associates with focused development in critical competency and business function areas as defined by the organization's Strategic Agenda; and

- Add economic value to the organization through the development of an executive leadership pipeline associated with measurably superior performance in the healthcare industry.

As evidenced by the program's strong reputation for accelerated development of hospital executives, the EDP is a highly selective leadership development program. Each of the EDP's program tracks—COO, CNO, and CFO development programs—attract high-achieving healthcare professionals with advanced degrees and established track records of industry experience. Ultimately, the EDP's mission is to establish a strong pipeline of leadership talent for hospital executive roles while also standardizing core HCA standards and processes across the company's network of hospitals. Sam Hazen, HCA's chief operating officer, remarked, "through participation in this program, executives not only distinguish themselves as candidates who may be tapped for future leadership advancement, but they further ensure that the standards, values, and processes that make HCA a leader in the industry are engrained and applied in our business."

Learning Model & Curriculum

The EDP's learning model and core curriculum are heavily weighted toward practical hospital management experience and multi-level executive mentoring. "Due to our Executive Development Program, our future CNOs, COOs, and CFOs are becoming HCA leaders through hands-on experience, extensive healthcare management training, and one-on-one mentorship by HCA executives," explains CFO and executive VP Bill Rutherford. Illustrated in figure 5.1, the EDP's learning model is anchored in a belief that 75 percent of leadership development occurs via experiential learning, while the remaining 25 percent should be delivered as part of didactic learning activities. The EDP's primary experiential activities include on-the-job training via placement as an 'associate' executive in an HCA hospital, and mentoring from HCA executives at both the local hospital and Nashville corporate office. For each of the EDP executive tracks (associate COO, associate CNO, and associate CFO), the participant is placed in an HCA hospital as an associate reporting to their respective functional chief executive. The remaining 25 percent of leadership development occurs via didactic learning activities, including a series of seminars delivered at HCA's Nashville corporate office, team action learning projects on a given facility or market strategy, and a series of individual leadership assessments and coaching sessions. The elements of the EDP's experiential and didactic learning activities are described below.

Program Tracks: Candidates for the EDP program include both high-potential, internal HCA employees and external hires who are geographically flexible and who possess both the aspiration and capability to succeed in hospital executive positions. EDP candidates for the associate CNO track include high-potential HCA employees with at least five years of leadership experience in healthcare, while associate CFO candidates must have at least one year of controller experience at HCA. For the associate COO track, EDP candidates include a mix of internal and external candidates who have recently graduated from an MHA, MBA, or a related degree program and possess at least two years of healthcare leadership experience. Based on HCA's annual talent strategy, executive turnover, and strategic objectives, a defined number of EDP candidates across the three tracks (COO, CNO, and CFO) are targeted for the program's integrated cohort. Given the EDP's emphasis on accelerated executive development, each candidate's 'graduation' from the program represents placement into an HCA hospital executive role as a COO, CNO, or CFO. The program lengths across the three tracks differ given the varying developmental needs of the talent pools for each track, as well as HCA's business needs for placements in vacant hospital C-suite roles. On average, the program length for associate CFOs is one to two years, while associate CNOs and associate COOs have a targeted program length of one to three years and two to three years, respectively.

Figure 5.1
Executive Development Program Learning Model

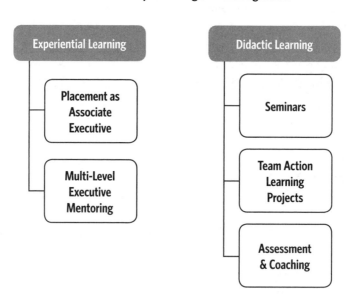

Executive Mentoring: The second element of experiential learning consists of multi-level mentoring, as each associate is paired with both a primary executive mentor—his or her chief executive supervisor—as well as a secondary mentor from HCA's corporate office. The associate's primary mentor and supervisor, who is an experienced CEO, CFO, COO, or CNO at an HCA facility, plays an invaluable role by ensuring that the executive team culture and hospital is supportive of the associate's development. The mentoring element of the EDP is critical for providing a structured, collaborative, and personalized relationship that focuses on developing each associate's leadership competencies. The mentoring process is designed to facilitate the transfer of a strategic perspective, organizational savvy, and HCA's core leadership competencies (see table 5.1) to the next generation of HCA leaders. The Nashville-based secondary mentor, an executive from HCA's corporate leadership team, provides the associate with ample exposure to the national office and demonstrates the company's strong commitment to executive development as a driver of operational excellence. Steve Otto, CEO of TriStar Skyline Medical Center, describes the mutual benefit of serving as a primary mentor for an EDP associate:

> *Participating as a mentor in HCA's EDP has been a rewarding opportunity to contribute to the development of our future leaders. The mentoring process is mutually beneficial as these talented individuals bring new ideas and fresh enthusiasm to challenges in the hospital. They will be significant contributors to the continued success of our organizations.*

Seminars: The EDP seminars are designed to provide associates with in-depth exposure to both the fundamentals of hospital management at HCA and the Nashville leadership team and corporate facility. Given that EDP associates are placed in full-time positions at HCA facilities across the country, the seminars provide opportunities for learning HCA's hospital management philosophy and networking with Nashville-based executive teams. Summarized below, there are five primary seminars that associates complete during their first twelve months in the program:

1. *Orientation:* This seminar introduces HCA's mission, vision, and strategic agenda. Associates learn about the leadership culture that drives the organization, including content focused on maximizing the value of their mentoring relationships; leading across multiple generations; leadership styles and their impact on performance outcomes; and an introduction to hospital operations, strategic planning, and project management at HCA facilities.

2. *Operations & Strategic Planning:* This seminar provides associates with the hands-on experience of applying HCA's strategic planning process to a given HCA facility or market. Associates are assembled into action learning teams for the purpose of assessing improvement opportunities

Table 5.1
HCA's Core Leadership Competencies

Leadership Competency	Definition
Building Strategic Relationships	- Developing and using collaborative relationships to facilitate the accomplishment of work goals.
Building Trust	- Interacting with others in a way that gives them confidence in one's intentions and those of the organization.
Business Acumen	- Using economic, financial, market, and industry data to understand and improve business results.
Coaching & Developing Others	- Providing feedback, instruction, and development guidance to help others excel in their current of future job responsibilities.
Compelling Communication	- Clearly and succinctly conveying information and ideas to individuals and groups in a way that captures and holds others' attention.
Customer Focus	- Ensuring that the customer perspective is a driving force behind business decisions and activities.
Driving Execution/Results	- Translating strategic priorities into operational reality by aligning organizational capabilities to yield measurable and sustainable results.
Quality Orientation	- Accomplishing tasks by considering all areas involved and accurately checking processes and tasks.

and revenue generating initiatives in an HCA market. The executive development team (EDT)—the professionals who operate the program—works directly with HCA's division presidents to identify a specific market that is experiencing operating challenges or growth opportunities that would serve as a valuable learning experience for the teams of EDP associates. Importantly, each team is assembled with a diverse mix of associates from each program track, thus ensuring that the team learning and application process is enriched with perspectives from clinical, operational, and financial professionals. Once the EDP teams are provided with an HCA market challenge or growth opportunity, they collect and assess clinical and operational data to support a facility or market strategy and execution plan. Because the market challenge presented to each team is a current issue facing a given HCA division or market, associates benefit from a learning experience that mirrors the actual divisional operating strategies and execution processes that are most critical to HCA's success. At the seminar's conclusion, each team delivers a capstone presentation of its findings and execution recommendations to a panel of judges that includes senior executives from HCA facilities, divisions, and the corporate office.

3. *Leadership:* The leadership seminar focuses on the developing associates' leadership competencies through exposure and skill-building in the following areas: crucial conversations, coaching and developing others, emotional intelligence, change leadership, diplomacy and negotiations, and marketing yourself and managing your career. As part of both the orientation and leadership seminars, associates are provided a series of leadership assessments and coaching sessions to further develop their leadership competencies. In addition to 360-degree assessment data, feedback from the associate's supervisor is utilized to inform the coaching process and development planning.

4. *Clinical/Physician Relations:* This seminar provides associates with education in physician relations and HCA's core quality initiatives from internal subject matter experts. Each year, the focal point of the seminar is updated according to HCA's current quality priorities or initiatives. The seminar also teaches associates how to navigate the challenges associated with developing strategic relationships with physicians, a key HCA stakeholder group. The specific topics addressed during this seminar include: improving patient safety, understanding the leadership role in quality compliance, providing national advocacy for HCA's clinical services agenda, developing a physician supply/demand analysis plan, and improving physician relations and retention rates to optimize quality performance outcomes.

5. *ACHE Congress on Healthcare Leadership:* The final seminar is an educational opportunity provided outside of HCA that allows associates to gain exposure to current issues, trends, and topics in healthcare while also facilitating networking opportunities with other healthcare leaders. Associates attend the annual American College of Healthcare Executives (ACHE) Congress on Healthcare Leadership,[95] which provides ample opportunities to learn from subject matter experts and network with healthcare leaders within and outside of HCA.

Evidence-Based Success Factors

While the EDP is consistent with research on healthcare executive development best practices, including the use of team-based action learning projects, role-based leadership training, and an assortment of leadership assessment and coaching sessions,[96] an evidence-based assessment is necessary to understand how the program has a sustained impact on HCA performance outcomes. In particular, effective execution of the EDP demands strong engagement from numerous stakeholders, including the executive development team, Nashville-based corporate leaders, group presidents, division presidents, and facility executive teams. In order to adopt an evidence-based approach for evaluating the execution success factors that drive the EDP's effectiveness, the executive development team initiated an independent and comprehensive program assessment (see About the Research for a summary of assessment methodology).

The assessment identified seven 'success factors' or sets of execution best practices across the three primary EDP phases: Candidate Assessment & Selection, Associate Education & Development, and Executive Placement & Onboarding. Illustrated in figure 5.2, consistent execution of these best practices drives key performance outcomes and establishes the EDP as a best-in-class executive development program. The success factors were identified via analysis of multiple assessment data sources such as archival data (program materials, curriculum modules, mentoring guides, etc.), dozens of stakeholder interviews, and performance metrics comparing EDP alumni and non-alumni across HCA. Overall, the EDP best practices offer a blueprint for implementing a highly effective executive development program for healthcare leaders. Each success factor is discussed below and illustrated by excerpts from HCA executives across levels and functions.

Figure 5.2
EDP Program Phases & Success Factors

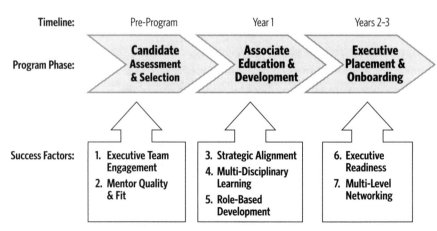

Candidate Assessment & Selection

Executive Team Engagement: Former CEO Jack Bovender's legacy of leadership development still reverberates throughout HCA. The depth and quality of executive team commitment to the EDP is critical for program execution and driving key outcomes. Many division presidents, hospital CEOs, and senior HR officers emphasize the importance of Bovender's explicit support of the program, and the legacy of current HCA executives who continue supporting the EDP as primary and secondary mentors, selection committee participants, team project sponsors and judges, and vocal advocates of the program's importance to HCA's talent strategy. Referencing the significance of Bovender's role as an EDP founder, San Antonio Division president Jaime Wesolowski remarked, "he started the [EDP] and chose ten CEO mentors to start the program. I was one of the first CEO mentors that he chose, and he talked about the importance of the program for not only getting the best talented young executives who want to pursue a career in healthcare administration, but also addressing our diversity opportunities. I think that the program has certainly done both of those things." Similarly, John Steele, HCA's senior vice president of Human Resources (SVP of HR), highlighted the importance of Bovender's role in clearly articulating the EDP as an HCA-wide strategic initiative. In describing the most important factors that explain the EDP's success, he stated, "the big driver is senior support at the top of the house. Jack made it clear when he was here that this program is a priority—we are going to make it work—so people make it work. Over his career, there were two or three things that he referred to as the 'North Bound Train' and this was one of them…and it made a difference."

One of the most important aspects of executive team support of the EDP is the breadth and depth of engagement from facility, divisional, and corporate HCA executives in the candidate selection process. The fifteen-member selection committee that assesses and ultimately selects EDP participants each year consists of facility CEOs and division presidents—as well as Nashville-based HR executives. For many executive participants on the selection committee, participation in the candidate assessment and selection process serves the best interests of both HCA and their respective hospital or division. Former Gulf Coast Division president Maura Walsh noted, "I personally feel that it is important to participate in developing talent for a selfish reason—I want to be sure I have bench strength in my division but I also want to help develop that talent to continue to lead HCA into the future." Cultivating a sense of EDP ownership amongst the division presidents and facility CEOs is critical to sustaining the program's success. Senior VP of HR John Steele remarked that "we have a lot of executive involvement—the selection is heavily weighted now to division president participation. I think that's made a huge difference over time. It used to be 'what black box does the HR team in Nashville have?' Now it's their choice. I think that is critically important. If this was an HR initiative and the operators were not owning it, it would die a slow painful death—it probably would be gone already."

Mentor Quality & Fit: Once candidates are selected for the EDP, one success factor is determining the ideal hospital facilities in which to place the healthcare leaders. The EDP's design places a strong emphasis on the primary mentoring relationship at the local hospital facility and on-the-job learning as the associates report directly to the hospital CEO, COO, CNO, or CFO, so the fit between the candidate and local executive mentor is key. The EDP selection panel carefully assesses each associate's developmental needs, the size and complexity of the hospital, and, perhaps most importantly, the depth of the local executive's mentoring capabilities. More than any other EDP success factor, the fit between the associate and his or her local executive mentor drives the ultimate program outcome—executive readiness for a hospital C-suite position. Walsh commented, "I think it's key to provide good mentors. If you put a COO [associate] in a hospital where the CEO doesn't enjoy mentoring or is not wanting to invest the time, I think we do a disservice to the candidate and we're not providing the right situation to develop talent for the company. I think the right mentor is important." The candidate assessment process facilitates a team approach to evaluating which hospital executive teams offer the best developmental opportunities for the pool of EDP candidates. The inclusion of multiple division presidents on the selection panel allows for a broader and more rigorous assessment of facility CEOs' fit with a given EDP candidate. As noted by Walsh, including these insights as part of the candidate placement process allows for much stronger fit between the candidate and his or her facility:

> *Those [executives] who have participated in this process will take candidates—we are invested in the process and we've spent a couple of days with them. There's not been a year that I have been on the selection panel that I have not accepted a candidate in my division. I've always had opportunities for candidates and I know which of my CEOs are strong mentors. [The executive development team] has worked with a lot of the CEOs, so they often have a feeling about which candidates would be a great fit for that opportunity.*

Associate Education & Development
Strategic Alignment: Another element of the EDP's design is the degree to which the curriculum and learning experiences are aligned with HCA's strategic

initiatives. As part of the process of annually reviewing and updating various elements of the program, the EDP team meets with HCA's group presidents to assess the overall curriculum and identify topics for the team action learning projects as part of the Operations and Strategic Planning seminar. Senior VP of HR John Steele explains the invaluable role of partnering with group presidents and their respective division presidents to identify the project topics that will drive the best combination of developmental value and relevance to one of HCA's current market opportunities or challenges:

> We always start by asking the group presidents—'is there something going on in your group?' Once given an idea, we go to the division presidents and ask if they are interested in sponsoring an EDP project. Who would not be interested in a group of smart, young people taking a look at an issue in your division and coming up with some ideas? We start with the group presidents because they are out doing monthly operations reviews, so both Chuck Hall (National Group president) and Jon Foster (American Group president) tell us where they have issues and where they need a fresh look at strategy.

As part of the development of the EDP's curriculum, a third success factor is ensuring that the seminars and team action learning project topics evolve with HCA's strategic initiatives and changes in the broader healthcare landscape. Importantly, strategic alignment of the EDP involves not only seminar content and team project topics, but the specific assignments that associates complete at their respective hospitals. Senior VP of HR John Steele remarked, "from a curriculum standpoint, we have evolved [the EDP] to keep up with our current strategic platforms around clinical integration, growth, and performance improvement. We have done a good job on the curriculum side and we try to ensure strategic alignment from an experience standpoint by building out a job that works well for [an EDP associate] to lead an expansion project or a service-line project that is very much aligned with how we think about our current strategy." The EDP excels at preparing future C-suite executives for managing the ongoing transition away from hospital-based care as well as the complexities of leading at HCA. Former Capital Division president Margaret Lewis emphasized the program's ability to create 'business leaders' who are knowledgeable of how HCA's strategic initiatives are executed within and across HCA's divisions and facilities:

> The whole shift in healthcare is outpatient and—from a hospital executive's standpoint—this is done by a different business unit within the company. It would be easy to say, 'Well, somebody else handles that.'

> But as part of the EDP, we want to produce business executives. We are in a large, heavily matrixed company, and we have a lot of HCA corporate directives, so we want to move the whole company in the same direction. If you don't know how all these people in a heavily matrixed environment have all the various business units that support your core business and how they operate collaboratively, then as [an associate executive] you're just stumbling through.

Multi-Disciplinary Learning: The integration of future hospital executives from multiple disciplines—finance, operations, and nursing—represents another critical EDP success factor. Healthcare's ongoing shift to value-based performance outcomes and increasing emphasis on the coordination of care, clinical quality measures, and cost containment demands executives who see 'the big picture' and work across functions and business units. EDP associates are provided powerful cross-functional, multi-disciplinary learning experiences via team action learning projects—comprised of associate COOs, CFOs, and CNOs—and on-the-job assignments that require collaboration with multiple hospital functional areas. San Antonio Division president Jaime Wesolowski noted, "I think [the integration of multiple disciplines] is very important because that's their future. For those who want to be CNOs, being able to understand and work with COOs as well as CEOs is critical. This is a big value-add of the program. This integration with young talented individuals is important because you need each other—it's all about team work, not individuals." Underscoring the increasing complexity of healthcare and the implications for the program's design, former Capital Division president Margaret Lewis noted that the EDP develops associates' ability "to negotiate and build strategic business relationships to reach the ultimate strategic objectives. The complexity of the environment is such that no one person can do it by themselves, and as obvious as it may be, it's the one thing that trips young executives up—going after something without identifying the unintended consequences and other affected areas outside of your span of control. That does happen when individuals are narrowly focused versus broad based—that is the biggest benefit [of the EDP program]."

The multi-disciplinary EDP design offers a related advantage regarding the fidelity of the team action learning projects and on-the-job assignments that represent the actual duties of hospital C-suite executives. These developmental experiences provide associates with exceptionally realistic settings in which to make strategically relevant decisions. Furthermore, these group experiences further develop associates' capabilities to work effectively in teams and, in some cases, identify important personal gaps that are reinforced via development plans. West Florida Division president Peter Marmerstein noted, "I think [the EDP's integrated disciplines] is the only way to create the kind of synergy that we need in order to be able to make informed decisions. How do you, in the healthcare arena, make decisions without some level of clinical input that you might get from the CNO's perspective or recognition of what goes on in the trenches and bedside dynamics that might not have been contemplated? Even the most sophisticated MBAs often lack the same level of financial acumen of the folks in our CFO track. As we are looking at developing economic models for a project, having input from people with that background is essential—it's almost hard to imagine how the program could have been effective without an integrated approach." Similarly, a hospital CNO who was recently placed into her role upon completing the EDP program observed the following:

> I think [the EDP's cross-disciplinary design] helped us learn to work with one another and see each other outside of preconceived silos— 'the COO only focuses on this' or 'the CNO only focuses on patient care.' I think it opened everybody's eyes. The CNO is a part of the budget and so is the COO. The CNO can be a part of a building project when the COO is definitely a part of the building project. In doing the team projects, people's natural strengths and weaknesses come out and you learn to work closely together, overcome some things, and let other team members grow. I felt like it helped us in a lot of ways—building relationships but also preparing us for how we're going to have to work to be successful when we're doing the role full time.

Role-Based Development: An important strength of the EDP's design is heavy emphasis on role-based learning and development as an associate executive placed at an HCA facility. The parallel learning that associates experience— on-the-job development as a direct report to a C-suite hospital executive coupled with EDP seminars and didactic learning experiences—affords HCA the dual benefits of accelerated executive development and C-suite placement at a time when many MHA programs and other graduate degree training fail to provide seasoned leadership talent. Former Capital Division president Margaret Lewis remarked, "the structure of the program—both on the content side relative to solving a real problem within a facility and working in a team—all are very valuable because not every candidate [for C-suite roles] has that depth or breadth of experience. On the COO side, there are only two MHA programs that offer or require a residency for a year in which you get a lot of this exposure. The EDP gives candidates that structure and the challenges of all these aspects of what senior leaders are going to be looking for in a hospital executive."

The structure and rigor of the team action learning projects as part of the operations and strategic planning seminar serve important roles for developing executive readiness for hospital C-suite roles. A recent EDP program graduate, who now serves as COO of a large hospital, described the primary drivers of the EDP's success as "the group project where the pressure cooker of working with people you have not necessarily worked with before, quickly working through information to come up with a good presentation, and then the opportunity to get up in front of the division presidents, CEOs, etc. Speaking in front of Sam Hazen (HCA's chief operating officer) and the other senior Nashville executives–I wouldn't trade that opportunity for anything." While the team action learning projects are intended to primarily provide associates with practical exposure to HCA's core administrative processes, including strategic planning, funding expansion and capital projects, new service line projects, and executing quality initiatives, the EDP teams provide senior HCA leaders with many actionable recommendations that ultimately deliver a lasting impact. West Florida Division president Peter Marmerstein describes the impact of an EDP team's set of recommendations on a hospital in his division:

> *One of our large hospitals was working on an expansion project and the division president asked that the EDP teams look at the issues surrounding this expansion project and build a recommended course of action. The multidisciplinary EDP teams really used the data, analyzed the environment, and came up with a different direction for this project than the local executive team. The executive team ended up changing direction on the basis of the analysis done by the EDP team. When you talk about [development programs providing] real-world experience, the EDP program gives a group of relatively inexperienced, young, bright, and enthusiastic budding executives a real-world problem for a hospital. They figured out which data are needed, analyzed the data, looked at the plan as it exists, and made recommendations. They took an entirely different approach to solve this problem and the company actually changed its direction based upon the finding of this EDP team. I don't know how much more real world you can get than that.*

Executive Placement & Onboarding

Executive Readiness: Once EDP associates have completed at least one year in the program, including all seminars, team projects, and mentoring activities, they are considered for placement in vacant C-suite positions throughout HCA's network of hospitals. While it is certainly expedient for HCA to immediately place EDP associates into open executive roles, the executive development team, division presidents, and facility CEOs carefully balance the needs of developing the candidate and meeting the talent needs of a given hospital.

Importantly, the developmental value of the EDP is not sacrificed for the sake of expediency and filling open C-suite roles. Indeed, a critical EDP success factor is the rigorous assessment of an eligible associate's 'executive readiness' for a given hospital C-suite opening. Emphasizing the importance of careful evaluation of executive readiness, National Group president Chuck Hall stated, "I [have to] approve any executive that's being placed into one of my hospitals. When working with the [executive] recruitment team to assess a candidate, we sometimes conclude that the person is simply not ready [for the C-suite role]. I'm more than happy to put that particular person in a different role, but I'm not going to support moving them into a chief operator role." Echoing a similar sentiment, many EDP alumni now working in C-suite positions assert the importance of balancing the program's developmental focus and the company's immediate needs for executive talent. The importance of this delicate balance is reflected in the following comments from EDP associates recently placed in hospital CFO and CNO roles, respectively:

> *I have some friends who work for competitors in leadership positions, and they say their [leadership development] program would promote people into positions when they were not ready. I firmly believe our program will not promote individuals into executive positions until you are ready and have the ringing endorsement from your mentor, from [the executive development team], and anybody else who has worked with you. I think that makes us more distinctive than the other programs. (Chief Financial Officer)*

> *If you are in the program longer, you have more time to take on more complex projects and learn from them. It should be more about the development of the candidate than filling a position because ultimately what happens is the candidate does not have the opportunity to really develop. It is a tough enough job as it is, and there is pressure to fill positions. I think we fill where people can succeed and not become overwhelmed or frustrated that people do not perform to level we thought they could. (Chief Nursing Officer)*

In concert with the executive development team and the associate's direct supervisor, division presidents exert tremendous influence on the ultimate decision to either place the candidate or allow him or her to continue development in the current associate role. The collaborative, team-based approach to assessing an associate's executive readiness is a critical EDP success factor. Describing his role in the assessment process, West Florida Division president Peter Marmerstein explains, "once EDP associates are in my division, I will sit down with them at least twice per year and take stock of where they are and what they see as their continuing developmental needs. I will chat with their direct mentor and supervisor to gain an assessment of the progress they are making, their readiness to move up, or their need to remain in the current capacity. I have a [CNO associate who has been] in my division for three years. I had conversations with her direct mentor, and we came to the conclusion that she just wasn't ready to move onto the next level. We worked with the mentor at the hospital to identify a targeted work plan to further develop her executive readiness." The EDP program maintains the discipline to avoid expediently placing an associate to fill a hospital opening at the expense of the individual's developmental needs.

Multi-Level Networking: The final EDP success factor is the multi-level network of HCA executives that newly placed associates leverage as part of their onboarding experience. Group presidents, division presidents, facility CEOs, Nashville-based corporate leaders, and fellow EDP associates comprise an incredibly influential network of HCA leaders that newly placed EDP associates can leverage as they onboard into their new C-suite roles. National Group president Chuck Hall remarked, "after [EDP associates] land their first job, I continue to follow up with them to see how things are going, and we'll schedule time for conversations as to things they're working on. Some [newly placed EDP associates] will call me and say, 'hey, I'm dealing with this issue, let me get your input as to how you would handle it.' HCA group presidents work to expand the networks of EDP candidates by exposing them to multiple hospitals and their local executive teams. Hall describes how he utilizes hospital operating reviews as learning experiences and networking opportunities for EDP candidates:

> I take [EDP associates] on what I refer to as road trips—when myself and my CFO go to various hospitals for operating reviews. I'll take them with me, let them see a number of hospitals, and get a sense as to what other management teams are doing, what they're thinking, and different management styles. They'll get exposed to at least three or four hospitals, the senior team, their strategies, their issues, and their opportunities, which I think is very helpful.

Importantly, development of EDP associates' professional network throughout HCA is a priority of division presidents and Nashville-based corporate leaders. Multiple division presidents commit to cultivating relationships with the EDP associates in their division, as well as facilitating connections with CEOs and division presidents in other HCA divisions. Describing her commitment to expanding the professional network of EDP candidates in her division, former Gulf Coast Division president Maura Walsh remarked, "I try to stay engaged with [EDP associates] while they are in my division. At least once or twice a year, I have a meeting with all of the COO associates, have them attend the COO meetings, and always include them in large management meetings. I try to give them exposure to leadership teams across the division. At least annually, I take them out for lunch and give a little face time with me." Similarly, SVP of HR John Steele describes networking as a critical driver of long-term success for EDP associates as they onboard into their executive roles:

> I think networking is a big driver [of the EDP's success]. The EDP candidates come in as cohorts, feed off each other, and have a network that other new executives don't have to draw on. They have the [EDP Team], a corporate mentor, and a once-a-quarter meeting with Milton Johnson. I think that really is the biggest difference in terms of the program's success—really a tight-knit group that has stayed that way over time and connected with each other. Having that long-term connection is huge.

Evidence-Based Evaluation: EDP's Impact on Key Metrics

An evidence-based approach for evaluating the EDP requires an analysis of the program's impact on key HCA performance metrics. In short, what is the evidence that the EDP is a best-in-class program that drives important performance outcomes? In an effort to present a clear, data-driven case for the program's efficacy to senior HCA leaders, the executive development team annually conducts an organizational impact analysis that focuses on several key metrics. The results of this analysis are summarized in an 'Organizational Impact Report' that is shared with group presidents, division presidents, Nashville-based corporate leaders, and facility CEOs. The primary metrics assessed as part of this analysis include: annual turnover of hospital C-suite executives, internal/external placement rate for hospital C-suite positions, number of hospital C-suite placements by hire source (EDP program, external hire, and internal promotion or transfer), and hospital C-suite executive gender and ethnic diversity. The following section describes the evaluation strategy and presents key results across each performance metric:

1. *Hospital C-Suite Executive Turnover (2010-2015):* The average annual turnover rate for HCA's C-suite executives who complete the EDP (4.8 percent) is less than half of the average annual turnover rate for those executives who did not complete the program (10 percent). For each of the executive roles (COO, CFO, CNO, and CEO), EDP alumni are significantly

more likely to remain in their C-suite position compared to executives who are promoted internally or are sourced externally. Impressively, fifty of the 113 (44 percent) HCA hospital COOs are EDP alumni, while none of the twenty-two CFOs sourced by the EDP have departed their roles. Furthermore, the average annual turnover rates for all C-suite executive roles are significantly lower than a national benchmark executive turnover rate of 8.7 percent, as reported by the Healthcare Talent Management Survey.[97] Overall, these results present compelling evidence of the EDP's impact on executive retention relative to alternative talent sources for C-suite roles, as well as a key industry benchmark for executive turnover.

2. *Internal/External Hospital C-Suite Placement Rate (2010-2015):* HCA's internal/external placement rate for C-suite executive positions has averaged 71 percent from 2010 to 2015. By comparison, results of the **Healthcare Talent Management Survey**[98] report an average 51 percent internal/external hiring ratio from a national sample of hospitals and health systems. For each of those years, HCA's reliance on internal executive talent for hospital C-suite positions has not only exceeded the national average but positioned the health system in the 90th percentile of this key leadership development metric.

3. *C-Suite Executive Placements by Hire Source (2010-2015):* The EDP program has remained a steady source of executive talent for HCA's hospital C-suite positions. During this period, one in five C-suite hires were sourced from the EDP program. The overall number of C-suite placements has maintained a steady increase while external hires have flattened. For 2014, seventeen of the eighty-seven hospital C-suite placements came out of the EDP, the highest number of executive placements since the program's inception. Across HCA's hospital C-suite teams, EDP alumni comprise 43 percent (50 of 115) of the COOs and 29 percent (46 of 159) of the CNOs. An impressive 21 percent (90) of hospital C-suite hires were sourced from the EDP, while 25 percent of all current C-suite executives (147 of 578) are EDP alumni. Overall, these metrics offer strong evidence of the EDP's track record as a reliable source of executive talent for HCA's hospital C-suite roles.

4. *Hospital C-Suite Executive Gender and Ethnic Diversity:* The final set of key metrics for assessing the EDP is gender and ethnic diversity for hospital C-suite roles. Given the program's origins and the founding commitment from former CEO Jack Bovender to enhance executive diversity, enhancing the representation of women and ethnic minorities in hospital

C-suites remains a critical performance outcome. The EDP has provided HCA with a C-suite talent pool comprised of a significantly greater number of women executives compared to executives sourced externally or via promotions and transfers. Overall, 47 percent (66 of 140) of EDP alumni in C-suite roles are women. As evidence of HCA's strong commitment to diverse executive teams, the overall percentage of women in executive roles exceeds the national benchmark of 42 percent, according to the **Healthcare Talent Management Survey**.[99] The EDP also provides a more ethnically diverse pool of C-suite executives compared to external hires and promotions or transfers. Overall, 16 percent (23 of 140) of EDP alumni placed in C-suite roles are non-white ethnic minorities. For CEOs, an impressive 25 percent of EDP alumni (7 of 28) are ethnically diverse. Overall, the percentage of ethnic minorities in C-suite roles for EDP alumni exceeds the national benchmark of 14 percent, according to the **Healthcare Talent Management Survey**.[100] Taken together, these results offer clear evidence of the EDP's effectiveness for enhancing the gender and ethnic diversity of HCA's hospital C-suite teams.

Lessons Learned

This case study described the primary phases and execution best practices of HCA's industry-leading executive development program for hospital C-suite leaders. The EDP's design and execution offers a series of lessons learned and practical recommendations for healthcare organizations seeking to develop a best-in-class executive development program.

1. *Engage Senior Executives at Multiple Program Phases:* A critical best practice for developing an exemplary leadership development program is engaging the health system CEO and other top executives at multiple points throughout the program development and execution phases. The CEO and senior executive team must clearly and persuasively articulate the program as an integral element of a broader, company-wide strategic initiative. Similarly, operator executives across levels (divisions, regions, hospitals, etc.) should be fully engaged as program owners via candidate selection, mentoring, project sponsorship, teaching seminars, and placement processes. Critically, program alumni should also be engaged through multiple opportunities for participation and program advocacy.

2. *Rigorously Assess Mentor Quality and Fit:* Best-in-class executive development programs ensure that mentors are carefully assessed for their interest and capabilities to serve in a critical coaching role for program

participants. In addition to establishing a clear evaluation process for vetting executive mentors, exemplary programs provide training, tools, materials, and best-practice guides to executive mentors that help facilitate high-quality mentoring relationships.

3. *Establish Local and Regional/Corporate Executive Mentors:* Provide program participants with executive mentors at both local (hospital or business unit) and regional or corporate levels. Early career healthcare leaders benefit from the tutelage and career feedback from C-suite executives at their local hospital, as well as the company-wide visibility provided by regional or corporate executive mentors. Importantly, executive mentors who operate outside of program participants' respective C-suite team are uniquely positioned to offer critical advice and feedback on 'managing up' and addressing challenges related to working effectively with their bosses.

4. *Annually Assess Program Curriculum for Strategic Alignment:* As part of the annual program development process, evaluate the program modules or seminars, project topics, assessment tools, and learning activities to ensure strong alignment with the health system's strategic initiatives. Given the massive and ongoing changes occurring in the healthcare industry, engage senior executives in annual discussions of the alignment between program curriculum and system-level strategies for evolving with the changing healthcare landscape. The ongoing shift from volume- to value-based hospital performance metrics, the transition from hospital-centric care to population management and the full spectrum of health services, and emphasis on collaborative leadership competencies, should influence program curriculum and learning activities. Best-in-class development programs continue evolving all aspects of the curriculum—targeted leadership competencies, modules, project-based experiences—from a focus on developing *hospital* executives to *healthcare* executives. Illustrating the company's strong commitment to evolving the EDP, HCA is currently expanding the program to build upon its outstanding reputation while incorporating program enhancements that address stakeholder feedback. Consistent with HCA's changing executive development needs, the EDP expansion will include a stronger emphasis on in-role development opportunities for internal candidates who are assessed via the talent review process as being six to eighteen months from readiness for promotion to CNO, CFO, and COO roles; virtual learning sessions that will be scalable for much larger internal candidate cohorts and leveraged with other internal roles or business lines; and enhanced ownership of

executive pipeline development by division presidents and facility CEOs.

5. *Create Program Cohorts Comprised of Multiple Functional and Clinical Disciplines:* Ensure that program cohorts consist of healthcare professionals from multiple functions and specialties, including operations, nursing, finance, and physicians. Best-in-class leadership development programs ensure that learning activities mirror the challenges associated with operating as part of a multi-functional C-suite team, develop participants' collaboration skills, and shed the 'silo' view of the organization.

6. *Partner with Regional and Local Executives to Design Team Action Learning Projects:* Engage with regional and local executives to identify topics for team-based action learning projects, such as hospital- or market-based challenges, the impact of emerging legislation or regulatory changes, competitive pressures, and other hospital-wide challenges that demand expertise and perspectives from multiple functional lenses.

7. *Provide Program Participants with Role-Based Assignments:* Emphasize on-the-job learning experiences, such as full-time hospital or regional administrative roles reporting directly to a C-suite executive, that require program participants to complete assignments (expansion, new service lines, quality initiatives, capital projects, etc.) that demand collaboration with multiple functions and diverse stakeholders.

8. *Utilize Executive Readiness Assessments for C-suite Placements:* Highly effective executive development programs resist the temptation to allow hospital C-suite vacancies to singularly drive executive placement decisions. A critical best practice is to engage the executive development program staff, regional or corporate leaders, and local hospital or business unit executives in a rigorous assessment of each candidate's readiness for a given C-suite role. As such, the focus should remain on each candidate's developmental needs and gaps in executive readiness while avoiding placement decisions driven primarily by hospital needs.

9. *Facilitate Multi-Level Networking Opportunities:* Exemplary executive development programs offer multiple opportunities for candidates to network with corporate, regional or divisional, and local facility executives throughout the program and after placement into their C-suite roles. As part of candidates' participation in the program, create post-program avenues for alumni to maintain an active network and provide one another career support and feedback.

Conclusion

As one of the nation's leading providers of healthcare services, HCA's ability to develop and retain a strong pipeline of healthcare executives has an incredibly broad and lasting impact on the quality of care for a vast number of US communities. As illustrated in this case, the company's strong commitment to developing executive leadership talent via the EDP drives several key leadership development metrics and C-suite diversity outcomes while advancing HCA's strategy to cultivate an unparalleled executive development capability. Looking to the future, the EDP will continue serving a critical role in developing leadership talent to effectively serve in increasingly complex C-suite roles.

About the Research

The research to support this case study was conducted by Kevin S. Groves, PhD and Groves Consulting Group during a twenty-month period that began in August 2014, and concluded in April 2016. The executive development team (EDT), an HR department located at HCA's Nashville headquarters in Nashville, initiated an independent and comprehensive assessment of the EDP program. The assessment's objectives included:

1. Evaluate the key EDP phases of candidate recruitment, selection, and placement; program design and execution; and onboarding into CNO, COO, and CFO positions;

2. Conduct semi-structured interviews with stakeholders across levels, including Nashville-based corporate leaders, group presidents, division presidents, facility CEOs, HR executives, and EDP alumni in hospital C-suite roles;

3. Identify critical stakeholder differences regarding the EDP's overall strategy, design principles, and execution practices; and

4. Assess the EDP's impact on key performance metrics, including executive placement, turnover, and diversity statistics.

The assessment strategy consisted of collected data from the following sources:

1. *EDT Professionals:* A series of open-ended interviews were conducted with EDT professionals to review and discuss all extant EDP program materials. The interviews were aimed at discussing the design and execution of all EDP program phases.

2. *HCA Corporate, Division & Hospital Executives:* HCA's two group presidents, senior HR corporate officers, five division presidents, and a large sample of EDP alumni in HCA hospital C-suite roles (CEO, COO, CFO, and CNO) participated in semi-structured interviews. The purpose of the interviews was to assess their level of engagement in the EDP program and their evaluation of the program's strengths and development areas.

The interviews were conducted in person or by phone with each executive and transcribed by an electronic recording service for the purpose of subsequent analysis.

3. *Observation:* Several EDP program sessions were observed for data collection, including the *Operations and Strategic Planning Seminar*, team coaching sessions delivered by EDT professionals, and the team action learning project presentations to HCA's senior executive team.

4. *Archival Data:* Archival data and information, including the EDP program annual reports, leadership competency model, EDP organizational impact reports, leadership assessment tools, mentoring materials, performance metrics, and other extant materials were obtained for review and analysis.

CHAPTER 6

Developing Leadership Talent through Strategy Execution: Kaiser Permanente's Strategic Leadership Program

What makes the Strategic Leadership Program (SLP) different and particularly valuable is its foundation in reality, its foundation in our strategy. The SLP connects that reality with both the projects that leaders complete and the residential experience. As I look back at the SLP projects, they're all substantive and important parts of our overall strategic agenda. These projects support Kaiser Permanente's strategic agenda while improving the performance of those specific work units. I think the broader SLP benefit is the continuing development of leaders who have better strategic context as they are driving, motivating, developing their teams and their areas.

Paul Swenson
Senior Vice President & Chief Strategy Officer
Kaiser Permanente

Kaiser Permanente

Founded in 1945 to meet the challenge of providing medical care to Americans during the Great Depression and World War II, Kaiser Permanente is one of the nation's largest not-for-profit health plans. The national health system serves 11.3 million members across seven regions, including Colorado, Georgia, Hawaii, Mid-Atlantic States (Virginia, Maryland, and Washington, DC), Northern California, Southern California, and the Northwest (Oregon and Washington[††]). Kaiser Permanente's rich history dates back to the late 1930s when a Pacific Northwest medical group was established to serve workers and their families during construction of the Grand Coulee Dam in northeastern Washington. Throughout World War II, the physicians comprising the medical group continued serving employees and their families at the Kaiser shipyards in Vancouver, Washington and Portland, Oregon. After the shipyards officially closed in 1945, Kaiser Permanente opened enrollment to the community. Currently operating as a fully integrated health system, Kaiser Permanente comprises the Kaiser Foundation Hospitals and their subsidiaries, Kaiser Foundation Health Plan, Inc. and The Permanente Medical Groups. With an annual operating revenue of $64.6 billion in 2016, the health system operates a network of thirty-eight hospitals, and has approximately 21,584 physicians and 199,320 employees. Kaiser Permanente's national business functions and many senior leadership teams reside at the health system's national headquarters in Oakland, California.

With a concerted focus on providing high quality healthcare services, including preventative and evidence-based care, Kaiser Permanente has established a venerated reputation. The Permanente Medical Groups, which provide care for Kaiser Permanente members, continuously develop and refine medical practices to help ensure that care is delivered in the most efficient and effective manner possible. Among the innovations it has contributed to US healthcare are prepaid health plans that spread costs to increase affordability; physician group practices that focus their abilities on preventing illness as much as caring for the sick; and an organized delivery system that places as many services as possible under one roof. Kaiser Permanente's health plans nationally rank among the best in terms of prevention, treatment, and patient experience, according to the National Committee for Quality Assurance.[101] In each state in which the health system operates, a Kaiser Permanente plan holds the top ranking for both commercial and Medicare plans. In California, its Medicare plan is the only plan to receive a 5-star rating from the Centers for Medicare & Medicaid Services[102] for five consecutive years. Impressively, nineteen of Kaiser Permanente's hospitals are listed among the nation's elite in *U.S. News & World Report*'s[103] annual 'Best Hospitals' rankings, while eight Southern California medical centers were named among 'Top Hospitals' by

---

[††] *The 2015 survey's factor analysis results and Cronbach alpha reliability analyses are available in the full report of survey findings at http://www.grovesconsultinggroup.com/wp-content/uploads/2015/07/ResearchReport.TalentMgmtPractices.20151.pdf.*

The Leapfrog Group.[104] Kaiser Permanente is nationally recognized as a thought leader and pioneer that is uniquely positioned for success amidst the Affordable Care Act (ACA) and ongoing healthcare reform efforts, particularly around the industry changes concerning quality improvement, efficiency of care, and population management. Kaiser Permanente's mission of preventative care and total patient health is strongly aligned with the ACA's requirements and incentives for healthcare providers, which has elevated the organization's national profile. Chairman and chief executive officer Bernard J. Tyson was ranked second on *Modern Healthcare*'s list of '100 Most Influential People in Healthcare 2016,'[105] only surpassed by President Barack Obama.

The following case study offers an analysis of Kaiser Permanente's Strategic Leadership Program (SLP), one of two national leadership development programs offered to Kaiser Permanente's leaders. The SLP serves a significant role in facilitating the execution of the organization's national business strategy across the regions, functions, and facilities. This case study is organized into the following sections. First, the primary SLP objectives and program phases, including the participant cohorts, curriculum, learning activities, and primary program outcomes, are discussed. Next, I present a set of evidence-based best practices or 'success factors' for designing a leadership development program that seeks to enhance strategic alignment and facilitate execution of national business strategy. The best practices and lessons learned are supported by the personal experiences of numerous SLP stakeholders, including Kaiser Permanente's senior leadership team, talent management and leadership development executives, and SLP alumni and their direct managers. Then, a set of key metrics are presented as evidence of the SLP's effectiveness and impact on Kaiser Permanente's performance outcomes, including the turnover, promotion, and job performance rates of program alumni. Finally, this case study concludes with the lessons learned and best-practice recommendations for designing a program that develops leadership talent by enhancing the strategic alignment of the organization's regions, functions, and business units.

Strategic Leadership Program

Program Objectives
The Strategic Leadership Program (SLP)—originally conceived as a development program for high-potential leaders—has evolved into a set of leadership development experiences that enhances participants' ability to align their respective functions and business units with Kaiser Permanente's national business strategy. The program's focus on business strategy execution and

strategic alignment is critical for supporting Kaiser Permanente's national leadership development. While the health system offers its leaders an impressive range of programs that meet various developmental needs, including helping leaders in transitionary roles, enhancing operational excellence, and developing the skills and competencies of high-potential leaders, the SLP serves a distinctive purpose by accelerating the strategic alignment of the organization's regions and functions. The SLP's fundamental purpose is to facilitate the execution of Kaiser Permanente's national business strategy by developing a critical core of mid-level leaders—directors, executive directors, and newly placed vice presidents—who are charged with aligning and executing the local strategies of their respective regions, functions, and departments. Of the four primary types of leadership development programs, which include individual skill development, socializing leadership vision and values, action learning initiatives, and strategic leadership initiatives, the SLP is an exemplary type of the latter.[106] Designed to be tightly integrated to an organization's strategic agenda, strategic leadership development programs "facilitate efforts to communicate and implement the corporate strategy, build strategic unity throughout the organization, and create a cadre of changes agents. They simultaneously build leadership capabilities while facilitating progress toward key strategic objectives," according to leadership development expert Jay Conger. As discussed below, the SLP's design elements are strongly aligned with industry best practices for creating and executing strategic leadership development initiatives.

Given the intensifying changes in the broader healthcare environment, particularly the short- and long-term effects of the Affordable Care Act (ACA) and ongoing healthcare reform efforts, the SLP serves an invaluable role in supporting Kaiser Permanente's efforts to continually evolve its strategic agenda. Robert Sachs, retired vice president of National Learning and Development‡‡, explains that "the SLP will continue to be an important focus because our [business] strategy will clearly continue to evolve as the environment evolves. Our chairman and CEO has begun to talk about how we are going from being a health *care* organization to a health *services* organization. The SLP is geared toward participants understanding of that broader strategic context and ensuring that the local strategy they are building has strong alignment to what the overall organization is trying to do." Overall, the SLP's primary objectives include the following:

1. *Enhance Ability to Think and Act Strategically:* Facilitate the ability to see the big picture; use frameworks, skills, and behaviors to improve critical thinking; and base decisions on broad external and internal factors.

---

‡‡ *Robert Sachs retired from Kaiser Permanente effective January 4, 2016.*

2. *Expand Understanding of Kaiser Permanente's Business Strategy:* Deepen understanding of Kaiser Permanente's national strategy and why the organization has adopted this strategy; identify ways to optimize strategic opportunities and manage risk; and establish critical linkages between strategy and implementation.

3. *Apply Ability to Think and Act Strategically:* Learn skills to develop, refine, and execute a strategic project; align the strategic project to Kaiser Permanente's national strategy; and facilitate the transition from thinking strategically to acting strategically.

4. *Connect and Network with Kaiser Permanente Leaders:* Develop relationships with Kaiser Permanente leaders across regions, facilities, and national functions; create thought partnerships to accelerate project execution; and collaborate with SLP peers, executive sponsors, managers, and other Kaiser Permanente leaders.

Program Participants

Given the SLP's primary focus on strategic alignment and the execution of Kaiser Permanente's national strategy, the selection criteria for participants and Kaiser Permanente's National Leadership Development (NLD) team, which includes the SLP manager, are equally important to the program's success. The NLD team focuses on talent development and succession planning for the entire enterprise. NLD team members assist their respective business functions and regions in the national nomination process, which takes place annually. The SLP nomination process focuses on directors, executive directors, and newly promoted vice presidents who meet the following criteria: currently driving a strategic initiative as part of his or her portfolio of responsibilities, the strategic initiative must be tied to his or her total performance evaluation, and possesses a consistent record of high performance evaluations. Although the SLP is not designed as a traditional high-potential leadership program focused on preparation for more senior leadership roles, typically two-thirds or more of the program's annual cohorts are comprised of individuals who have been rated as high-potential leaders via Kaiser Permanente's annual talent review process. The vetting process for SLP cohorts, which are limited to thirty-six participants per cohort and two cohorts per year, ensures robust learning and development outcomes, as well as strengthening relationships with executive teams across Kaiser Permanente's regions, functions, and national headquarters. According to Gregg Servis, the SLP's program manager, the vetting process for each cohort involves careful assessment of multiple factors and stakeholders.

"We ask the regions and functions to rank in priority order the list of nominees they put forward for consideration. All nominees are required to write a statement of interest explaining how they imagine the program will serve them at this time, what strategic initiative they're driving, and what they as leaders hope to gain from the program. The value Kaiser Permanente holds around diversity and inclusion is also a fundamental building block that informs the final composition of each cohort."

The SLP program manager and supporting SLP team members examine the capacity for the candidates' direct managers to support their experience in the program. The SLP team utilizes a checklist that assesses managers' willingness to support their direct reports throughout the SLP. The checklist asks the local HR business leader to rate the manager along several dimensions: the extent to which the managers can support the participants, whether or not they create time for their direct report's development, and if they have a track record for supporting the development of his or her teams. Given the significant portion of time that the strategic projects demand from each participant—on average a third of their time—rigorous assessment of manager support enables the SLP's success. "We've learned from experience that oftentimes the mindset of the manager would be, 'I'm going to send my person off to this leadership training and they're going to come back a leader. In the meantime, I'm going to continue to overload them with requests,'" explains Servis. The managers of SLP participants are incorporated into the program at various points to facilitate greater manager engagement and support. Servis explains that "beginning with interviews that include both participants and managers, we're very clear about what's needed [in terms of manager support]. Managers get multiple touchpoints at the start and middle of the program, and then attend graduation to see all of the other participants. This approach has generated a lot of momentum in terms of managers being actively involved and engaged in the talent development process. The day-long graduation event provides managers and participants with a peer-to-peer experience where the talent development process is palpably present." Before the SLP team finalizes each cohort, Kaiser Permanente's succession management team offers important input to ensure that high-potential Kaiser Permanente leaders with developmental needs that match the program's learning activities are considered.

Program Phases & Curriculum

Delivered across a span of eight months, the SLP comprises three distinct phases that include a mix of learning and development activities; they are illustrated in figure 6.1.

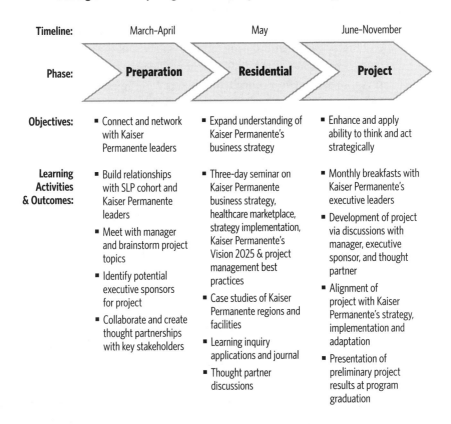

Figure 6.1

Strategic Leadership Program Phases, Objectives & Learning Activities

Preparation Phase: Once the cohort is formed, the program kicks off in late March with a virtual session designed to welcome the participants, outline the primary program activities and deadlines, and begin building the participants' networks. During this phase, participants meet with their direct manager to begin brainstorming strategic project topics that they will execute throughout the program. Participants are coached to have a series of conversations with their manager concerning their respective goals for SLP participation and how managers can best support their direct reports' participation in the program. In conversations with their direct manager, participants identify a project topic that both responds to a specific business/function or regional need and is also linked to their development plan and their performance evaluation. Participants and their managers discuss the necessary resources and support for executing their projects, including the role of executive sponsors. The process for identifying and creating the scope of work for the strategic project is an important SLP design element that must strike a balance between being 'executable' while also delivering developmental value to the participant. Paul Swenson, senior vice president and chief strategy officer, notes that "the projects need to be something that are real, agreed upon, and part of the strategic agenda of the participants' business, function, or region. The participant must have a role of significance in the project, and must be able to measure progress within the time frame of the SLP program." While project execution and strategic alignment are key criteria for project scoping, Dan Cousins, vice president of Talent and Organizational Performance, explains that the developmental value of the project is increasingly critical as the SLP evolves to meet Kaiser Permanente's changing leadership development needs. "A lot of growth comes out of challenging yourself to do something that initially looked impossible. In the context of our company's strategic direction, we're going to need people who can think around corners, so staying within an easily managed scope of work will probably not lead to the leadership development we are going to need. We need people who are thinking creatively about new kinds of partnerships and new ways of realizing opportunities that will cross boundaries of authority and responsibility within the organization and external to the organization."

Indeed, Kaiser Permanente executives who have sponsored multiple SLP projects underscore the importance of this balance. Kristy LoRusso, vice president of National Direct Marketing and executive sponsor for several strategic projects, says that "those participants who try to broaden the project scope in order to make it harder for themselves to grow as a leader are more satisfied and get more out of the program. They were also the most engaged with me so I had more line of sight as to what they were doing." Kaiser Permanente executives who have supported numerous direct reports' SLP participation and also served as executive sponsors for SLP projects cite examples of exemplary strategic projects. Irene Chavez, senior vice president and area manager for the San Jose market in Kaiser Permanente's Northern California region, served as executive sponsor for an SLP project led by a pharmacy director in her service area. Addressing two pillars of Kaiser Permanente's strategic plan—affordability and membership growth—the project was designed to "help the affordability initiative and continue to serve a growing number of members without adding additional pharmacy space or additional pharmacists," says Chavez. The project scope included establishing a 'Lean' approach to four pharmacy areas (inpatient, discharge, outpatient, and clinical) within a medical center that had traditionally operated in silos. The project included developing multiple Kaizen events in which each of the four pharmacy areas would work with each other to identify cost savings and eliminate redundant or inefficient practices. "When [the pharmacy director] came back from SLP and had fully fleshed out his project, he was able to execute in a very expeditious manner. Now there is great cross coverage by his managers and directors, great knowledge growth within each one of those previously siloed areas and incredible cost savings," says Chavez. While pharmacy costs are soaring across many medical centers, the San Jose facility's pharmacy continues to perform well against its annual budget. Impressively, the project's impact has provided numerous benefits to Kaiser Permanente beyond the local facility as these best practices have been disseminated to other medical centers within the service area. Chavez reports that "we've just seen remarkable savings and remarkable management growth to the point where two of the folks have been chosen to move out of our shop and advance to management roles. Because they've been so successful at the local level, three of my folks lead peer groups at the regional level to move in the direction of what we've accomplished at San Jose."

Residential Phase: This SLP phase consists of an off-site, three-and-a-half-day residential program that primarily focuses on expanding participants' understanding of Kaiser Permanente's national strategy and its implications for their respective regions, functions, and departments. Conducted in mid-May to allow participants sufficient time for discussions with their managers and prospective executive sponsors regarding strategic project topics, the residential program includes four primary learning activities:

1. *Strategy Sessions by Kaiser Permanente Executives:* A diverse faculty of national headquarters executives facilitate interactive discussions and active learning and applications across the following topics: the healthcare industry marketplace, Kaiser Permanente's 2015 Strategic Plan, Kaiser Permanente's Vision 2025, business strategy development and implementation best practices, and Kaiser Permanente's community benefit and total health strategy. Central to the SLP's design, these sessions are facilitated by national headquarters executives from Corporate Planning, Strategic Planning, Business Development, Community Health, and other business functions. In addition to senior vice president and chief strategy officer Paul Swenson, other senior executives who regularly serve as SLP faculty include executive vice president and chief medical officer Patrick Courneya, MD, and senior vice president and chief diversity and inclusion officer Ronald Copeland, MD. Engaging several of Kaiser Permanente's most senior, system-level executives to lead the residential sessions is an SLP design element that enhances the program's credibility and ultimate impact. Dr. Copeland, who also serves as the SLP's executive co-sponsor and teaches a seminar on diversity and inclusion, says, "I think [the residential program] creates an awareness of the challenges of healthcare reform. Participants get their strategy content and time

away from the day-to-day to reflect, learn, and appreciate our strategy. Their awareness level goes way up in terms of understanding what healthcare reform really means for the healthcare industry, including Kaiser Permanente." Fundamentally, the sessions expand and deepen the participants' perspectives regarding the macro changes in the healthcare industry and Kaiser Permanente's strategic positioning.

2. *Strategy Applications—Kaiser Permanente Case Study:* Interspersed throughout the three-and-a-half-day residential program, participants apply the concepts and frameworks provided in the strategy sessions via a Kaiser Permanente case study. The full-length case study centers on the fundamental strategic questions facing the executive team of a Kaiser Permanente region. Led by executives from Kaiser Permanente's corporate planning and strategic planning units, the case study session engages participants in practical applications of Kaiser Permanente's strategic plan and strategy implementation best practices. Consistent with traditional case study pedagogy, participants are asked to evaluate the strategic decisions and processes executed by the regional executive team described in the case. Participants evaluate and reflect on the region's new market expansion opportunities, threats to the region's sustainability, and strategic actions that the executive team should adopt the next three to ten years. Laura Long, an SLP alumna and executive director of systems alignment and integration in the national Diversity and Inclusion office, discusses the importance of the case study as part of the residential program. "The case study was really helpful to enrich our understanding of Kaiser Permanente's strategy. It included so many different parts of the business, growth of the business, and the importance of regional alignment to the strategic plan. It addressed affordability, growth, acquisition opportunities, labor management, and all the other areas you must think about when making a strategic decision. As a director, you are very focused in your area and do not always have line of sight to the overall business strategy. The case study was so helpful to broaden my perspective."

3. *Strategy Applications—Learning Inquiry and Learning Journal:* In addition to the Kaiser Permanente case study, participants engage in learning inquiry applications and complete a learning journal whereby they reflect and record how key learnings from the strategy sessions can be applied to the day-to-day operations of their respective regions, functions, and departments. These exercises ask participants to reflect on how they can communicate Kaiser Permanente's strategy and the strategic frameworks to their respective teams. As an extension of the learning

inquiry and learning journal applications, senior executives engage participants in informal, 'fireside chat' format discussions that take place in the evenings. This aspect of the residential program offers participants unique moments to meaningfully engage senior executives with difficult questions, ideas, probing issues, complexities, and innovative solutions. Paul Miller, SLP alum and senior director of Medicare at national headquarters, credits these applications for helping to sustain his strategic thinking over time and align his team's work activities to the national Kaiser Permanente strategy. "The SLP's overall emphasis on mapping our work activities to the overarching strategy of the organization, and using that as the compass, was very effective. When developing an operating plan, if any of the work activities or initiatives do not map back to the overall strategy, then I pause and question whether that activity is valuable and whether we should be spending time doing that." Miller notes that participation in the SLP has reinforced his efforts to "be cognizant of any decision that I'm making or being asked to make—how does that tie to the strategy of the organization? It was really helpful for me to be more cognizant and deliberate about that connection."

4. *Tools and Resources for Project Execution:* A final element of the residential program is a series of tools and resources designed to support execution of the strategic projects. The first of these tools is a set of project scoping and project management best practices, including the elements of a project work plan, delineation of project audiences and stakeholders, core work group and setting committee membership, project milestones and update reporting, and major project deliverables. Participants are also provided guidelines for identifying executive sponsors as well as processes for requesting data sources (e.g., membership data, patient satisfaction scores, patient visit encounters, operating costs, market fundamentals, etc.) that will serve as key inputs for the project teams. Finally, participants establish 'thought partnerships' to serve as a resource to support project execution and establish mutual accountability. SLP participants pair with one another during a networking reception that takes place during the first evening of the residential program. While the SLP team provides guidelines for selecting a thought partner, the SLP participants ultimately use their strategic project ideas and personal intuition for contracting with them. The thought partnerships provide participants with a resource for honest feedback, identifying other resources throughout Kaiser Permanente's complex system, and helping to collaboratively link leaders and strengthen networks across the enterprise. Mari Hern, an SLP alumna and executive director of IT Asset Management in the

Mid-Atlantic States Region, noting the importance of the thought partnership for her business says, "that whole connection has been very beneficial, and not just for my projects but other projects as well. We've been able to help other people that have reached out to me for certain things that are not my area, but I know a contact for it and we're able to partner or direct them to the right person. It's been hugely beneficial, especially in regions and organizations that aren't familiar with each other." Chuck Larson, vice president of Product Management at national headquarters, highlights the importance of relationship building throughout the program. A direct manager of three SLP alumni during the last five years, Larson asserts that "one of the most beneficial aspects of the program is the relationships and connectivity you build with other leaders of the organization. For the staff that I send through the program, I really emphasize the importance of building relationships during the residential phase. I actually say, 'I want you going out every night with your peers during the residential phase. I want you to go out with your peers and build personal relationships with these folks.' If you have those personal relationships, you are much more effective as a leader. As you go further in your career, those relationships are more and more meaningful in terms of being successful than many other things."

Project Phase: The final SLP phase consists of a series of learning and networking activities that culminate with the strategic project presentations and graduation ceremony in November. Upon completing the residential phase, participants continue development of the work plan for their respective strategic projects. They focus on executing their project work plans and conducting ongoing conversations with their executive sponsor(s), direct manager, thought partner, and other key project stakeholders. The strategic project presentations, which are attended by the participants' direct managers, executive sponsors, and senior Kaiser Permanente leaders, serve as a valuable learning objective by expanding participants' understanding of the breadth and depth of Kaiser Permanente's leadership roles and functions. James Schroeder, SLP alum and executive director of Medicaid at national headquarters, underscores the importance of gaining a deeper appreciation for the work of his fellow SLP participants. "The biggest benefit of the program is networking and understanding what other people do in the different units of Kaiser. It's not just meeting people, but having those people to reach out to and getting a better understanding of what different people do. A couple of the people that I got to know through the program I've later partnered with on projects. I probably got the most out of the poster session at graduation and hearing about what everybody did on their projects." The poster session format allows participants to practice their strategic project elevator pitches in a timed, fast-paced environment. As part of the session, senior executives and SLP participants vote on the best-in-class and most impactful projects, which are formally acknowledged at the graduation ceremony. Not only do participants gain a deeper appreciation for the work of their peers and Kaiser Permanente's complexity, but they also learn how various regions, functions, and departments are seeking strategic alignment across the enterprise; Dan Cousins, vice president of Talent and Organizational Performance, says, "At graduation, participants get the opportunity to see a lot of different expressions of what strategic alignment looks like from different parts of our organization and see Kaiser Permanente's strategy through many different lenses, not just their own. This part of the program is very important, especially when we get to succession, because we want to develop leaders who have more than a single perspective or expertise."

Throughout the project phase, 'Monthly Breakfasts with Leadership' offer participants an opportunity to meet with Kaiser Permanente's national leaders in a more intimate setting. Limited to just twelve attendees, SLP participants attend up to six monthly breakfast sessions beginning in June and ending in October. The purpose of these informal meetings is to provide participants with greater visibility and exposure to Kaiser Permanente's senior executives, as well as an opportunity to briefly share the topics and progress of their strategic projects. The colloquial format of the setting allows small groups of participants to engage in informal, authentic leader-to-leader conversations with Kaiser Permanente's top executives. For SLP participants, the breakfast sessions serve the dual purpose of validating their understanding of Kaiser Permanente's national strategy while also creating a welcoming forum to discuss innovative ideas. Asma Saif, executive director of Care Delivery, Technology, and Strategy, says, "I found the in-person senior leader sessions to be incredibly helpful because they were dedicated in-person time. It was very productive to be able to just clear some space in my brain to listen, learn, and validate what I had already heard about our national strategy as well as absorb some 'up close and personal time' with senior leaders." As underscored by Kristen Janes, director of Program Development, Laboratory Strategy, and Implementation, the intimate discussion forums often mark the beginnings of much stronger and long-term working relationships between SLP participants and Kaiser Permanente's senior leaders. "The relationships that you develop with the other [SLP participants] and with our senior leadership are one of the most important benefits of the program. I have been able to reach out to Vivian Tan (vice president of Strategy and Transformation at national headquarters, and an SLP faculty member) and share with her some of what I am doing in terms of the next project I am working on and how that will relate to our Vision 2025 strategy."

Evidence-Based Success Factors

Research findings on leadership development best practices[107] are highly consistent with the SLP's design and execution. Of the four primary types of leadership development programs, the SLP is an exemplary case of a strategic leadership development initiative. According to Conger[108] and other executive development experts, strategic leadership development initiatives should be established according to several key design elements for optimal impact: clear strategic framework driving program content; curricula designed to elicit group discussions between units and across levels; trained facilitators provide critical process assistance; learning experiences cascade across multiple levels; and active feedback mechanisms. To rigorously evaluate the SLP according to these design elements and measure the program's impact on key performance metrics, Kaiser Permanente's National Leadership Development (NLD) team initiated an independent and comprehensive program assessment (see About the Research for a summary of assessment methodology).

Overall, the assessment results indicate that the Strategic Leadership Program's effectiveness is driven by the five primary success factors presented in table 6.1, each represents a set of key program design and execution best practices. Identified via analysis of a rich mix of data sources including archival data (program materials, curriculum modules, faculty presentations, etc.), dozens of stakeholder interviews, and performance metrics comparing SLP alumni and comparable Kaiser Permanente leaders, these success factors offer healthcare organizations a set of practical building blocks for designing a strategic leadership development program.

National Strategy-Driven Curriculum

The first success factor is the clarity and consistency with which Kaiser Permanente's national business strategy drives the program's curriculum and learning activities. The SLP's sustained success is dependent upon how Kaiser Permanente's national business strategy and supporting materials, including Kaiser Permanente's Strategic Plan and Vision 2025, motivates basic curriculum and pedagogical choices concerning session content, project scope of work and support, stakeholder engagement, and related learning activities. In his analysis of best practices driving successful strategic leadership development programs, Conger asserts that "the foundational feature of these programs is a clearly articulated strategic framework that guides the organization's collective efforts. If the new strategy is vague or clouded by competing initiatives, the development efforts will simply surface underlining conflicts, create frustration, and ultimately increase opposition to the change effort."[109] Senior vice president, chief strategy officer, and SLP executive co-sponsor Paul

Table 6.1

Strategic Leadership Program Success Factors and Critical Design Elements

Success Factor	Critical Design Elements
National Strategy-Driven Curriculum	▪ Program curriculum and learning experiences driven by Kaiser Permanente's national business strategy ▪ Kaiser Permanente's Strategic Plan, Vision 2025, and Marketplace Scan as key inputs for curriculum design
Executive Team Engagement	▪ Program curriculum co-designed by Corporate Planning to ensure alignment to Kaiser Permanente's Strategic Plan ▪ Senior executives from multiple national business units engaged as residential program instructors, speakers, and project sponsors
Role-Based Development Experiences	▪ Identification and completion of a project that aligns with Kaiser Permanente's Strategic Plan and addresses a specific business/function or regional need ▪ Alignment of broader departmental and direct reports' work activities with Kaiser Permanente's Strategic Plan
Development of Strategically Aligned Leadership Competencies	▪ Enhance participants' ability to collaborate with peers and executive teams across functions, regions, and facilities ▪ Develop participants' strategic mindset and enterprise-wide perspective on critical issues ▪ Heighten participants' self-efficacy and poise to step up to broader leadership challenges
Expansion and Leveraging of Kaiser Permanente Leader Network	▪ Broaden and deepen participants' network of Kaiser Permanente professionals and executives across functions, regions, and facilities ▪ Facilitate opportunities for participants to engage with Kaiser Permanente executives for vetting project ideas ▪ Leveraging leader network for project execution and dissemination of project findings

Swenson, emphasizes the importance of Kaiser Permanente's national strategy as the SLP's foundational feature. "What makes the SLP different and particularly valuable is its foundation in reality, its foundation in our strategy. The SLP connects that reality with both the projects that leaders complete and the residential experience. As I look back at the kinds of SLP projects the participants chose, they're all substantive and important parts of our overall strategic agenda." Equally important for driving program success is the nimbleness of the SLP curriculum, which is designed in step with Kaiser Permanente's evolving strategic response to an increasingly complex and challenging healthcare landscape.

For SLP participants who are on the front lines of the enterprise-wide strategy, the SLP curriculum effectively balances the structure and rigor of Kaiser Permanente's strategic framework while also leveraging the real-time challenges and opportunities associated with delivering on the organization's mission.

Along a similar vein, Robert Sachs, retired vice president of National Learning and Development, highlights the importance of the SLP remaining focused on strategic alignment and avoiding the pursuit of multiple and potentially conflicting program goals. "The fundamental focus of the SLP is using the national strategy to develop direction for your team. The focus is understanding what is our strategy, how does our strategy get developed, and how do you use that understanding and related tools to develop the local strategy that you are responsible for. It's all about helping people sort through difficult strategic decisions—since strategy isn't about easy choices, it's about hard choices." Indeed, a key design element driving the SLP's success is the laser focus of the curriculum and learning activities on alignment with the national business strategy rather than the pursuit of multiple program outcomes. The SLP's design reflects very clear choices about strategic alignment and execution as primary program outcomes that are not diluted by additional curricula and learning activities (e.g., individual skill development, action learning initiatives, new leader transitions, etc.) which may result in a different set of leadership development outcomes.

Executive Team Engagement

The nature and magnitude of senior executive team engagement is the next critical success factor since the responsibility of program design, execution, and delivery is co-owned by chief executives from Kaiser Permanente's national headquarters, including Corporate Planning (Paul Swenson, senior vice president and chief strategy officer) and National Diversity and Inclusion Strategy and Policy (Ronald Copeland, MD, senior vice president and chief diversity and inclusion officer). Director of National Leadership Development, Alice Chen, notes the distinctiveness of her team's partnership with executives from Corporate Planning. "The SLP is one of only two enterprise-wide programs to which we invite participants from all regions and all functions, giving our leaders a true cross section of the entire organization. The program is primarily led by our strategy executives—it's not an HR-run development program— who are people from the business talking about our strategy, the framework that we use, and Kaiser Permanente's national strategy. The SLP creates strong alignment across all the participants coming from a strategy point of view, which is really unique."

SLP alumni overwhelmingly laud the credibility and expertise provided by Kaiser Permanente's senior executives who perform multiple roles throughout the program and beyond, including residential program instructors, breakfast series speakers, project sponsors, and mentors. In addition to Corporate Planning leaders, chief executives from multiple functions and businesses are actively engaged in one or more SLP roles. Patrick Courneya, MD, (executive vice president and chief medical officer), Janet Liang (chief operating officer), Dick Daniels (executive vice president and chief information officer), and Chuck Columbus (senior vice president and chief HR officer) represent a sample of national headquarters executives who remain actively engaged in a variety of SLP roles. The engagements between SLP participants and senior Kaiser Permanente executives during the program are a starting point for building stronger partnerships moving forward. Asma Saif, executive director of Care Delivery, Technology, and Strategy, underscores the long-term value of exposure to senior leaders from multiple businesses and functions. "As I started putting our care delivery strategy together, it was really important that I understand our enterprise strategy. I connected with Paul Swenson (chief strategy officer) and Vivian Tan (vice president, Strategy and Transformation) very early on in my work, and they were great supporters. They saw the value of the work I was doing and then actively included me in their work. I do not have any formal reporting relationship to our strategic planning colleagues, but I would say that it is a positive mutual partnership based on an understanding of how our contributions complement each other." Overall, the varied settings, formats, and roles in which senior leaders from multiple business units are engaged with the SLP's design and delivery are critical drivers of the program's long-term impact across Kaiser Permanente.

Role-Based Development Experiences

More than any other success factor or set of best practices, the SLP's effectiveness hinges on astutely leveraging role-based development experiences for leaders charged with executing Kaiser Permanente's national strategy. While numerous leadership scholars and abundant research findings confirm the integral role of job experiences in the leadership development process,[110] relatively few organizations adopt an approach that strategically utilizes job experiences to develop leadership talent. Indeed, most organizations fail to gain the most from their leadership development efforts due to overreliance on classroom-based training programs, utilizing tactical rather than strategic job experiences, or adopting a 'survival of the fittest' strategy of placing leaders in stretch roles and simply promoting those who succeed. While these practices may prove useful in some contexts, "they seldom achieve the potential that could be attained with a rigorous, comprehensive approach that systematically builds experiences into the heart of the organizational talent management system," concludes leadership development experts Paul Yost and Mary Plunkett.[111] Indeed, the SLP strategically leverages the projects as critical job experiences for a core group of Kaiser Permanente's leaders. Organizations that effectively use job experiences for developing leadership talent utilize a framework or taxonomy, as illustrated in table 6.2, that identifies the job experiences, competencies, key stakeholders, and learning capabilities that leaders require as they transition throughout various job assignments and roles in the organization.[112]

Table 6.2
Talent Management Taxonomy for Kaiser Permanente Leaders

Experiences	Competencies	Key Stakeholders	Learning Capabilities
Business Experiences • Lean project design and execution • Development of new service lines • Development of new market or geographic service areas • Turnaround of underperforming business unit **Perspective-Building Experiences** • Rotation to new region, medical center, or national headquarters • Labor management partnership • Kaiser Foundation Health Plan and Permanente Medical Group partnership **Functional Experiences** • Sales and marketing role • Information and digital technology role • Shared services role	• Strategic thinking • Enterprise-wide view of Kaiser Permanente • Leadership self-efficacy • Collaboration and alignment skills • Inclusive style leveraging diversity • Healthcare industry knowledge • Kaiser Permanente's integrated model and strategy acumen • Results orientation • Negotiation and influence skills • Influencing and working across business units	• Board of Directors • National Leadership Team • Regional executives • Community relations • Government relations • Labor leaders • Permanente Medical Group leaders • Mentors • SLP thought partners • Key consumer/payer groups • Key suppliers	• Cognitive ability • Integrity • Learning agility • Openness to feedback • Emotional intelligence • Cultural intelligence

The leadership development experiences that SLP participants complete vis-à-vis the strategic projects include business experiences, key functional or disciplinary experiences, and perspective-building experiences. Throughout the process of executing their strategic projects, SLP participants develop a range of leadership competencies and knowledge bases that are critical for executive performance at Kaiser Permanente. Each participant's work plan specifies the key stakeholder relationships that must be cultivated to drive successful execution of the strategic project. This element of the role-based developmental experience is vital for the participant's development as well as project success. Prominent leadership development organizations such as the Center for Creative Leadership[113] and the Corporate Leadership Council[114] have consistently found that relationship-building remains one of the most important drivers of a leader's development. Learning capabilities include those stable traits and personal characteristics that facilitate participants' ability to gain the lessons learned from their experiences and thoughtfully apply them to subsequent leadership roles. These enabling capabilities comprise personal characteristics and self-regulatory mechanisms, such as learning agility,[115] cognitive ability,[116] emotional intelligence,[117] and cultural intelligence,[118] enabling top leadership performance in highly dynamic, uncertain environments such as healthcare delivery organizations. For Kaiser Permanente and other best-practice organizations that leverage job experiences to drive strategic leadership development outcomes, the benefits of developing a talent management taxonomy include the following:

- Assess individual leaders' strengths and development opportunities, and identify job assignments and projects that will address their weaknesses or gaps.

- Assess the extent to which various leadership roles and project-based assignments across the enterprise provide leaders with the requisite developmental experiences.

- Identify and codify the experiences, competencies, stakeholder relationships, and learning capabilities that are aligned with the strategic plan and can be developed in various business units, functions, and project-based assignments.

- Enhance the developmental value of roles, job assignments, projects, and other leadership development experiences.

Development of Strategically Aligned Leadership Competencies

The fourth SLP success factor is the development of leadership competencies that are strongly aligned with Kaiser Permanente's national business strategy. The core pillars of Kaiser Permanente's national strategy—driving affordability and membership growth, enhancing the consumer digital experience, and ensuring consistency of healthcare services throughout the network—dictate the competencies that leaders must develop as well as the SLP's development experiences and projects. The three sets of role-based development experiences—business, perspective-building, and functional—in column one of the talent management taxonomy (table 6.2) enable the development of leadership competencies (listed in column two) that are aligned with Kaiser Permanente's strategic plan. Summarized in table 6.3, SLP alumni and their direct managers highlight how the SLP's learning and development activities allow participants to enhance these leadership competencies—a core set of skills and knowledge bases that sustain executive performance well beyond the SLP program—developed through the completion of the strategic project and other learning experiences.

Consistent with Kaiser Permanente's strategy of driving affordability by coordinating health services across business units and enhancing the consistency throughout Kaiser Permanente's network, SLP alumni and their direct managers laud the program's ability to develop strong collaboration skills. Paul Miller, SLP alum and senior director of Medicare at national headquarters, states that "with the Kaiser culture around consensus-building and alignment, the opportunity to develop these skills was a big takeaway and reinforcement from the program. When it comes to presenting a strategic plan, or presenting a business case, SLP helped us ensure that there is work done in the background to build alignment. It's very difficult to build that alignment on the spot when people are seeing something for the first time. Doing that work strategically with a variety of individuals in the background and drawing out concerns and other ideas is really important." Kaiser Permanente executives whose direct reports have participated in the SLP consistently reference the program's efficacy for enhancing participants' executive readiness, ability to transition from tactical to strategic work activities, and overall leadership self-efficacy. Perhaps more than any other competency or learning capability, SLP stakeholders stress the program's ability to increase participants' beliefs in their ability to confidently and collaboratively drive meaningful strategic change. In addition to offering a deep dive into the healthcare industry's dynamics and Kaiser Permanente's integrated delivery model, the program ultimately succeeds by creating leaders with the confidence and tools to embrace complex projects that demand engagement from multiple business units. Debbie Zuege, the Colorado Region's executive director of Clinical Operations, summarizes the SLP's impact on a key leader in her unit. "I think what participation in the SLP did was to help her have the tools to speak with the medical group, our strategic management department, and our marketing department. She worked with people who were not her direct reports to get her project going, which shows the ability to cross lines of accountability and responsibility. The program has continued to solidify her leadership style and given her more tools and more confidence to take more chances. She is the

Table 6.3
The SLP Leadership Competencies & Executive Excerpts

Competency	Executive Excerpts
Strategic Thinking	The SLP allows some of our major strategic initiatives to start to cross-pollinate. Instead of us marching down a path where we're just looking at how we access services and places of service, it makes us build into our plan [such issues as] how do we enable telemedicine as a digital service into our delivery of care? The SLP brings a component of connecting major strategic initiatives that probably would be much more difficult to execute on if we didn't have this type of program. (Chuck Larson, Vice President, Product Management)
Influencing & Working across Business Units	This program allowed me to have a structure around conversations with leadership—fairly sensitive topics and labor related. The program helped me connect with the right executives in various areas to get their input, which prior to the program was much more challenging. So that has been the greatest thing. (Motz Feinberg, Executive Director, Supply Chain Operations)
Enterprise-Wide View of Kaiser Permanente	What I enjoyed the most from our SLP program was that the participants were from all over the place. I'm in IT, which is where our technology risk office resides, but they were from across the organization. I got to partner up with folks that were anywhere from a hospital administrator to someone in the quality assurance side of care delivery. I found that to be a great way to have a broader understanding of the business. (Jason Zellmer, Vice President, Technology Risk Management)
Collaboration & Alignment Skills	When you think about the organization, we work extremely cross functionally. The way you get things done in our organization is largely through your ability to build relationships, influence outcomes, and collaborate on strategy and create change. My SLP experience allowed me to work with these different functions—audit, legal, our compliance partners, and the corporate controller function—which was a great opportunity for me to partner with these groups and incorporate their input. (Okorie Ramsey, Vice President, Finance Compliance Officer & Sarbanes-Oxley (SOX))
Leadership Self-Efficacy	You really see yourself as an emerging leader who is going to be part of the transformation instead of being on the recipient end. It was as though we were called forth—you are chosen to be here. You have projects that can have impact. We saw ourselves as the new generation really moving Kaiser Permanente forward. (Dexter Borrowman, Director, Kaiser Permanente National Service and Quality)
Leveraging Diversity & Inclusion Skills	One of the most important aspects of the program was appreciating how much Kaiser Permanente embraces diversity. I think there was a consistent level of speakers in communicating how much we embrace diversity and how much we want to make space for that diversity. For example, one of the key themes of one of the dinners was making space for the quiet ones such that diversity is not just in the context of culture or creed, but also in the space of how people think and how people process information. That has proven to be very helpful. (Cyrus Yang, Executive Director, Delivery System Planning)

one that I always think of first to take on kind of big projects that need a strategic thinker and a region-wide view."

Expansion and Leveraging of Kaiser Permanente Leader Network

The final success factor that drives the SLP's effectiveness is the focus on expanding and leveraging participants' leader network across Kaiser Permanente. Participants establish and cultivate new relationships with a diverse set of Kaiser Permanente executives, including fellow SLP participants, program faculty, guest speakers, strategic project executive sponsors, and Kaiser Permanente's national leadership team via the monthly breakfast series. Thoughtfully expanding the participants' leader networks serves several important purposes, including expediting strategic project execution, broadening access to leaders, business units, and resources throughout Kaiser Permanente, and exposure to national and regional executives for career advancement and succession management. Many SLP stakeholders emphasize the short- and long-term value of the program's focus on networking. "The SLP, of everything we have, is probably the best use of relationships and the most comprehensive program for connecting individual participant's aspirations, input and guidance from their managers, and exposure to our company's executives," says Dan Cousins, vice president of Talent and Organizational Performance. The mix of networking sessions and opportunities are "not just a 'sage on the stage' perspective where they listen to a presentation. SLP participants are exposed repeatedly in informal settings where they have an opportunity to meet different leaders, ask questions, and calibrate what they're hearing from different leaders from across the organization." The ultimate value of leader networking as a central SLP focus extends well beyond the confines of the program and the strategic projects. Program alumni emphasize the practical value of their expanded Kaiser Permanente leader network well after graduation from the program. The following include representative excerpts from SLP alumni extolling the post-program networking benefits:

> If I have an issue or somebody says, 'Hey, Laurie, I have some assets over in this medical building,' then I know exactly who to talk to. The connections developed in the program have been amazing and very beneficial—not just for my projects, but other projects as well. We've been able to help other people that have reached out for certain things that are not my area but I know a contact for it and we're able to partner in that space or connect them with the right person. That's been hugely beneficial. (Mari Hern, executive director, IT Asset Management)

The networking really helped me because I have been able to reach out to a number of people since completing the SLP in my day-to-day job; I've been able to remember those people and actually partner with them in different ways. For instance, I was doing something with individuals moving to charitable lines of business and I remembered that one of my fellow SLP participants was from community benefit. I was able to reach out, talk to her, and come up with some different plans. Overall, I believe that the relationships I developed in SLP helped me to just be a more well-rounded executive. (Tina Weiss, executive director, Individual and Family Plans)

When you have a similar and common experience that you are able to draw from, it just brings a sense of commitment to support one another, whereas if you did not have the connection, you wouldn't necessarily get that same level of attention. I can tap on a colleague who participated in the program and say, 'Hey...could you just look at this?' When you have that relationship, they want to support you not only because you're a colleague but because we have a personal relationship from the experiences that we shared. (Okorie Ramsey, vice president, Finance Compliance Officer & Sarbanes-Oxley)

Evidence-Based Evaluation: SLP's Impact on Key Metrics

While the preceding discussion offers strong support for the success factors that drive the SLP's effectiveness, an evidence-based approach for evaluating the program requires analysis of key quantitative performance metrics. The SLP's long-term success depends upon a clear, evidence-based approach that clearly demonstrates the SLP's impact on strategically aligned performance metrics. As such, Kaiser Permanente's National Leadership Development (NLD) team adopts a three-pronged evaluation strategy. First, the direct managers of SLP participants complete survey-based evaluations of the strategic projects as they are presented at the graduation session. Second, SLP participants complete self-assessment surveys after the residential and graduation sessions that assess program quality and the level of engagement provided by faculty and guest speakers. At the graduation session, SLP participants also complete survey items that measure multiple dimensions of their learning and performance outcomes. These dimensions and representative assessment items include learning effectiveness ("SLP enhanced my ability to think and act strategically"); job impact ("What I learned at SLP will help me perform better as a leader, particularly in executing on a specific business strategy"); business results ("Estimate how much of your job performance related to "strategy and business execution" will improve based on your SLP experience"); and return on investment ("This program was a worthwhile investment in my professional career development").

While the survey-based evaluation results from SLP participants and their direct managers are overwhelmingly positive, the NLD team recognizes the limitations of exclusively relying on self-assessment and perception-based data to evaluate the SLP's long-term efficacy.[119] Therefore, the third and final part of the evaluation strategy consists of assessing the SLP's sustained impact across three performance metrics: annual turnover, annual promotions, and annual performance reviews. In order to evaluate the program's impact over a sustained period, three groups of Kaiser Permanente leaders were compared across those three metrics. The three comparison groups included the following: 943 directors, executive directors, and vice presidents designated as high-potential leaders via Kaiser Permanente's talent review process but have not completed the SLP, the HiPo group; sixty-five SLP alumni who had not been assessed as high-potential leaders and who were at least one year removed from program graduation, the SLP group; and ninety-six leaders who were both designated as high-potential leaders via Kaiser Permanente's talent review process and also at least one year removed from program graduation, the group labeled as Both. These Kaiser Permanente leaders were assessed over a three-year period (2013-2015) to isolate the SLP's impact on annual turnover, annual promotions, and annual performance reviews. The following section presents key results across each performance metric:

1. *Annual Turnover (2013-2015):* Illustrated in figure 6.2, the 2013 turnover rate for the SLP group was 4.6 percent compared to 2.2 percent for the HiPo group, while the Both group had a 1 percent annual turnover rate. Interestingly, the variance in turnover rates across the three groups increased in 2014 and 2015. The impact of SLP participation by Kaiser Permanente's high-potential leaders was magnified in each successive year following completion of the program. In 2014, the annual turnover rate the Both group was an impressive 0 percent compared to 5.9 percent for the HiPo group and 6.8 percent for the SLP group. These trends continued in 2015 with the annual turnover rate surging to 8.3 percent for the HiPo group, 6.3 percent for the SLP group, and only 2.1 percent for the Both group. Given the exceedingly high and increasing costs associated with healthcare executive turnover,[120] these data offer strong evidence of the SLP's sustained impact on the retention of Kaiser Permanente's leadership talent.

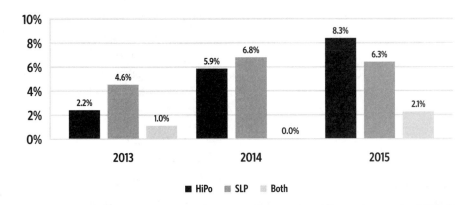

Figure 6.2
Annual Turnover of SLP Alumni versus Comparison Groups of Kaiser Permanente Leaders (2013-2015)

Notes: The 'HiPo' group (n = 943) includes executives who were designated as high-potential leaders via Kaiser Permanente's annual talent review process but have not completed the SLP program; the 'SLP' group (n = 65) incudes executives who completed the SLP but have not been designated as high-potential leaders via Kaiser Permanente's talent review process; the 'Both' group (n = 96) consists of executives who completed the SLP and were also designated as high-potential leaders via Kaiser Permanente's talent review process.

2. *Annual Promotions (2013-2015):* Presented in figure 6.3, the annual promotion rate over a three-year period for the three comparison groups offers strong support for the SLP's positive impact. The HiPo and SLP groups experienced a sharp decline in the percentage of leaders promoted from 2013 through 2015, while those Kaiser Permanente leaders in the Both group experienced a strong upward trend in annual promotions. Tellingly, the promotion rate for the HiPo group declines from 17.5 percent in 2013 to 10.2 percent in 2015 while the Both group's promotion rate grew from 8.4 to 12.5 percent during the same three-year period. These findings suggest an important lagged effect of the SLP on career advancement once alumni are three years removed from the program. Overall, the promotion rate differences across the three comparison groups offer evidence of the SLP's impact on Kaiser Permanente's leadership bench strength and succession management efforts.

3. *Annual Performance Review (2013-2015):* The final performance metric that offers strong evidence of the SLP's impact is the annual performance review, which evaluates job performance on a scale of 1 (low) to 5 (high). Presented in figure 6.4, the performance review mean score for

the HiPo and SLP groups gradually declines from 2013 through 2015. For the HiPo group, the score dipped from 3.75 in 2013 to 3.60 in 2015 and the SLP group experienced a sharp decline from 3.57 to 3.29 in the same three-year period. By comparison, Kaiser Permanente leaders in the Both group maintained the highest mean annual performance review rating from 2013 (3.77) to 2015 (3.69). Furthermore, the Both group achieved the highest mean job performance rating across all groups over that same three-year period. Reflecting a trend observed with the annual turnover and promotion rates, the sharpest differences between the groups were observed during the third year (2015), which offers more support for the SLP's lagged impact on job performance.

Lessons Learned

The preceding case study outlined the primary phases, objectives, learning activities, and performance outcomes of Kaiser Permanente's Strategic Leadership Program. Designed to support the execution of Kaiser Permanente's national business strategy through alignment of the organization's regions and functions, the SLP's distinctive design offers a series of lessons learned and practical recommendations for healthcare organizations seeking to develop leaders through strategic initiatives:

1. *Maintain Disciplined Program Focus:* An important best practice is maintaining sharp focus on the primary program outcomes while resisting the temptation to pursue multiple goals and potentially dilute both program quality and ultimate impact across the organization. Rather than trying to achieve conflicting program goals, such as individual skill development, leader role transitions, and action learning initiatives, exemplary leadership development programs are designed to align learning activities with clear objectives and program outcomes. As illustrated by Kaiser Permanente, best-practice organizations adopt a portfolio approach to executive development whereby a menu of programs is created to meet the different developmental needs that leaders experience throughout their career. Strategic leadership development programs like the SLP are designed to achieve greater strategic alignment in a rapidly changing business environment. Healthcare organizations seeking to design a strategic leadership development program should carefully evaluate the trade-offs—such as comparative program objectives, benefits, and costs—associated with the various types of leadership development programs and their relative effectiveness for meeting different developmental needs for healthcare leaders.

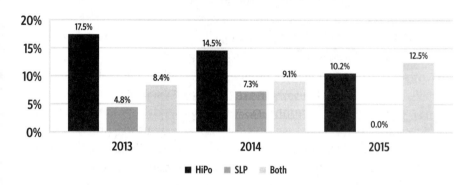

Figure 6.3

Annual Promotions of SLP Alumni versus Comparison Groups of Kaiser Permanente Leaders (2013-2015)

Notes: The 'HiPo' group (n = 943) includes executives who were designated as high-potential leaders via Kaiser Permanente's annual talent review process but have not completed the SLP program; the 'SLP' group (n = 65) incudes executives who completed the SLP but have not been designated as high-potential leaders via Kaiser Permanente's talent review process; the 'Both' group (n = 96) consists of executives who completed the SLP and were also designated as high-potential leaders via Kaiser Permanente's talent review process.

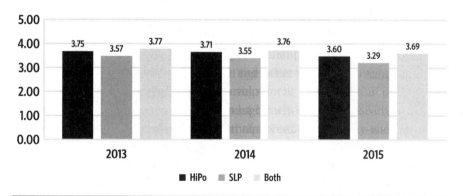

Figure 6.4

Annual Performance Review of SLP Alumni versus Comparison Groups of Kaiser Permanente Leaders (2013-2015)

Notes: The 'HiPo' group (n = 943) includes executives who were designated as high-potential leaders via Kaiser Permanente's annual talent review process but have not completed the SLP program; the 'SLP' group (n = 65) incudes executives who completed the SLP but have not been designated as high-potential leaders via Kaiser Permanente's talent review process; the 'Both' group (n = 96) consists of executives who completed the SLP and were also designated as high-potential leaders via Kaiser Permanente's talent review process.

2. *Ensure Co-Ownership of Program Design and Execution by Business Owners:* An invaluable lesson learned is the importance of ensuring that strategic development programs are co-owned by business owners and senior leadership teams, particularly the chief strategy officer and other system-level leaders charged with business planning responsibilities. The foundational design of exemplary strategic leadership development programs, and the learning activities and job experiences therein, is based upon the health system's strategic plan and senior leaders' ability to clearly articulate the enterprise-wide strategy. For many stakeholders, and particularly participants, the program's relevance and credibility are driven by the engagement of senior leaders as program sponsors, program faculty, project advisors, guest speakers, and mentors. While human resource and organization development professionals perform important co-ownership roles in program design and execution, strategic development programs must be driven by the senior leaders responsible for strategy development and business planning.

3. *Leverage Role-Based, Strategically Aligned Development Experiences:* As the central learning experience that comprises strategic development programs, best-practice organizations strategically utilize job experiences to develop leadership talent. While most organizations fall short of maximizing gains from leadership development programs, exemplary organizations use a range of job experiences to develop leadership competencies tied to the business strategy. As exemplified by the SLP, healthcare organizations should develop a talent management taxonomy that assesses the job experiences, competencies, key stakeholders, and learning capabilities that leaders will need as they transition throughout various job assignments and roles. The development of such a tool will help identify those roles, job experiences, and projects that offer the greatest developmental value for the participants and strategic alignment for the organization.

4. *Assemble Diverse Program Cohorts with Strong Project Support:* Another critical lesson learned is the importance of selecting program participants according to several key criteria, including functional, regional, and departmental diversity; alignment with the talent review process and high-potential leader designation; and strong project support. The assembly of program cohorts comprised of leaders from multiple levels, regions, and functions, as well as a mix of clinical and administrative leaders, provides a rich learning environment in which to deepen participants' understanding of national business strategy and strategic alignment from multiple perspectives. Exemplary programs also assess the level of

support provided by the participants' direct managers. The ultimate success of strategic development programs is strongly moderated by at least two critical factors: (1) the extent to which participants have 'ready now' projects that are primed for strategic alignment, and (2) supportive direct managers who provide participants with time away from other day-to-day duties, encouragement, and guidance throughout the program. As such, the selection process for program cohorts should include careful evaluation of the candidates' entire job context and support system.

5. *Expand and Cultivate the Participants' Leader Network*: A final lesson learned is the importance of thoughtfully expanding and leveraging the participants' leader networks across the organization. The expansion and active cultivation of leader networks through multiple program activities provide numerous short- and long-term benefits, including expediting execution of strategic projects, broadening access to leaders throughout the organization, facilitating post-program job assignments and projects, and providing invaluable exposure to senior leaders concerning succession and career advancement.

Conclusion

As one of the nation's largest and most successful fully integrated health systems, Kaiser Permanente's Strategic Leadership Program is a testament to the organization's strong commitment to developing leadership talent. In the midst of an increasingly uncertain business environment that will continually drive changes to its national business strategy, Kaiser Permanente has created an exemplary leadership development program that serves the distinctive purpose of enhancing the strategic alignment of its regions and functions. As illustrated in this case, the SLP effectively develops a core of mid-level healthcare leaders—directors, executive directors, and newly placed vice presidents—who are charged with aligning the local strategies of their respective regions, functions, and departments. Moving forward, the SLP will continue serving a critical role in Kaiser Permanente's efforts to develop leadership talent and evolve its business strategy to reflect the dynamics of the healthcare industry.

About the Research

The research to support this case study was conducted by Kevin S. Groves, PhD, and Groves Consulting Group during a 6-month period that began in August 2015, and concluded in January 2016. As part of an annual program evaluation process, Kaiser Permanente's National Leadership Development initiated an independent and comprehensive assessment of the Strategic Leadership Program (SLP). The assessment strategy consisted of collecting data from the following sources:

1. *NLD Professionals:* A series of open-ended interviews were conducted with NLD executives and professionals to review and discuss all extant SLP materials. The interviews were aimed at discussing the SLP's design and execution best practices.

2. *SLP Alumni & Managers:* SLP graduates and their director managers participated in semi-structured interviews to assess their perspectives on the program's design and execution best practices. The interviews were conducted in person or by phone with each executive and transcribed by an electronic recording service for the purpose of subsequent analysis.

3. *SLP Executive Sponsors:* The program's two corporate-level executive sponsors participated in semi-structured interviews to collect their views on the SLP's design and execution best practices.

4. *Archival Data:* Archival data and information, including Kaiser Permanente's Strategic Plan and Vision 2025, SLP residential presentations and supporting materials, SLP performance metrics, and other extant materials were obtained for review and analysis.

CHAPTER 7

Assessing and Developing Your Organization's Talent Management Capabilities (TMCs)

The primary premise for this book is an evidence-based case for succession management capabilities that help address many of the pressing business challenges facing healthcare executives. Summarized in chapter 1, the challenges facing hospitals and health systems, including industry consolidation, massive workforce demographic shifts, legal and regulatory changes, and the ongoing transition from volume- to value-based care, demand a far more strategic and proactive approach to managing leadership talent. Despite the clear 'business case' for leveraging exemplary talent management practices to meet these unprecedented healthcare industry changes, many hospitals and health systems have overlooked this investment. Of all the drivers of hospital and health system performance that CEOs, executive teams, and boards can directly impact, succession management capabilities are simultaneously the most important, yet most frequently neglected, asset for many organizations. As illustrated in this book, rigorous research across national benchmarking surveys, intensive case studies of leading health systems, and numerous consulting engagements presents a compelling, evidence-based rationale for the importance of talent development and succession planning practices for healthcare organizations.

The following concluding chapter presents an integrative summary of talent development and succession management principles that characterize best-practice organizations, including a series of recommendations for CEOs, executive teams, and boards seeking to enhance their respective organization's capabilities. Before presenting the integrative principles and best-practice recommendations, this chapter provides a diagnostic tool to assess an organization's strengths and development opportunities across the **Talent Management Capabilities (TMCs)**. Executives whose organizations utilize some of the **TMCs** may use this tool to create an action plan for improvement. For those with well-developed talent management strategies, this chapter provides a checklist to measure their progress. On the other hand, executive teams and boards of organizations with underdeveloped or non-existent talent management capabilities may use this chapter as an efficient diagnostic tool for assessing their primary strengths and development opportunities.

Talent Management Capabilities (TMCs) Assessment

Let's start with a brief reflection on your organization's critical talent management challenges as a prelude to formally assessing talent development and succession planning practices. In order to capture the challenges associated with managing leadership talent across your organization, complete the brief exercise in table 7.1.

This exercise is designed to facilitate reflection on the primary talent management challenges facing your organization, and how your leadership team is currently positioned to address them. The purpose of this exercise is to capture the critical challenges associated with your organization's talent management landscape and use this contextual data for establishing an executive agenda and action planning priorities.

The next step for assessing your organization's talent development and succession management practices is completing the **Talent Management Capabilities (TMCs)** assessment in table 7.2 while keeping in mind your organization's primary talent management challenges[§§]. This diagnostic tool is designed to assess the frequency and importance of all eight **TMCs** and their associated best practices across your organization. Illustrated in chapter 2, the eight **TMCs** represent building blocks in the foundation of an exemplary succession management strategy. The semi-annual **Healthcare Talent Management Survey**[121] allows for benchmarking of **TMC** utilization rates across multiple

---

[§§] *Note that the Talent Management Assessment and related succession management and talent development diagnostic tools are available at http://www.grovesconsultinggroup.com/index.php/gcgassessments/*

Table 7.1
Your Organization's Critical Talent Management Challenges

In the space provided, list your organization's critical talent management challenges across the four processes. Next, list your specific objectives for addressing these challenges.

Critical Challenges	Objectives to Address Challenges
1. Attracting/Acquiring Leadership Talent:	
2. Identifying/Assessing Leadership Talent:	
3. Developing Leadership Talent:	
4. Retaining Leadership Talent:	

Table 7.2
Talent Management Capabilities (TMCs) Assessment

This assessment is designed to provide you with feedback and insights about your organization's talent management practices. First, provide a rating according to the scale below that captures the *Frequency* with which the *TMCs* are utilized in your organization. Next, indicate the level of *Importance* of the *TMCs* for addressing your organization's current talent management challenges—identified in the reflection exercise (table 7.1).

Frequency Rating Scale:
- 1 = Not at All
- 2 = Rarely
- 3 = Sometimes
- 4 = Usually
- 5 = Always

Importance Rating Scale:
- 1 = Not Important
- 2 = Slightly Important
- 3 = Important
- 4 = Very Important
- 5 = Extremely Important

	Frequency Rating	Importance Rating
Top Management Team Support		
The senior leadership team describes talent management as a strategic priority.		
The senior leadership team actively participates in the talent review process.		
The senior leadership team communicates a sense of urgency for investing in talent management practices.		
The senior leadership team supports the integration of talent management practices into our operations.		
The senior leadership team teaches in our leadership development programs several times per year.		
The senior leadership team spends at least 20 percent of its time on mentoring and developing other leaders in our organization.		
Average Rating (Total/6)		
Performance Appraisal Practices		
The performance management system is deemed credible by managers across our organization.		
The performance management system is deemed credible by employees in key positions.		
Managers meet with their superiors at least twice per year for a formal discussion of their performance.		
High-potential employees meet with their superiors at least twice per year for a formal discussion of their performance.		
Managers annually receive 360-degree feedback that is development-based (not part of their formal performance appraisal).		
Average Rating (Total/5)		

TMC Assessment *contd.*

Frequency Rating Scale:
1 = Not at All
2 = Rarely
3 = Sometimes
4 = Usually
5 = Always

Importance Rating Scale:
1 = Not Important
2 = Slightly Important
3 = Important
4 = Very Important
5 = Extremely Important

	Frequency Rating	Importance Rating
Talent Assessment Practices		
Talent review sessions are characterized by authentic, non-politicized dialogue.		
Talent review sessions consist of cooperative and collaborative decision-making.		
High-potential employees are identified in the context of our organization's strategic priorities.		
Formal assessments (e.g., nine-box tools) are utilized to plot employees in key positions according to job performance and leadership potential.		
High-potential employees are formally assessed at front-line levels of management (e.g., supervisor, shift leader, etc.).		
Average Rating (Total/5)		
Selection & Onboarding Practices		
The selection process for managerial positions involves behaviorally based interviews linked to leadership competencies.		
The distinctiveness of our organization is made clear to external candidates for key positions.		
Employees promoted into managerial positions or roles that are new to our organization complete a formal onboarding program.		
Managers hired from outside our organization complete a formal onboarding program.		
Average Rating (Total/4)		
Leadership Development Culture		
Managers across our organization view the process for designating high potentials as fair and equitable.		
Our organization seeks to achieve transparency with the high-potential designation process.		
Our organizational culture de-emphasizes the status associated with high-potential designations.		
Employees view the process for designating high potentials as fair and equitable.		
Managers are trained to formally communicate high-potential designations to employees.		
Average Rating (Total/5)		

TMC Assessment *contd.*

Frequency Rating Scale:
1 = Not at All
2 = Rarely
3 = Sometimes
4 = Usually
5 = Always

Importance Rating Scale:
1 = Not Important
2 = Slightly Important
3 = Important
4 = Very Important
5 = Extremely Important

	Frequency Rating	Importance Rating
Incentive Pay Practices		
The incentive pay structure for our senior leadership team incentivizes support for talent management practices.		
Performance appraisal practices incentivize managers to support talent management practices.		
The board of directors advocates an incentive pay structure that incentivizes CEO support of talent management practices.		
Average Rating (Total/3)		
Role-Based Leadership Development		
Our organizational culture discourages talent hoarding—managers keeping high-potential employees from leaving their current positions.		
Our organizational culture encourages managers to 'release' high-potential employees for developmental assignments elsewhere in the hospital or across our health system.		
Our organization employs an action learning program in which high-potential employees learn new skills by completing team projects that address critical, organization-wide problems and reflecting on their experiences in a facilitated session.		
Our organization employs job rotations whereby leaders are re-assigned on at least a half-time basis to temporary roles for skill development.		
Average Rating (Total/4)		
Talent Management ROI		
Our organization utilizes metrics and ROI analyses to evaluate the effectiveness of our talent management practices.		
Our organization's talent management metrics are reviewed by the governing board.		
Our organization's talent management metrics are clearly communicated to management teams across the hospital or health system.		
Average Rating (Total/3)		

types of healthcare delivery organizations, including academic medical centers or health systems, community-based or independent hospitals, private or faith-based health systems, government institutions, and for-profit or investor-owned health systems. Note that any single organization may not possess all of these capabilities, yet all of the talent development and succession management practices that comprise the **TMCs** can be effectively developed through a thoughtful and targeted action plan.

Executive Agenda: Courses of Action

The assessment results recorded in table 7.2 may be used to diagnose your organization's relative strengths and development areas across the **Talent Management Capabilities (TMCs)**. For each of the eight **TMCs**, plot the average frequency and importance ratings for your organization on the graph in figure 7.1. The vertical y-axis represents the average importance ratings while the horizontal x-axis represents the average frequency ratings. The quadrants allow for analysis of the **TMCs** according to their relative importance to your organization as well as priorities for action-planning moving forward. The quadrants represent the following priorities with respect to determining next steps for enhancing your organization's talent development and succession management practices:

- **Quadrant A** *(Development Areas)*: The talent management practices placed into this quadrant likely demand immediate attention and action planning for remediation. In contexts with limited resources and/or insufficient political support for talent management, these practices should be targeted for immediate development.

- **Quadrant B** *(Strengths)*: The talent management practices positioned in this quadrant represent your organization's primary strengths and core competencies. As such, these should be maintained, reinforced, and modeled throughout the organization.

- **Quadrant C** *(Low Priority)*: The talent management practices represented in this quadrant are executed less frequently and also considered less critical to your organization; they are low priority and therefore do not require additional resources.

- **Quadrant D** *(Possible Overuse)*: These talent management practices are executed with high frequency yet considered less important for addressing your organization's critical talent management challenges. Strong consideration should be given to devoting fewer resources to these practices in favor of those practices represented in Quadrants A and B.

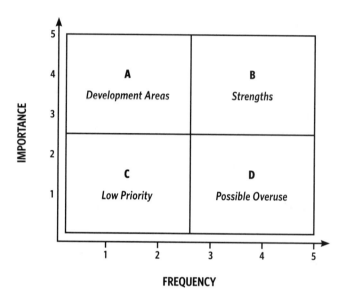

Figure 7.1
Talent Management Capabilities (TMCs) Assessment Results & Action-Planning Priorities

The ultimate purpose of the **TMC Assessment** is to establish a clear and compelling executive agenda that includes priorities for an action plan that targets both strengths and development areas. While all healthcare organizations would benefit from deep capabilities across the eight **TMCs** and their associated best practices, the often-limited resources of executives' time and attention requires a more direct action plan that leverages current strengths and enhances specific development areas. Most importantly, an effective action plan should target those succession management practices that are closely aligned with your organization's business strategy. For example, health systems experiencing tremendous growth through acquisitions and the resulting pressures on leadership team transitions may target **Selection & Onboarding Practices** for action planning. Alternatively, healthcare organizations that are in the nascent phases of establishing a talent management strategy may focus on establishing **Top Management Team Support** and fundamental building blocks such as **Performance Appraisal Practices** and **Talent Assessment Practices**. As you review your **TMC Assessment** results and action-planning priorities plotted on figure 7.1, reflect on the following questions to further guide the development of your action plan:

- What overall patterns do you detect in the **TMC** frequency/importance ratings plotted in the graph above?

- Do you notice any common themes for those practices represented in Quadrant A *(Development Areas)* and/or Quadrant B *(Strengths)*?

- Are there trends or patterns in the types of **TMCs** clustered in Quadrant A and/or absent from Quadrant B?

- For those **TMCs** represented in Quadrant A, how can you leverage the necessary resources and political support for an action plan to enhance these development areas?

The final section of this chapter concludes with an integrative summary of talent development and succession management principles that characterize best-practice organizations, including a series of recommendations for CEOs, executive teams, and boards seeking to enhance their respective organization's capabilities. For healthcare executives seeking to craft an action plan for leveraging their organization's strengths and improving development areas, the following discussion provides a series of practical recommendations across the **TMCs**. Supported by the rigorous research findings summarized in this book, the following best-practice recommendations include the talent management policies, processes, and strategies that distinguish high-performance healthcare organizations.

Talent Development & Succession Management Principles

Illustrated throughout this book, talent management systems and practices are increasingly utilized by hospitals and health systems to confront the myriad challenges facing healthcare organizations. The earlier chapters have referenced many healthcare organizations, including academic medical centers, community hospitals, investor-owned healthcare companies, and prominent faith-based health systems, that have successfully implemented talent development and succession management best practices. An integrative analysis of the talent development and succession management systems described in this book reveals a set of five critical themes or principles that healthcare executives should utilize to guide their strategy and craft a practical, strategically-aligned development plan. Summarized below are the five principles and their key elements:

1. **Strong Alignment between Business Strategy & Talent Management Capabilities**

    ✓ **Identify strategic talent pools.** An essential best practice in the current environment of limited resources is to clearly identify the talent and positions that are critical to execution of the business strategy. For many healthcare organizations, strategically critical positions include hospital or facility C-suite roles—CEO, COO, CFO, and CNO—as well as physician alignment, CMO and Clinical Integration positions. The allocation of resources to talent pools that have the greatest strategic impact is a distinguishing practice of high-performance organizations across industries.[122]

    ✓ **Elevate the strategic priority of talent management practices.** Create a sense of urgency amongst board members and senior management teams by clearly articulating the strategic priority of talent development and succession management practices. Executive teams must elevate the strategic priority of talent management by generating greater awareness of the impact of talent management capabilities on clinical quality, cost containment, workforce productivity, employer of choice designations, and other strategic metrics.[123] High-performing healthcare organizations implement strategic initiatives aimed at enhancing clinical quality metrics, such as the Centers for Medicare and Medicaid Services' (CMS) value-based purchasing program, through targeted application of talent management practices.

    ✓ **Assess leadership development program curricula for strategic alignment.** As part of an annual appraisal process, evaluate all leadership development program modules or seminars, project topics, assessment tools, and learning activities to ensure strong alignment with your organizations' strategic initiatives. Engage senior executives in annual discussions of the alignment between leadership development program curricula and your organization's strategic initiatives. The ongoing shift from volume- to value-based hospital performance metrics, the transition from hospital-centric care to population management and the full spectrum of health services, and continuing industry consolidation should drive the design of leadership development program curricula.

    ✓ **Leverage role-based, strategically aligned development experiences.** Utilize role-based job experiences or temporary assignments as core elements of your leadership development strategy. Healthcare organizations with exemplary performance outcomes utilize a range of permanent job experiences and temporary assignments to develop leadership competencies that are tied to the business strategy. As part of an annual process for refining your organization's leadership development strategy, develop a talent management taxonomy that assesses the job experiences, competencies, key stakeholders, and learning capabilities that leaders must demonstrate as they advance throughout their career. The development of such a tool will help identify those roles, job experiences, and projects that offer the greatest developmental value for the participants and strategic alignment for the organization.

2. **Substantive Engagement of Board Members and Executive Teams across Talent Management Capabilities**

   ✓ **Engage executive teams in leadership assessment and development practices.** Fully engage senior leaders in the design and execution of succession management capabilities, particularly talent assessment practices and leadership development programs. Executive teams should be intimately involved in rigorous assessments of their direct reports, the results of which are utilized to drive talent review meetings. Human resource leaders should partner with executive teams to identify a range of leadership development experiences that are aligned with the business strategy. The health system CEO and other senior executives should be engaged with leadership assessment and development activities at multiple points throughout the program.

   ✓ **Develop multiple mentoring and teaching opportunities for senior leaders.** Create a range of engaging opportunities for senior leaders to serve as mentors and teachers through formal mentoring programs, sponsorship of action learning projects, and teaching modules as part of internal leadership development programs or 'leadership academies,' or standalone courses.

   ✓ **Compel board members to participate in talent reviews for the top management team.** Exemplary succession management systems meaningfully engage key board members, including the board chair and the HR or compensation committee, in the annual talent review process for the CEO's direct reports and emerging system-level executives. Ensure that the annual talent review process provides the board chair and other key board members or committees with the opportunity to participate in talent reviews for the CEO's direct reports, identify developmental needs, and craft development opportunities for potential successors.

✓ Partner with regional and facility executives to design action learning projects. Ensure that core leadership development program elements, such as team-based action learning projects, are vetted and co-owned by executives at the regional and local or facility levels. Executive teams operating in a given region and across diverse medical centers or facilities offer invaluable local insights on the effective design of leadership development activities, such as identify topics for team-based action learning projects.

3. Robust Talent Management Metrics and ROI Measures

✓ **Illustrate the looming retirement wave and workforce demographics.** Conduct annual forecasting analyses that illustrate anticipated retirements and leadership bench strength across executive roles and other critical leadership positions. Emphasize the practical value of superior talent management practices for maintaining stability in critical executive roles and avoiding the substantial difficulties associated with unexpected retirements or exits. Conduct annual retirement forecasts that plot employees in leadership positions (e.g., supervisor, manager, director, and executive) across key age groups (< 30, 30-34, 35-39, 40-44, 45-49, etc.). For each leadership position or management level, report and discuss the following metrics with senior executive teams and board members: (a) overall percentage of leaders who are 55 or older (or at your organization's retirement age), and (b) percentage of leadership positions that have at least one 'ready now' candidate (leadership bench strength).

✓ **Establish an evidence-based evaluation strategy to sharpen the business case.** As part of the process for gaining executive team support, present a data-driven case for the positive impact of succession management capabilities on key performance metrics. Collect baseline (pre-program) data and post-program outcomes across a set of performance metrics identified by human resource leaders and senior executive teams as strongly aligned with the business strategy. Design talent management initiatives as 'living labs' in which real-time data are collected to improve the program and calculate ROI analyses that enhance the program's reputation amongst key organizational stakeholders.

✓ **Benchmark your talent management capabilities against comparable organizations.** Annually participate in benchmarking surveys for the purpose of comparing your talent development and succession management capabilities to industry peers and establishing (or enhancing) an 'employer of choice' distinction in key labor markets.[124] Participating in annual benchmarking surveys allows for direct comparison of your organization's talent management practices and performance outcomes to hospitals and health systems that are most similar in size and type of healthcare delivery model (academic, specialty, for-profit/investor-owned, community, governmental, etc.).

✓ **Communicate the ROI of talent management practices to key stakeholders.** Utilize your organization's benchmarking study results to populate internal balanced scorecards or dashboards that are discussed with key stakeholders. Cultivate an organization-wide appreciation for the value of highly developed succession management capabilities by annually reporting your scorecard results to multiple internal stakeholders, including the governing board and management teams across the organization.

4. **Rigorous Leadership Assessment, Development, and Succession Management Practices**

   ✓ **Conduct comprehensive talent reviews.** Design and conduct annual talent review sessions with the same rigor and discipline as the budgeting, strategic planning, performance management, and other core business processes. A highly effective talent review is a standardized, data-driven process across medical centers or facilities that begins with the system leadership team and proceeds sequentially throughout each management level. In partnership with senior executive teams, clearly establish that the goal of the talent review process is not replacement planning—the identification of the most likely direct report to replace an incumbent leader—but to cultivate strong succession plans for strategically critical positions and create a central, searchable repository of leadership talent. Highly effective talent reviews are full-day sessions facilitated by human resource professionals in which management teams assess their direct reports, calibrate ratings across team members, and discuss personalized development plans for employees rated as high potentials and high performers. Ensure that talent review sessions are conducted following the completion of the annual performance review process to avoid the many drawbacks associated with asking management teams to simultaneously assess job performance and leadership potential.

   ✓ **Utilize formal leadership assessment tools.** Equip the focal participants of talent review sessions—management teams—with formal leadership assessment and calibration tools to enhance the quality and objectivity of the discussion. Adopting validated instruments, such as high-potential leadership assessments, 9-box grids that plot employees according to job performance and leadership potential, and executive readiness assessments for C-suite placements, significantly minimizes or eliminates the risk of talent review discussions degrading into politics and talent hoarding. Utilizing formal, validated assessment tools sends a clear message to management teams regarding the objectivity and rigor of the talent review process. Partner with senior executive teams to clearly define each dimension of the 9-box grid and the career development implications for employees falling within each box. Engage human resource professionals and the relevant hiring executives in a rigorous assessment of each candidate's readiness for the C-suite or other critical leadership role. Maintain the focus of the placement decision on each candidate's developmental needs and gaps in executive readiness while avoiding placements driven *exclusively* by position vacancies.

✓ **Link leadership assessment results to targeted leadership development experiences.** Ensure that talent assessment activities balance the discussion of assessment results along with specific developmental experiences for leaders moving forward. Best-practice talent review sessions consist of facilitated discussions that calibrate the high-potential ratings of employees while also including dialogue regarding the relevant developmental assignments, training, and other career experiences for employees across 9-box grid. Human resource professionals and senior executive teams must collectively develop a range of leadership development experiences that are strongly aligned with the hospital or health system's strategic initiatives, such as an internal leadership academy, team-based action learning projects that address organization-wide challenges, job rotations or temporary job transfers, Lean projects, system-wide task forces, and specialized courses or training programs. For many prominent health systems, internal leadership academies serve as invaluable leadership development experiences for high-potential leaders.[125]

✓ **Align leadership assessment and development practices with diversity initiatives.** Accelerate workforce diversity initiatives by seeking consistency and transparency with talent review practices, specifically the high-potential leadership assessment process. Ensuring that employees are assessed using a validated, standardized assessment of high-potential leadership is critical for enhancing diversity metrics across management and executive positions. Highly effective talent review practices utilize validated leadership potential assessments that measure the traits and leadership competencies associated with performance in future leadership roles. When consistently applied over time, these practices cultivate a more diverse pipeline of leadership talent that can effectively accelerate an organization's diversity initiative.

5. **Consistent Cultivation of a Leadership Development Culture**

   ✓ **Facilitate multi-level and cross-disciplinary networking and development opportunities.** Offer multiple opportunities for employees and particularly high-potential leaders to network with system, regional, and local facility executives. Develop numerous avenues for leadership development program participants or 'alumni' to maintain an active network and provide one another career support and feedback. Design talent management practices and programs to expand and cultivate the networks of high-potential leaders. When developing internal leadership academies or leadership development programs, ensure that program cohorts consist of professionals from multiple functions and specialties, including operations, nursing, finance, and physicians. Best-in-class leadership development programs ensure that learning activities mirror the challenges associated with operating as part of a multi-functional leadership team by enhancing collaboration skills and helping participants shed the 'silo' view of the organization.

   ✓ **Ensure co-ownership of program design and execution by HR and business owners.** Require co-ownership of the design and execution of succession management practices and programs by human resource professionals and business owners. Enhance the relevance, credibility, and strategic alignment of talent development and succession planning practices by placing business owners, executive teams, and functional heads in co-ownership roles charged with program design and execution.

   ✓ **Adopt a flexible talent management software platform.** Utilize a flexible, user-friendly talent management software solution that seamlessly engages multiple stakeholders—including human resource professionals, executive teams, and job incumbents, in the development of a repository of talent data. In addition to creating talent profiles, the platform should provide a central, searchable warehouse of talent data on high-potential assessment results, 9-box grid results, risk and impact of loss in critical roles, potential future positions or job roles for high-potential leaders, development planning, and potential successors. Utilize the software platform as a dynamic tool that must be developed and updated by multiple stakeholder groups—not only HR professionals—throughout the year.

✓ **Craft leadership development strategy and programs with targeted outcomes.** Develop a comprehensive leadership development strategy that coherently aligns clear learning objectives and targeted outcomes. Resist the temptation to pursue multiple leadership development program goals and potentially dilute both program quality and ultimate impact across the organization. Rather than trying to achieve conflicting program goals, such as individual skill development, leader role transitions, and action learning initiatives, exemplary leadership development programs align learning activities with clear objectives and program outcomes. Carefully evaluate the trade-offs—such as comparative program objectives, benefits, and costs—associated with the various types of leadership development programs (individual skill development, leader transitions, action learning initiatives, etc.) and their relative effectiveness for meeting different developmental needs for healthcare leaders.

Conclusion

The purpose of this book was to offer an accessible, practical, and evidence-based resource to healthcare executives and boards contending with the industry's unprecedented succession planning and talent management challenges, including the imminent wave of executive retirements, lack of leadership bench strength in critical roles, integration of nursing and physician leaders into executive development programs, surging need for greater ethnic and gender diversity in executive ranks, and the industry's ongoing transition from volume- to value-based performance metrics. To help address these challenges, this book offers practitioners a practical framework and a series of best practices, tools, and strategies for designing and executing an effective succession management system. The **Talent Management Capabilities** framework is distinctive in its focus on healthcare organizations and the unique contextual challenges faced by healthcare executives.

In closing, I hope that this book has provided you with practical tools and a compelling, evidence-based business case for succession management capabilities in your organization. For human resource professionals seeking to establish stronger strategic partnerships with executive teams and boards members, I hope that the benchmarking data, value-based performance metrics, and case studies offer a useful foundation for investing in talent development and succession planning practices. It is also my sincere hope that this book has not only communicated the urgency of confronting succession planning and talent management challenges immediately, but also offered encouragement and strengthened your confidence to establish exemplary succession management capabilities in your own organization.

Acknowledgments

I am deeply indebted to a great number of family members, friends, colleagues, clients, and hundreds of healthcare organizations for their important contributions to this book. I would like to extend my sincere appreciation to the many people who have offered counsel, support, and encouragement throughout the research and writing for this book. I offer my heartfelt thanks to a number of individuals who deserve special recognition.

To the hundreds of hospital and health system executives who have participated in the semi-annual **Healthcare Talent Management Survey**, I thank you for your participation and for your commitment to advancing our field's understanding of talent management practices in healthcare. Your willingness to share your succession management and talent development practices and workforce performance metrics is greatly appreciated. To the many healthcare executives who provided insights, case examples, and feedback on various chapters and sections of this book, I offer my genuine thanks and gratitude for your contributions. I am deeply indebted to Debra Canales (Providence St. Joseph Health) for providing steadfast support and encouragement of my work in healthcare. The incredible depth of her experiences across healthcare institutions and her unwavering commitment to talent management has greatly influenced my thinking about leadership development and succession planning. I would also like to extend my sincere thanks to the many healthcare executives who read an early version of the manuscript and offered their invaluable comments and feedback. These prominent healthcare leaders include Sister Carol Keehan (Catholic Health Association), John Figueroa (Genoa), Thomas Priselac (Cedars-Sinai Health System), Gary Burnison (Korn Ferry), Dan Borton (McLaren Health Care), Andrew Garman, PsyD, (National Center for Healthcare Leadership & Rush University), Matthew McElrath, EdD, (Keck Hospital of USC), Jim Dunn, PhD, (Parkland Health & Hospital System), Jim Gauss (Witt/Kieffer), Jack Schlosser (Spencer Stuart), David Lawrence, MD, (Kaiser Foundation Health Plan & Hospitals), Deb Canales (Providence St. Joseph Health), and Mike Helm (Sutter Health). I greatly appreciate your generous commitment of time, energy, and expertise to the project.

I am especially grateful for the support and partnership provided by Jim Gauss and the executive search professionals at Witt/Kieffer for their important contributions to the semi-annual **Healthcare Talent Management Survey**. Thank you for sharing your experiences and perspectives on healthcare leadership, and for identifying executive participants who represent healthcare organizations with exemplary talent management practices. I am indebted to Jim and our mutual friend Nick Fraunfelder for turning my attention to the healthcare industry many years ago and for supporting research on succession management.

I would also like to acknowledge the thoughtful contributions and perspectives shared by many healthcare executives in the research studies that formed the foundation of this book, including Victor Buzachero (Scripps Health), Herb Vallier (Ascension Health), Deanna Kenard (Methodist Health System), Marguerite Samms and Christine Homer (Intermountain Healthcare), Debbie Kiser (Novant Health), and many others. Thank you for your willingness to share your important insights, experiences, and perspectives on healthcare's talent management landscape.

I am very grateful for the support and encouragement provided by my academic colleagues, friends, and graduate student associates at the Graziadio School and across the academy. These include Jason Pinegar, Michelle Guzman, Ann Le, Tamarra Allen, Sarah Iskander, Nancy Dodd, Charles Vance, Mark Allen, Gary Mangiofico, Ann Feyerherm, Miriam Lacey, and Stephen McGuire. Thank you all for your many valuable insights and contributions to the development of this book.

I would like to thank Jerry Pogue, and the entire publishing and editorial team at Second River Healthcare. I am sincerely grateful for your willingness and enthusiasm to support this book and for your encouragement, advice, and feedback throughout the project. Thank you for believing in the value of this project for the healthcare leaders and for preparing hospitals and health systems for the challenges that lay ahead.

I am deeply grateful for my wife, Jill, and our daughters—Anna and Kate—for their patience, love, and support throughout the writing of this book project. Thank you for tolerating the disruptions to our family time and for supporting me every step of the way. I am also profoundly thankful to my parents for their unwavering encouragement, guidance, and love.

For the many stakeholders at each of the four case studies presented in this book, I offer my sincere gratitude for your time, insights, and many contributions to gaining a deeper understanding of your organization's talent management practices. Listed alphabetically, I would like to acknowledge the many contributors across each health system:

Cleveland Clinic Health System. I am deeply grateful to Cleveland Clinic's Office of Learning and Performance Development (OLPD) professionals who supported the research conducted for this case study. My sincere thanks to Carrie Hill for her tireless work in shepherding the research project from beginning to end, and for providing access to the many stakeholders and data sources that were necessary for presenting a full picture of the executive onboarding program. I would also like to offer my sincere thanks and appreciation for the gracious support and project stewardship provided by Jim Dunn (formerly Cleveland Clinic's executive HR and chief learning officer, currently executive VP and chief talent officer at Parkland Health & Hospital System). Finally, I thank the many hiring executives, newly hired executives, and clinical managers and caregivers across Cleveland Clinic for offering their invaluable contributions to this research and helping to deepen our collective understanding of exemplary onboarding practices in healthcare organizations.

Hospital Corporation of America (HCA). I am grateful for the project partnership and support provided by HCA and the professionals of the Executive Development Team. I would like to offer my sincere thanks for their support of the research conducted for this case study. I would like to especially thank Dell Oliver, assistant vice president of Executive Development, for her work in spearheading the project. I am grateful for the executive sponsorship provided by John Steele (executive vice president, Human Resources) throughout the project. I would also like to thank Carla Worthey, assistant vice president of Strategic Analytics, for her work in providing the performance metrics and impact statistics used to assess the EDP's outcomes. I thank Ann Hatcher (VP, Key Talent Acquisition & Development) for her efforts to push the project across the finish line. I would also like to acknowledge the contributions of the many other HCA professionals who contributed to this project, including Joe Hill, Jennifer Tomlin, and Scott Samale. Finally, I thank the many senior HR executives, group presidents, division presidents, and hospital CEOs, COOs, CFOs, and CNOs for their interview participation and for helping advance our knowledge of healthcare executive development practices.

Kaiser Permanente. I offer my sincere thanks to Kaiser Permanente and the many professionals and executives that comprise the National Leadership Development team for their unwavering support of the research conducted for this case study. I am deeply grateful for the executive sponsorship provided by Robert Sachs (retired VP of National Learning & Development) and the ongoing support of SLP program manager Gregg Servis and learning lead Alison Lopriore throughout the project. I offer my thanks to SLP executive co-sponsors Dr. Ronald Copeland, MD, (senior vice president, chief diversity & inclusion officer) and Paul Swenson (senior vice president, chief strategy officer) for their support of this case study. I would also like to thank Marjorie Kleerup (lead consultant, Workforce Information Management) for her work in providing the SLP evaluation metrics. Finally, I am thankful for the many SLP alumni executives and their managers for participating in the interviews and offering many important insights on the program's design and impact on their careers and business units.

Sutter Health. I offer my sincere thanks to Sutter Health and the many professionals of Sutter Health University (SHU) for their support of the research conducted for this case study. I am grateful for the executive sponsorship provided by Mike Helm (former CHRO) and Yvonne Gardner (former VP of Talent Management) throughout the project. I would like to especially acknowledge Erika Duffy, who heads Sutter Health's talent review and succession management process, for her relentless support in shepherding the project from beginning to end. My sincere thanks to the many SHU professionals, including Glenda Adachi, Sue Gotelli, Christine Cress, Corinne Boulanger, and Dorothy Lingren, who provided numerous materials, performance data, and access to key stakeholders across the health system. Finally, I thank the many system, service area, and affiliate executives across Sutter Health for their interview participation and for helping advance our knowledge of talent review and succession management practices.

Glossary

Accountable Care Organizations (ACOs) – Groups of physicians, hospitals, or clinics, and other healthcare providers who voluntarily come together to provide coordinated high-quality care to Medicare patients. The goal of ACOs is to coordinate healthcare delivery by ensuring that patients receive the right care at the right time while avoiding unnecessary duplication of services, preventing medical errors, and achieving cost savings.

Action Learning Projects – Team-based leadership development approach that allows diverse groups of high-potential leaders to address organization-wide challenges or problems through a team project. After completing a structured data collection process, each team of high-potential leaders presents its findings to the project's executive sponsors and the senior leadership team.

Affordable Care Act (ACA) – The Patient Protection and Affordable Care Act is a United States federal statute that was signed into law by President Barack Obama on March 23, 2010. The ACA requires hospitals and primary physicians to transform their practices financially, technologically, and clinically to drive better health outcomes, lower costs, and improve methods of distribution and accessibility. Nicknamed Obamacare, the ACA was designed to increase health insurance quality and affordability, lower the uninsured rate by expanding insurance coverage and reduce the costs of healthcare.

American College of Healthcare Executives (ACHE) – ACHE is an international professional society of forty thousand healthcare executives who lead hospitals, healthcare systems, and other healthcare organizations. The organization's mission is to advance its members and healthcare management excellence through education and research.

American Hospital Association (AHA) – AHA is the national organization that represents and serves all types of hospitals, health care networks, and their patients and communities. AHA is comprised of nearly five thousand hospitals, health care systems, networks, other providers of care, and forty-three thousand individual members.

American Hospital Association's *Environmental Scan* – An annual review of healthcare trends, insights, and information about market forces that have a high probability of impacting the healthcare field. Published by Hospitals & Health Networks and the American Hospital Association (AHA), the Environmental Scan is designed to help hospital and health system leaders understand the healthcare landscape and the critical issues and emerging trends in the foreseeable future.

AMN Healthcare – A healthcare staffing solutions company that provides a range of workforce solutions, including managed services, recruitment process outsourcing, and consulting services to increase efficiency and improve patient outcomes.

Annual Turnover Metrics – The percentage of the overall workforce or a specific job group (nurses, executives, physicians, etc.) that departs the position during a fiscal or calendar year. Annual turnover may be driven by termination, retirement, death, resignations, or any combination of these factors.

Baby Boomers – The demographic group born during the post-World War II baby boom between approximately 1946 and 1964. Many demographers have described this generation as generally valuing material success, traditional values, consensus-building, work ethic, and social values and change.

Behavioral Interview – An interview technique in which the job applicant, either an internal employee seeking a promotion/transfer or an external applicant, is asked to describe past behaviors, actions, decisions, or experiences that are appropriate for determining whether he or she is suitable for the position. A behavioral interview for a leadership position is a structured interview that is created after a thorough assessment of the leadership skills and competencies needed for the position.

Benchmarking Surveys – A survey that allows an organization to compare its business processes and performance metrics to industry norms and best practices from other companies.

Board of Governors (BOG) – A body of members who jointly oversee the activities of an organization, typically a non-profit organization. The BOG for a non-profit organization is analogous to the board of directors of a company.

Center for Creative Leadership (CCL) – A non-profit, global provider of leadership development programs and related services. CCL is located in ten offices across the globe and provides professional development services that transform individual leaders, teams, and organizations.

Centers for Medicare and Medicaid Services (CMS) – CMS is a federal agency within the US Department of Health and Human Services (HHS) that administers the Medicare program and works in partnership with state governments to administer the Medicaid program and other state insurance programs and health insurance portability standards.

Cohort – A group of employees or leaders who collectively participate in an organization's training or development program. Leadership development programs or leadership academies often adopt a cohort model in which a group of employees complete the program as a single cohort or group of participants.

Integrated Cohort – An integrated cohort is a group of employees or leaders that represent a diverse mix of functions, regions or business units, clinical and administrative roles, and other forms of diversity.

Construct Validity – The degree to which an assessment or survey measures what it claims or purports to be measuring. The construct validity of an assessment used for talent management applications, such as an assessment of high-potential leadership, is established by conducting a series of studies that collect data on the assessment's internal consistency (reliability of the assessment's items or questions), content validity (legitimacy of the assessment's items or questions in terms of content and substance), and predictive validity (accuracy of the assessment's ability to predict relevant performance outcomes).

Corporate Leadership Council – As part of the Corporate Executive Board (CEB), the Corporate Leadership Council is a consulting firm that provides advisory services to chief HR officers who seek to optimize the performance of their HR function and business.

C-Suite Executives – Chief executives who comprise the chief executive officer's or president's cabinet, including the chief executive officer, chief operating officer, chief financial officer, chief nursing officer, chief medical officer, and chief human resource officer.

- **Chief Executive Officer (CEO)** – A chief executive officer describes the position of the most senior corporate officer, executive, leader, or administrator in charge of managing an organization.

- **Chief Administrative Officer (CAO)** – Chief administrative officers are top-tier executives who supervise the daily operations of a business and are ultimately responsible for its performance. Found across all industries and in both the non-profit and publicly traded sectors, these management professionals are experts at maintaining numerous functions of the businesses they serve.

- **Chief Operating Officer (COO)** – A chief operating officer is one of the highest-ranking executive positions in an organization. The COO is responsible for the daily operation of the company, and routinely reports to the highest-ranking executive, usually the chief executive officer (CEO). The COO is usually the second in command at the firm, especially if the highest-ranking executive is the chairman and CEO.

- **Chief Financial Officer (CFO)** – The chief financial officer is a corporate officer primarily responsible for managing the financial risks of the organization and also responsible for financial planning, record-keeping, and financial reporting to higher management.

- **Chief Nursing Officer (CNO)** – The chief nursing officer is a C-suite executive that serves as the head of the nursing staff and often the hospital's or health system's top clinical quality officer.

- **Chief Medical Officer (CMO)** – The chief medical officer is the primary leader of all medical divisions and physician staff in a hospital or health system. The CMO is inevitably a physician, as opposed to the COO or CAO, who is often a non-medical professional.

- **Chief Human Resource Officer (CHRO)** – The chief human resources officer is a corporate officer who oversees all aspects of human resource management policies, practices, and operations for an organization.

Diversity – Acknowledging, understanding, accepting, and valuing differences among people with respect to age, class, race, ethnicity, gender, disabilities, religion, and other group differences.

- **Ethnic Minority** – A circumstance or outcome in which a particular ethnic group (Asian-Americans, African-Americans, Hispanics/Latinos, etc.) comprises a minority of a particular population.

- **Racial Minority** – A circumstance or outcome in which a particular race (Asian, Caucasian, Black or African-American, etc.) comprises a minority of a particular population.

- **Culturally Diverse** – The existence of diverse or different cultures in a group, organization, or community. Organizations that are culturally diverse are comprised of different group cultures (gender, ethnicity, profession, region, etc.) that respect each other's differences.

Domain Score – The Centers for Medicare and Medicaid Services (CMS) executes the Value-Based Purchasing Performance program, which assesses hospitals' performance across four domain scores. These domain scores include the Clinical Process of Care Domain, Patient Experience of Care Domain, Outcome Domain, and Efficiency Domain. A hospital's total score across these four domains are calculated to determine hospital reimbursements for healthcare services to Medicare patients.

Empirical – A description of primary research methods that collect original data. Empirical research is the knowledge or source of knowledge that is acquired through direct observations and experimentation.

Evidence-Based Research – The process of utilizing the best available research evidence that illustrates whether and why a given treatment or practice is effective. Evidence-based research projects seek to gather original, empirical research findings to inform a given practice, program, or treatment.

Executive Coaching – A leadership assessment and coaching process that provides support, feedback, and developmental planning for executives and executive teams. Executive coaching is often one element of a comprehensive leadership development program or leadership academy for business leaders.

Executive Development Program (EDP) – A formal leadership development program for an organization's executives or high-potential leaders that often includes learning modules or classroom-based learning, 360-degree feedback, mentoring or coaching, and team-based action learning projects.

Executive Development Team (EDT) – A group of human resource and organization development professionals who design and deliver a range of executive development programs. The professionals are responsible for working with the organization's executive team to design and implement the programs.

Executive Leadership Team (ELT) – An organization's top leadership team or C-suite executives, normally comprising the chief executive officer, chief financial officer, chief operating officer, chief nursing officer, chief medical officer, and chief human resource officer.

Executive Onboarding Program (EOP) – A formal program and set of activities for onboarding executives into their new positions. The executive onboarding process normally includes orientation activities, stakeholder analyses, new leader assimilation activities, and a series of individual and group meetings to establish working relationships within the first year of hire.

Executive Sponsor – A member of the senior executive team or other influential organizational leader who sponsors a project or program for the purpose of enhancing the project or program's visibility, credibility, and access to resources. The team-based action learning projects that often comprise internal leadership development programs are normally assigned an executive sponsor to spearhead the project and provide support to the team members.

Executive Team Diversity – The degree of gender, ethnic, functional, professional, clinical/administration, and other forms of group diversity that characterize an executive team.

Healthcare Talent Management Survey – A semi-annual national survey of hospitals and health systems that assesses talent management and succession planning practices and their performance outcomes. Conducted by Groves Consulting Group, LLC, and the Graziadio School of Business and Management, the survey establishes national benchmarks for the quality and impact of talent management and succession planning practices in hospital organizations.

Health Research Institute – A research-based division of Pricewaterhouse-Coopers (PwC) that supports executives in healthcare organizations by providing new intelligence, perspectives, and analysis on trends affecting all health-related industries.

Health Resources and Services Administration (HRSA) – An agency of the US Department of Health and Human Services that serves as the primary federal agency for improving health and achieving health equity through access to quality services, a skilled health workforce and innovative programs. HRSA's programs provide healthcare to people who are geographically isolated, and economically or medically vulnerable.

High-Potential Leader – a high-potential employee is defined as "someone who is capable of rising to and succeeding at a more senior, critical role. An employee's potential is defined in terms of their personal aspirations, functional ability, and engagement."

Hospital Consumer Assessment of Healthcare Providers and Systems Survey (HCAHPS) – The survey that assesses patient satisfaction as part of the Centers for Medicare and Medicaid Services (CMS) methodology for measuring the quality and value of healthcare services for Medicare and Medicaid patients. The survey consists of ten items that asks patients to rate the quality of their inpatient stay along several dimensions, including the clarity of discharge instructions, quietness and cleanliness of the hospital room and facility, quality and consistency of communication from nurses and physicians, and pain management.

HCAHPS Score – The Hospital Consumer Assessment of Healthcare Providers and Systems Survey, which is a national, standardized survey that that measures patient satisfaction. The results of this survey determine a hospital's score on the Patient Experience of Care Domain, which is one dimension of the Affordable Care Act's Value-Based Purchasing Program that determines hospital reimbursement rates for services to Medicare patients.

IBM Institute for Business Value – A research division of IBM that focuses on thought leadership by conducting a range of research studies and producing numerous white papers and industry reports on emerging business trends, business innovations, and success patterns across such diverse topics as talent and change, cognitive computing, customer experience and market strategy, cloud computing, and electronics.

Internal/External Placement Rate – The ratio of internal promotions to external hires for executive-level positions whereby a high internal/external placement rate (70 percent or higher) indicates that most vacant executive roles are filled by internal candidates. This ratio is a very common metric for assessing the effectiveness of an organization's talent management practices, and is often part of a 'balanced scorecard' for communicating talent management outcomes with the board and other key stakeholders.

KRONOS – A workforce solutions company that provides a suite of tools and services to manage and engage the workforce from pre-hire to retire. These tools and services include time and attendance applications, payroll and benefits administration, and workforce analytics.

Leadership Academy – An internal leadership development program that often includes multiple leadership development activities, including 360-degree assessment, classroom-based learning sessions facilitated by external experts and senior executives, case studies featuring current business challenges facing the organization, and team-based action learning projects.

For many organizations, a leadership academy represents a core succession planning program for developing future senior executive team members.

Leadership Bench Strength – The percentage of critical leadership positions for which there is at least one 'ready now' internal candidate. Leadership bench strength is a common metric for assessing the efficacy of an organization's succession management practices.

Leadership Development Institute – An organization's internal leadership programs, learning and development practices, and other training programs are often grouped under a single entity called a 'Leadership Institute' or 'Corporate University.'

Lean Project – A methodology for identifying opportunities to reduce costs and eliminate redundancies or inefficiencies in any business process. The main principle of a Lean project is to make changes to a business process or practice that delivers greater value with less waste in a project context. Many healthcare organizations are increasingly adopting Lean projects as a leadership development tool or set of experiences for high-potential leaders.

Learning Journal – A learning and development tool that is often used as part of a leadership development program for executives or high-potential leaders. The learning journal allows program participants to capture their reflections, insights, observations, and questions in a journal that is completed throughout the program.

Longitudinal Research Project – A longitudinal study or research project is a quasi-experimental research design that tracks repeated observations of the same variables (e.g., people, processes, practices, policies, etc.) over long periods of time. These studies offer many advantages and greater confidence in the validity of research findings because they allow researchers to control or hold constant the differences observed in the study participants that are unrelated to the goals of the study.

Millennials – The demographic group born between approximately 1982 and 1999. Many demographers have described this generation as being tech-savvy and impatient while valuing diversity, change, social awareness and activism, and work/life balance.

National Center for Healthcare Leadership (NCHL) – A not-for-profit organization that works to ensure that high-quality, relevant, and accountable leadership is available to meet the needs of 21st century healthcare. NCHL's vision is to optimize the health of the public through leadership and organizational excellence.

National Leadership Development (NLD) Team – A group of human resource and organization development professionals who design and deliver leadership development programs on a national scale. The professionals are responsible for working with the organization's executive team to design and execute programs for which participants will be drawn from across the organization's national network of hospitals, regions, facilities, and other business units.

New Leader Assimilation (NLA) – A leadership and team development process that facilitates the rapid development of strong relationships between a newly placed executive or leader and his/her direct reports. This development process is facilitated by a human resource or organization development professional and involves a series of interviews with the new executive, each of his/her direct reports, and facilitated sessions with the entire team.

New Leader Orientation (NLO) – A new employee orientation program designed specifically for leaders (internal promotions and external hires) who are transitioning into new managerial roles. New Leader Orientation programs often consist of comprehensive reviews of organizational policies, processes, and supporting systems (payroll, performance management, budgeting, staffing, project management, etc.) as well as modules on the organization's history, culture, mission, values, and vision.

Nine-Box Tools – An assessment tool used as part of talent review sessions that plots all managers or employees in a given work unit or team according to two dimensions: job performance and leadership potential. The resulting grid illustrates all employees across nine cells or boxes that each represent a different set of leadership development implications.

Office of Learning and Performance Development (OLPD) – A department of human resource and organization development professionals who design and implement a range of learning, training, and development programs for employees across the organization. The OLPD office typically provides a range of services and programs for employees across the organizations, including new employee orientation, training programs, courses and other learning modules, firm-wide leadership academy programs, performance management tools, and other resources.

Onboarding Practices – An organization's onboarding practices normally include all activities from an employee's acceptance of an employment offer (Day 1) through the first ninety days of employment. These activities usually include welcome packets of new hire materials (welcome letter, benefits package, company info, etc.), orientation programs, personal introductions to colleagues and business units across the organization, building tour, detailed work plan for the first ninety days, and assignment of a peer sponsor to provide facilitate socialization into the organizational culture.

Oracle Taleo – Oracle Taleo is a talent management software program or platform that allows organizations to store, codify, and utilize a wide range of data that inform numerous talent management practices such as talent acquisition, performance management, learning and development, high-potential assessment, and succession planning.

Orientation – New employee or new leader orientations are designed to provide all new staff members with standard information about the organization and their new role, including the organization's strategy, history, operations, culture, administrative systems and processes, and governance.

Pedagogy – Pedagogy is the science of teaching and specifically the educational and instructional methods that teachers adopt for accomplishing learning outcomes. The pedagogical choices or strategies that teachers employ involve the mix of educational and instructional methods (e.g., case studies, lecture-based discussions, experiential exercises, team-based projects, etc.) for optimizing learning outcomes for a given group of students or program participants.

Performance Success and Development Process (PSDP) – The PSDP is a key part of the data collection process for an organization's annual talent review meeting. The PSDP provides management teams with a standard form or set of questions on which to measure each of the positions or high-potential leaders who are being assessed as part of the talent review session.

Pre-boarding – The pre-boarding phase of the new employee onboarding process normally consists of all activities that take place before the employee's first day on the job. These activities include the new hire materials (welcome letter, benefits package, company history, and background information, etc.) that are sent to the candidate soon after acceptance of the job offer.

Qualitative – Qualitative research is a broad method of inquiry that involves collecting information, observations, statements, and other data that are unstructured, not easily quantifiable. Common qualitative research methods in organizational research include document analysis, individual interviews, group interviews or focus groups, observational analysis, case studies, and ethnographic studies.

Quantitative – Quantitative research is the systematic empirical investigation of observable phenomena or data via statistical, mathematical, or computational techniques. Common quantitative research methods in organizational research includes analysis of survey data, operational data, financial data, clinical data, and other forms of data that are quantifiable.

Return on Investment (ROI) – A metric that is used to measure or assess the rate of return on a given investment of some resource over a specific period of time. The ROI of leadership development and other talent management practices is assessed through various metrics, including the financial savings from lower executive turnover, higher patient satisfaction, higher employee productivity, and other financial outcomes.

Revenue Cycle Management – Utilizing medical billing software programs, revenue cycle management is the financial process that healthcare facilities use to track patient care episodes from registration and appointment scheduling to the final payment of a balance.

Selection and Onboarding Practices – As one of the eight Talent Management Capabilities (TMCs), Selection and Onboarding Practices include activities aimed at selecting and socializing leaders into critical leadership roles. These practices include selection processes for key leadership positions that consist of behaviorally based interviews that are aligned with key leadership competencies. These practices also include the quality and frequency with which managers and executives who are selected into key leadership roles, both internal and external candidates, complete a formal onboarding program.

Standard & Poor's 500 – An American stock market index based on the market capitalizations of five hundred large companies having common stock listed on the NYSE (New York Stock Exchange) or NASDAQ (National Association of Securities Dealers Automated Quotations). The Standard & Poor's 500 is one of the most commonly followed equity indices, and many consider it one of the best representations of the US stock market.

Strategic Leadership Program (SLP) – A type of leadership development program that is designed to be tightly integrated to an organization's strategic agenda. This type of development program effectively facilitates the top executive team's efforts to communicate and implement the corporate strategy and develop alignment across the organization. The overarching goal of strategic leadership programs is to advance progress toward strategic objectives while also developing the participants' leadership capabilities.

Stretch Assignments – A project or task given to an employee, high-potential leader, or established executive which is beyond the person's current knowledge, skills, or competencies in order to developmentally "stretch" the employee. Stretch assignments challenge employees by placing them into uncomfortable or unfamiliar situations and contexts that provide powerful learning and growth opportunities.

Succession Management – The process of identifying those jobs or roles that are strategically critical for the organization and creating a formal plan and set of supporting processes to replace the incumbents of these jobs with experienced and capable employees. Critical succession management processes or practices include high-potential leadership assessment, talent review sessions, forecasting talent needs, and establishing succession management metrics to measure performance outcomes.

Talent Assessment Practices – As one of the eight Talent Management Capabilities (TMCs), Talent Assessment Practices include the formal processes through which high-potential leaders and successors to critical leadership roles are identified via standardized assessment instruments, nine-box grids, and other tools. Talent assessment practices include the use of formal assessment tools such as validated assessments of high-potential leadership competencies and nine-box grids, which plot leaders at a given level (system, region, facility) across quadrants according to job performance (y-axis) and leadership potential (x-axis).

Talent Management Capabilities (TMCs) – A set of talent management and succession planning best practices that drive exemplary performance outcomes in organizations. These practices include Top Management Team Support, Talent Assessment Practices, Performance Appraisal Practices, Incentive Pay Practices, Leadership Development Culture, Role-Based Leadership Development, Selection & Onboarding Practices, and Talent Management ROI.

Talent Profile – An assessment form or chart that requires executives to provide a series of data points for each of their direct reports in critical positions. The talent profile represents a comprehensive assessment of both the job incumbent and the position across several critical dimensions, including the job incumbent's leadership potential, promotability, risk and impact of loss (if the incumbent should vacate the position), and the ideal next position or job assignment for the incumbent. The assessment also asks the executive to rate the job incumbent's readiness to succeed one or more specific roles across the organization.

Talent Review Sessions – Facilitated executive team meetings in which each executive or manager shares and discusses his/her direct reports in terms of leadership potential, readiness for advancement, leadership strengths and development opportunities, and other talent information. The talent review session or meeting is often a core element of an organization's annual succession management process.

Taxonomy – The study of the general principles of scientific classification, which involves the process or system of describing the way in which different things are related by placing them into groups.

360-Degree Leadership Assessment & Feedback – A popular leadership assessment and development process in which a manager is provided feedback across a series of leadership competencies from direct reports, peers, supervisors, and external stakeholders. Also known as multi-rater feedback or multi-source feedback, 360-degree feedback is used by organizations to solicit data (both quantitative ratings and comments) from a diverse group of workplace sources on a manager's work-related behavior and/or performance.

Value-Based Performance Metrics – These hospital performance metrics include the four domain scores (Clinical Process of Care Domain, Patient Experience of Care Domain, Outcome Domain, and Efficiency Domain) that comprise the Affordable Care Act's (ACA) Value-Based Purchasing program. Administered by the Centers for Medicare and Medicaid Services (CMS), the Value-Based Purchasing Program incentivizes hospitals to deliver higher quality and more efficient healthcare services.

Value-Based Purchasing – Hospital value-based purchasing (VBP) is part of the Centers for Medicare & Medicaid Services' (CMS) effort to improve healthcare quality by linking Medicare's payment system to the clinical quality outcomes of participating hospitals. Participating hospitals are paid for inpatient acute care services based on the quality of care provided to Medicare patients, not only the quantity of healthcare services. Congress authorized the Value-Based Purchasing program as part of the Affordable Care Act (ACA).

Volume- to Value-Based Metrics – The healthcare industry's transition from fee-for-service to value-based care that is intended to increase the quality of care while reducing the inefficiencies and excess procedures and overtreatment that characterizes US healthcare overall. Value-based purchasing metrics links the payment for healthcare services to the quality of care rather than the volume of services.

Workforce Metrics – Workforce metrics include common performance outcomes or measures that reflect the quality of the employees and other important characteristics such as employee productivity (net revenue/FTEs), annual turnover, and employee engagement.

About the Author

Kevin S. Groves, PhD, is president of Groves Consulting Group, LLC, and associate professor of Organizational Theory and Management at Pepperdine University's Graziadio School of Business and Management. The consultancy supports businesses, non-profit organizations, and government agencies with leadership and organization development solutions, including 360-degree assessment tools, executive development program design and facilitation, succession planning systems, and high-potential identification and development practices. Supporting clients across multiple industry sectors, the firm focuses on developing evidence-based solutions that are anchored by rigorous research. A sample of healthcare clients includes St. Joseph Health System, Mayo Clinic Scottsdale, HCA, SCAN Health Plan, HealthStream, Inc., Kaiser Permanente, and Sutter Health.

As an associate professor at the Graziadio School, Dr. Groves teaches a range of graduate courses including leadership competency development, organization design, and organization development and change. He primarily teaches in the Graziadio School's full-time and part-time MBA programs at the Malibu and West Los Angeles campuses. Prior to joining the Graziadio School faculty, Dr. Groves served as an assistant professor of Management and director of the PepsiCo Leadership Center at California State University, Los Angeles. As director, he managed a $1.45 million PepsiCo Foundation grant that served the leadership development needs of students, community members, and local business leaders. Prior to his academic career, Dr. Groves worked as a management consultant in the Strategy & Organization practice at Towers Perrin (now Towers Watson).

An active leadership scholar, Dr. Groves' research is currently focused on talent management and succession planning practices, particularly the ROI of such practices across industry sectors. He conducts national benchmarking survey studies, including the semi-annual **Healthcare Talent Management Survey**, intensive case studies of organizations with exemplary talent management practices, and quantitative assessments of the financial impact of talent management best practices. Dr. Groves' research is widely published in business, leadership, and healthcare management journals, including *Health Care Management Review, Journal of Management, Journal of Business Ethics, Journal of Leadership and Organizational Studies, Academy of Management Learning & Education, Group & Organization Management, Human Resource Development Quarterly*, and many others.

An active speaker, Dr. Groves regularly delivers presentations, keynote addresses, and facilitation of executive team sessions. Adopting a collaborative approach with clients, he delivers engaging presentations that integrate best practices from industry leaders, rigorous research findings, and business environment trends.

Dr. Groves holds a bachelor's degree in psychology and business administration from Eastern Washington University. He earned his master of arts (MA) and doctor of philosophy (PhD) degrees in organizational behavior from Claremont Graduate University.

He resides with his wife, Jill, and their daughters, Anna and Kate, in Hermosa Beach, California. You can learn more about Dr. Groves at his website, www.grovesconsultinggroup.com, or contact him at kevin.groves@grovesconsultinggroup.com.

Notes

CHAPTER 1

[1] Teresa Thrall, "Finding Your Next CEO," *Hospitals & Health Networks* 82, no. 12 (2008): 24-37.

[2] Vicki A. Darnell and Kathy M. Noland, "Growing Tomorrow's Talent Today: Succession Planning a Critical Strategy in Healthcare," B. E. Smith, accessed January 1, 2017, https://www.besmith.com/sites/default/files/Growing%20Tomorrow%27s%20Talent%20Today-Succession%20Planning%20a%20Critical%20Strategy%20in%20Healthcare_web.pdf.

[3] Tim Ringo et al., "Integrated Talent Management: Part 3; Turning Talent Management into a Competitive Advantage: An Industry View," IBM Global Business Services/IBM Institute for Business Value, accessed January 1, 2017, http://www-935.ibm.com/services/us/gbs/bus/pdf/gbe03083-usen-talentpart3.pdf.

[4] Robert E. Lewis and Robert J. Heckman, "Talent Management: A Critical Review," *Human Resource Management Review* 16, no. 2 (2006): 139-154.

[5] Rob Silzer and Ben E. Dowell, "Strategic Talent Management Matters," in *Strategy-Driven Talent Management: A Leadership Imperative*, ed. Rob Silzer and Ben E. Dowell (San Francisco: Jossey-Bass, 2010), 3-72, quote on p.18.

[6] Mark A. Huselid, "The Impact of Human Resource Management Practices on Turnover, Productivity, and Corporate Financial Performance," *Academy of Management Journal* 38, no. 3 (1995): 635-672.

[7] Jeffrey Pfeffer, *Competitive Advantage Through People: Unleashing the Power of the Workforce*, (Boston: Harvard Business Review, 1994).

[8] Matthew Guthridge and Asmus B. Komm, "Why Multinationals Struggle to Manage Talent," *The McKinsey Quarterly* (2008), accessed January 1, 2017, https://www.slideshare.net/KamelionWorld/why-multinationals-struggle-to-manage-talent.

[9] Paul R. Bernthal and Scott E. Wellins, *Leadership Forecast 2005-2006: Best Practices for Tomorrow's Global Leaders*, (Pittsburgh, PA: Development Dimensions International, 2005).

[10] Elizabeth L. Axelrod, Helen Handfield-Jones, and Timothy Welsh, "War for Talent, Part Two," *The McKinsey Quarterly*, accessed January 1, 2017, http://www.andersonpeoplestrategies.com/sites/default/files/uploads/McKWarforTalentArticle.pdf.

[11] Shawn Fegley, *Succession Planning: Survey Report*, (Alexandria, VA: Society for Human Resource Management, 2006); William J. Rothwell, *Effective Succession Planning: Ensuring Leadership Continuity and Building Talent from Within*, (New York: AMACOM, 2016).

[12] Kevin S. Groves, "Impact of Talent Management Practices on Hospital Clinical, Financial, and Workforce Metrics," Groves Consulting Group (2013), www.grovesconsultinggroup.com/index.php/gcgresearch/; Kevin S. Groves, "Impact of Talent Management Practices on Financial, Workforce, and Value-Based Purchasing Metrics," Groves Consulting Group (2015), same website as above.

[13] David A. Nadler, "The CEO's Second Act," Harvard Business Review 85 (Jan 2007): 66-72; Corporate Leadership Council, Models and Methodologies for On-boarding Programs, Corporate Leadership Council, 2003.

[14] Kevin S. Groves, "Impact of Talent Management Practices on Financial, Workforce, and Value-Based Purchasing Metrics," Groves Consulting Group (2015), www.grovesconsultinggroup.com/index.php/gcgresearch/.

[15] Karen O'Leonard and Jennifer Krider, "Leadership Development Factbook 2014: Benchmarks and Trends in U.S. Leadership Development," Bersin by Deloitte (2014), accessed June 1, 2015 http://www.bersin.com/Practice/Detail.aspx?docid=17478&mode=search&p=Leadership-Development ; Fegley, *Succession Planning: Survey Report*, (see note 11, item 1).

[16] Mark A. Huselid, "The Impact of Human Resource Management Practices on Turnover, Productivity, and Corporate Financial Performance," *Academy of Management Journal* 38, no. 3 (1995): 635-672.

[17] O'Leonard and Krider, "Leadership Development Factbook 2014," (see note 15).

[18] Ibid.

[19] Corporate Leadership Council, *Models and Methodologies*, (see note 13, item 2).

[20] Corporate Leadership Council, *Workforce Turnover and Firm Performance: The New Business Case for Employee Retention*, Corporate Executive Board (1998).

[21] Nadler, "The CEO's Second Act," (see note 13).

[22] Gretchen Michals, "Turnover Surprise," *NACD Directorship* 34, no. 6, (Dec 2008/Jan 2009): 17.

[23] "What Works: Healing the Healthcare Staffing Shortage," *PricewaterhouseCoopers' Health Research Institute*, accessed January 1, 2017, http://www.pwc.com/us/en/healthcare/publications/what-works-healing-the-healthcare-staffing-shortage.html.

[24] Leslie A. Athey and Andrew N. Garman, "White Paper; How Senior Leadership Teams are Changing: A Survey of Freestanding Community Hospital CEOs," ACHE: Division of Member Services, Research, (Fall 2014): 9, accessed January 1, 2017, http://www.ache.org/pubs/research/pdf/CEO-White-Paper-2014.pdf.

[25] American College of Healthcare Executives, "Hospital CEO Turnover Rate Remains Elevated," press release, March 11, 2016, http://www.ache.org/pubs/Releases/2016/Hospital-CEO-Turnover-Rate-Remains-Elevated.cfm.

[26] Lee Ann Jarousse, ed., "2016 American Hospital Association Environmental Scan," *Hospitals & Health Networks* (Sep 15, 2015): 2, http://www.hhnmag.com/articles/3199-american-hospital-association-environmental-scan.

[27] "Labor Force Statistics from the Current Population Survey," Bureau of Labor Statistics, accessed January 1, 2017, https://www.bls.gov/cps/demographics.htm#age.

[28] "Top Health Industry Issues of 2015: Outlines of a Market Emerge," PricewaterhouseCoopers' Health Research Institute (Dec 2014): 1-18, https://www.pwc.com/us/en/health-industries/top-health-industry-issues/assets/pwc-hri-top-healthcare-issues-2015.pdf.

[29] Allan Schweyer, "The State of Talent Management in the Healthcare Industry," *Human Capital Institute* (May 2009): 3, 13, http://www.hci.org/hr-research/state-talent-management-healthcare-industry.

[30] "2014 Hospital CEO Survey on Succession Planning," *Healthcare Executive* 29, no. 4 (2014): 74.

[31] Ibid.

[32] Ann Scheck McAlearney, "Executive Leadership Development in U.S. Health Systems: Exploring the Evidence," American College of Healthcare Executives, (Apr 2008), accessed June 1, 2015, https://www.ache.org/pubs/research/McAlearney_HMRA_Report.pdf.

[33] Andrew N. Garman and J. Larry Tyler, "Succession Planning Practices & Outcomes in U.S. Hospital Systems: Final Report," American College of Healthcare Executives, (Aug 20, 2007), accessed January 1, 2017, http://www.ache.org/pubs/research/succession_planning.pdf.

[34] Yan Zhang and Nandini Rajagopalan, "CEO Succession Planning: Finally at the Center Stage of the Boardroom," Business Horizons 53, no. 5 (2010): 455-462.

[35] Ken Favaro, Per-Ola Karlsson, and Gary L. Neilson, "CEO Succession 2000-2009: A Decade of Convergence and Compression," *Strategy & Business*, originally published by Booz & Company, Issue 59 (Summer 2010).

[36] Linda Wilson, "Inner Strength: Top-Performing Hospitals are More Apt to Promote from Within and Take a More Strategic Approach When Recruiting Executives," *Modern Healthcare* (Jul 2005): 8-25.

[37] ACHE, "Hospital CEO Turnover Rate Remains Elevated," (see note 25).

[38] Darnell and Noland, "Growing Tomorrow's Talent Today," (see note 2).

[39] Thrall, "Finding your next CEO," p. 26, (see note 1).

[40] Amir A. Khaliq, Stephen Walston, and David M. Thompson, "The Impact of Hospital CEO Turnover in U.S. Hospitals: Final Report," American College of Healthcare Executives, (Feb 27, 2006), http://www.ache.org/pubs/research/pdf/hospital_ceo_turnover_06.pdf.

[41] Darnell and Noland, "Growing Tomorrow's Talent Today," (see note 2).

[42] "The Future of the Nursing Workforce: National- and State-level Projections, 2012-2025," *U.S. Department of Health and Human Services, Health Resources and Services Administration, National Center for Health Workforce Analysis*, Rockville, MD, (Dec 2014), http://bhpr.hrsa.gov/healthworkforce/supplydemand/nursing/workforceprojections/index.html.

[43] AMN Healthcare, "2015 Survey of Registered Nurses: Viewpoints on Retirement, Education, and Emerging Roles," The Center for the Advancement of Healthcare Professionals (2015), http://www.amnhealthcare.com/uploadedFiles/MainSite/Content/Workforce_Solutions/2015_Survey_Registered_Nurses_FOR_WEB_SingPage.pdf.

[44] Jarousse, ed., "2016 AHA Environmental Scan," (see note 26).

[45] Bonnie L. Atencio, Jayne Cohen, and Bobbye Gorenberg, "Nurse Retention: Is It Worth It?" *Nursing Economics* 21, no. 6: 262-268.

[46] American Medical Association's Physician Masterfile, accessed January 1, 2017, https://www.ama-assn.org/life-career/ama-physician-masterfile.

[47] "2016 Survey of Physicians 55 and Older: Based on 2015 Data," AMN Healthcare, accessed January 1, 2017, http://www.amnhealthcare.com/uploadedFiles/MainSite/Content/Healthcare_Industry_Insights/Industry_Research/2016%20Survey%20of%20Physicians%2055%20and%20older.pdf.

[48] Society for Healthcare Strategy & Market Development for the AHA, eds., *Futurescan™ 2015: Healthcare Trends & Implications 2015-2020*, Health Administration Press, (2015): 29.

[49] "Labor Force Statistics," (see note 27).

[50] American College of Healthcare Executives, "A Comparison of the Career Attainments of Men and Women Healthcare Executives," ACHE: Division of Member Services, Research (Dec 2012): 16, http://www.ache.org/pubs/research/2012-Gender-Report-FINAL.pdf.

[51] "Diversity and Disparities: A Benchmark Study of U.S. Hospitals in 2013," Institute for Diversity in Health Management, accessed January 1, 2017, http://www.hpoe.org/Reports-HPOE/Diversity_Disparities_14_Web.pdf.

[52] American College of Healthcare Executives, "A Racial/Ethnic Comparison of Career Attainments in Healthcare Management," ACHE: Division of Member Services, Research, (2015): 23, http://www.ache.org/pubs/research/2014-Race-Ethnicity-Report.pdf.

CHAPTER 2

[53] Charles Goretsky, "Talent Management in Healthcare: Meeting the Challenge," Bersin by Deloitte, Nov 21, 2012; Claudio Fernandez-Aroaz, Boris Groysberg, and Nitin Nohira, "How to Hang on to Your High Potentials," *Harvard Business Review* (Oct 2011): 76-83.

[54] Silzer and Dowell, "Strategic Talent Management Matters," (see chap. 1, note 5).

[55] Brian E. Becker, Mark A. Huselid, and Richard W. Beatty, *The Differentiated Workforce: Transforming Talent into Strategic Impact*, (Boston: Harvard Business Review Press, 2009); Mark Allen, *The Corporate University Handbook: Designing, Managing, and Growing a Successful Program*, (New York: AMACOM, 2002).

[56] Silzer and Dowell, "Strategic Talent Management Matters," (see chap. 1, note 5).

[57] Groves, "Impact on Hospital Clinical, Financial, and Workforce Metrics," and "Impact on Financial, Workforce, and Value-Based Purchasing Metrics," (see chap. 1, note 12)

[58] Kevin S. Groves, "Integrating Leadership Development and Succession Planning Best Practices," *Journal of Management Development* 26, no. 3 (2007): 239-260; Kevin S. Groves, "Talent Management Best Practices: How Exemplary Health Care Organizations Create Value in a Down Economy," *Health Care Management Review* 36, no. 3 (2011): 227-240.

[59] "Best Practices in Healthcare Leadership Academies," National Center for Healthcare Leadership, (2010), http://nchl.org/Documents/Ctrl_Hyperlink/doccopy5381_uid6102014456192.pdf.

[60] Groves, "Impact on Hospital Clinical, Financial, and Workforce Metrics," and "Impact on Financial, Workforce, and Value-Based Purchasing Metrics," (see chap. 1, note 12)

[61] John C. Scott, Steven G. Rogelberg, and Brent W. Mattson, "Managing and Measuring the Talent Management Function," in *Strategy-Driven Talent Management: A Leadership Imperative*, edited by Rob Silzer and Ben Dowell, (San Francisco: John Wiley & Sons, 2010), chap. 12; Mark Allen, *The Corporate University Handbook: Designing, Managing, and Growing a Successful Program*, (New York: American Management Assn, 2002); Jack J. Phillips, *Return on Investment in Training and Performance Improvement Programs—2nd ed.* (Woburn, MA: Routledge, Aug 2011).

[62] J. Deane Waldman, et al., "The Shocking Cost of Turnover in Health Care," *Health Care Management Review* 29, no. 1 (2004): 2-7; Larry Johnson, "Cutting Costs by Managing Nurse Turnover," *Balance* 3, no. 5 (Sept/Oct 1999): 20-23; Alastair M. Gray, Victoria L. Phillips, and Charles Normand, "The Costs of Nursing Turnover: Evidence from the British National Health Service," *Health Policy* 38, no. 2 (1996): 117-128.

[63] Scott, Rogelberg, and Mattson, "Managing and Measuring the Talent Management Function," (see chap. 2, note 61, item 1).

CHAPTER 3

[64] "2016-2017 Best Hospitals Rankings and Ratings," *U.S. News & World Report*, Aug 2, 2016, http://health.usnews.com/best-hospitals/rankings.

[65] "NCHL Identifies BOLD Organizations That are Preparing Leaders to Transform Healthcare," National Center for Healthcare Leadership, press release, (Chicago, Oct 17, 2016), http://nchl.org/Documents/NavLink/10.17.16_NCHL_Bold_Recognition_uid10262016932001.pdf.

[66] Michael D. Watkins, *The First 90 Days, Updated and Expanded: Proven Strategies for Getting Up to Speed Faster and Smarter*, (Boston, MA: Harvard Business Review Press, May 2013).

[67] David Dotich, James Noel, and Norman Walker, *Leadership Passages: The Personal and Professional Transitions That Make or Break a Leader*, (San Francisco: Jossey-Bass, Sep 2004); Ira M. Levin, "New Leader Assimilation Process: Accelerating New Role-Related Transitions," *Consulting Psychology Journal: Practice and Research* 62, no. 1 (Mar 2010).

[68] Alan M. Saks, Krista L. Uggerslev, and Neil E. Fassina, "Socialization Tactics and Newcomer Adjustment: A Meta-Analytic Review and Test of a Model," *Journal of Vocational Behavior* 70, no. 3 (Jun 2007): 413-446; Helena D. Cooper-Thomas and Neil E. Anderson, "Organizational Socialization: A New Theoretical Model and Recommendations for Future Research and HRM Practices in Organizations," *Journal of Managerial Psychology* 21, no. 5 (2006): 492-516; Russell Korte and Shumin Lin, "Getting on Board: Organizational Socialization and the Contribution of Social Capital," *Human Relations* 66, no. 3 (Mar 2013): 407-428.

[69] "Adopting a Systematic Approach to Bringing Healthcare Leaders Into a New Position or Organization (Policy Statement)," ACHE: Healthcare Executive 30, no. 3 (May/Jun 2015): 110-111; Marjorie Derven, "Management Onboarding: Obtain Early Allegiance to Gain a Strategic Advantage in the War for Talent," T&D, (Apr 2008): 49-52; L. Rita Fritz, "The First 100 Days: How to Accelerate the Learning Curve for Executives," *ACHE: Healthcare Executive* 22, no. 6 (Nov/Dec 2007): 8-14.

[70] Watkins, *The First 90 Days*, (see chap. 3, note 66).

[71] Kim Lamoureux, "Strategic Onboarding: Transforming New Hires into Dedicated Employees," *Bersin by Deloitte; Research Bulletin* 3 (Jan 2008): 1-16; Daniel Cable, Francesca Gino, and Bradley R. Staats, "Reinventing Employee Onboarding," *MIT Sloan Management Review* 54 (Mar 19, 2013): 23-28; Cheryl Ndunguru, "Executive Onboarding: How to Hit the Ground Running," The Public Manager, (Sep 15, 2012): 6-9.

CHAPTER 4

[72] "2016-2017 Best Hospitals Rankings and Ratings," (see chap. 3, note 64).

[73] "Doctors Name America's Top Residency Programs," *U.S. News & World Report*, accessed January 1, 2016, http://health.usnews.com/health-news/top-doctors/articles/2014/02/20/doctors-name-americas- top-residency-programs.

[74] "BOLD Recognition," National Center for Healthcare Leadership, accessed June 15, 2015, http://www.nchl.org/static.asp?path=6531.

[75] "Sutter Health University Talent Management and Succession Planning," SHU document shared

with author via e-mail January 30, 2016.

[76] "From Rising Stars to Successful Leaders: Identify and Develop Your Top Talent with Rigorous Program Management Based on Proven Best Practices," Corporate Leadership Council, accessed May 10, 2015, http://www.clc.executiveboard.com.

[77] Rothwell, *Effective Succession Planning*, (see chap. 1, note 11, item 2); Groves, "Impact on Financial, Workforce, and Value-Based Purchasing Metrics," (see chap. 1, note 14).

[78] Tequia Burt, "Leadership Development as Corporate Strategy: Using Talent Reviews to Improve Senior Management," *Healthcare Executive* 20, no. 6 (Nov/Dec 2005): 14-18; Allan H. Church and Christopher T. Rotolo, "How are Top Companies Assessing their High-Potentials and Senior Executives? A Talent Management Benchmark Study," *Consulting Psychology Journal: Practice and Research* 65, no. 3 (2013): 199-223; Rob Silzer and Allan H. Church, "The Pearls and Perils of Identifying Potential," *Industrial and Organizational Psychology* 2, no. 4 (Dec 2009): 377-412.

[79] Mark A. Huselid, Brian E. Becker, and Richard W. Beatty, *The Workforce Scorecard: Managing Human Capital to Execute Strategy*, (Boston, MA: Harvard Business School Press, Mar 2005).

[80] John Black with David Miller, *The Toyota Way to Healthcare Excellence: Increase Efficiency and Improve Quality with Lean*, (Chicago: Health Administration Press, May 2008).

[81] Rothwell, *Effective Succession Planning*, (see chap. 1, note 11, item 2); Silzer and Church, "The Pearls and Perils of Identifying Potential," (see chap. 4, note 78, item 3).

[82] Gail Dutton, "High Potentials: Tell Them or Not?" *Training Magazine* 52 (2015): 26-31; Marie LaMarche and Kim E. Ruyle, "Point—Counterpoint: Should You Tell Employees They're Part of a Succession Plan?" *HR Magazine* 60 (Jan 2015): 26-27.

[83] Groves, "Impact on Financial, Workforce, and Value-Based Purchasing Metrics," (see chap. 1, note 14).

[84] Ibid.

[85] Ibid.

[86] Michael M. Lombardo and Robert W. Eichinger, "High Potentials as High Learners," *Human Resource Management* 39, no. 4 (Winter 2000): 321-329.

[87] "White Paper: Best Practices in Healthcare Leadership Academies," National Center for Healthcare Leadership, (copyright 2010), http://www.nchl.org/Documents/Ctrl_Hyperlink/doc-copy5381_uid6102014456192.pdf .

CHAPTER 5

[88] "Fortune 500 Companies," *Fortune*, accessed March 1, 2017, http://beta.fortune.com/fortune500/hca-holdings-63.

[89] The Joint Commission, "Joint Commission Certified Organizations," accessed August 15, 2015, https://www.jointcommission.org/accreditation/top_performers.aspx. Publisher's Note: The "Top Performers on Key Quality Measures®" on The Joint Commission website is in hiatus status beginning Jan 2016.

[90] "Truven Health 100 Top Hospitals," Truven Health Analytics™, accessed August 15, 2015, http://100tophospitals.com/.

[91] "World's Most Ethical Companies® Honorees," Ethisphere Institute, http://worldsmostethical-companies.ethisphere.com/honorees/.

[92] Merrill Goozner, "Leaders Who Took the Difficult Path," *Modern Healthcare* 45 (2015): 1.

[93] Adam Rubenfire, "Jack Bovender: Rebuilding a Quality Culture at HCA," *Modern Healthcare* 45 (2015): 2-4, quote on p. 3.

[94] "Preparing the Best for Success: Executive Development Program Annual Report," Hospital Corporation of America internal report, (HCA Executive Development, 2016).

[95] "Congress on Healthcare Leadership," American College of Healthcare Executives, http://www.ache.org/congress/.

[96] McAlearney, "Executive Leadership Development in U.S. Health Systems," (see chap. 1, note 32); NCHL, "White Paper: Healthcare Leadership Academies," (see chap. 4, note 87); Andrew N. Garman, et al., "High-Performance Work Systems in Health Care Management, Part I: Development of an Evidence-Informed Model," *Health Care Management Review* 36, no. 3 (Jul-Sep 2011): 201-213; Mark Brenner, "Mentoring's Role in Succession Planning," *Talent Management* (2008): 1-4.

[97] Groves, "Impact on Financial, Workforce, and Value-Based Purchasing Metrics," (see chap. 1, note 14).

[98] Ibid.

[99] Ibid.

[100] Ibid.

CHAPTER 6

[101] "NCQA Health Insurance Plan Ratings 2015-2016—Summary Report (Private)," National Committee for Quality Assurance, http://healthinsuranceratings.ncqa.org/2015/default.aspx.

[102] "Five-Star Quality Rating System," Centers for Medicare & Medicaid Services, accessed September 1, 2015, https://www.cms.gov/Medicare/Provider-Enrollment-and-Certification/CertificationandComplianc/FSQRS.html

[103] "2016-2017 Best Hospitals Rankings and Ratings," (see chap. 3, note 64).

[104] "2016 Top Hospitals," The Leapfrog Group, accessed January 1, 2017, http://www.leapfroggroup.org/compare-hospitals.

[105] "100 Most Influential People in Healthcare 2016," *Modern Healthcare*, http://www.modernhealthcare.com/community/100-most-influential/2016/.

[106] Jay Conger, "Developing Leadership Talent: Delivering on the Promise of Structured Programs," in *Strategy-Driven Talent Management: A Leadership Imperative*, ed. Rob Silzer and Ben E. Dowell, chap. 6, quote p. 301, (San Francisco: Jossey-Bass, 2010).

[107] Robert J. Thomas, Claudy Jules, and David A. Light, "Making Leadership Development Stick," *Organizational Dynamics* 41, no. 1 (Mar 2012): 72-77, DOI: 10.1016/j.orgdyn.2011.12.009; Paul R. Yost and Mary Mannion Plunkett, "Developing Leadership Talent Through Experiences," in *Strategy-Driven Talent Management: A Leadership Imperative*, ed. Rob Silzer and Ben E. Dowell, chap. 7, (San Francisco: Jossey-Bass, 2010); NCHL, "White Paper: Healthcare Leadership Acade-

mies," (see chap. 4, note 87); McAlearney, "Executive Leadership Development in U.S. Health Systems," (see chap. 1, note 32).

[108] Conger, "Developing Leadership Talent," (see chap. 6, note 106).

[109] Ibid., p. 302.

[110] Morgan McCall, Michael M. Lombardo, and Ann M. Morrison, *The Lessons of Experience: How Successful Executives Develop on the Job*, (New York: The Free Press, 1988); Morgan McCall, High Flyers: Developing the Next Generation of Leaders, (Boston: Harvard Business School Press, 1998); Gail S. Robinson and Calhoun W. Wick, "Executive Development That Makes a Business Difference," Human Resource Planning 15, no. 1 (Mar 1992): 63-76.

[111] Yost and Plunkett, "Developing Leadership Talent," (see chap. 6, note 107, item 2): quote on p. 314.

[112] Ibid.

[113] Esther H. Lindsey, Virginia Homes, and Morgan McCall, *Key Events in Executives' Lives*, (Greensboro, NC: Center for Creative Leadership, 1987).

[114] Corporate Leadership Council, *Voice of the Leader: A Quantitative Analysis of Leadership Bench Strength and Development Strategies*, (Washington, DC: Corporate Executive Board, 2001).

[115] Lombardo and Eichinger, "High Potentials as High Learners," (see chap. 4, note 86).

[116] Timothy A. Judge, Amy E. Colbert, and Remus Ilies, "Intelligence and Leadership: A Quantitative Review and Test of Theoretical Propositions," *Journal of Applied Psychology* 89, no. 3 (Jun 2004): 542-552.

[117] Daniel Goleman, *Emotional Intelligence: Why It Can Matter More Than IQ*, (New York: Bantam Books, 1995).

[118] Kevin S. Groves and Ann E. Feyerherm, "Leader Cultural Intelligence in Context: Testing the Moderating Effects of Team Cultural Diversity on Leader and Team Performance," *Group & Organization Management* 36, no. 5 (Oct 2011): 535-566.

[119] Scott, Rogelberg, and Mattson, "Managing and Measuring," (see chap. 2, note 61, item 1).

[120] Joan Almost, "Review: The Consequences of Executive Turnover," *Journal of Research in Nursing* 16, no. 6 (Oct 2011): 515-517; Daniel J. Sinnott, "Leadership Turnover: The Health Care Crisis Nobody Talks About," *Trustee* 61, no. 7 (Jul 2008): 29-32; Khaliq, Walston, and Thompson, "Impact of Hospital CEO Turnover," (see chap. 1, note 40).

CHAPTER 7

[121] Groves, "Impact on Hospital Clinical, Financial, and Workforce Metrics," and "Impact on Financial, Workforce, and Value-Based Purchasing Metrics," (see chap. 1, note 12).

[122] Huselid, Becker, and Beatty, *The Workforce Scorecard*, (see chap. 4, note 79); Huselid, "Impact on Turnover, Productivity, and Performance," (see chap. 1, note 6).

[123] Groves, "Impact on Financial, Workforce, and Value-Based Purchasing Metrics," (see chap. 1, note 14); Silzer and Dowell, "Strategic Talent Management Matters," (see chap. 1, note 5); Gray, Phillips, and Normand, "The Costs of Nursing Turnover," (see chap. 2, note 62, item 3); Waldman,

et al., "The Shocking Cost of Turnover in Health Care," (see chap. 2, note 62, item 1).

[124] NCHL, "BOLD Award," (see chap. 4, note 74).

[125] NCHL, "White Paper: Healthcare Leadership Academies," (see chap. 4, note 87).